THE HISTORY OF WORLD WAR I

GALLIPOLI &
THE MIDDLE EAST
1914–1918

THE HISTORY OF WORLD WAR I

GALLIPOLI &
THE MIDDLE EAST
1914–1918

FROM THE DARDANELLES TO MESOPOTAMIA

EDWARD J. ERICKSON

FOREWORD BY PROFESSOR GARY SHEFFIELD

amber BOOKS

Dedicated to the memory of my mother, Edith Cullen Erickson

This edition first published in 2008

Published by
Amber Books Ltd
Bradley's Close
74–77 White Lion Street
London N1 9PF
United Kingdom
www.amberbooks.co.uk

ISBN: 978-1-906626-04-4

Series Commissioning Editor: Charles Catton
Editorial: Ilios Publishing, Oxford, UK
Picture Research: Terry Forshaw and Susannah Jayes
Design: Hawes Design
Cartography: Patrick Mulrey
Indexer: Margaret Vaudrey

For editorial or picture enquiries please contact editorial@amberbooks.co.uk

Printed in Dubai

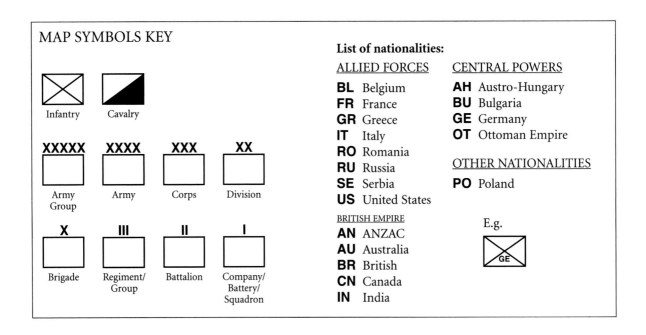

MAP SYMBOLS KEY

Infantry

Cavalry

XXXXX Army Group

XXXX Army

XXX Corps

XX Division

X Brigade

III Regiment/Group

II Battalion

I Company/Battery/Squadron

List of nationalities:

ALLIED FORCES

BL Belgium
FR France
GR Greece
IT Italy
RO Romania
RU Russia
SE Serbia
US United States

BRITISH EMPIRE

AN ANZAC
AU Australia
BR British
CN Canada
IN India

CENTRAL POWERS

AH Austro-Hungary
BU Bulgaria
GE Germany
OT Ottoman Empire

OTHER NATIONALITIES

PO Poland

E.g.

GE

Contents

Foreword

When the Berlin Wall came down in 1989, it triggered the beginning of the end of a period of history that began with the assassination of Archduke Franz Ferdinand in Sarajevo 75 years earlier. The death of the heir to the thrones of Austria-Hungary fanned the smouldering embers of international rivalry into life, and within six weeks most of Europe was at war. World War I destroyed the existing international balance; brought down mighty empires; created the conditions that led to the rise of fascism and communism; made a second global conflagration likely, if not inevitable; and even sowed the seeds of the Cold War. When, after the collapse of the Soviet Union in 1991, historians looked back, they readily identified 1914, the outbreak of World War I, as the beginning of the 'Short Twentieth Century', the bloodiest period in history.

Such a critical era demands to be properly understood, and I am delighted that such a distinguished Anglo-American team of historians – all of them acknowledged experts in their fields – have written a series of admirably accessible books on the war. As it happens, all of them are colleagues, past or present. They have succeeded magnificently in presenting accounts of the key campaigns that skilfully interweave narrative with some incisive analysis incorporating up-to-date research. This is grown-up history for the 21st century.

Gary Sheffield
Professor of War Studies
Centre for First World War Studies
University of Birmingham

Captain Alfred Shout, posthumous Australian winner of the Victoria Cross, Gallipoli.

The Road to War

Many conventional ideas about the Ottoman forces engaged in World War I in the Mediterranean and Middle East are unbalanced, such as their army being inherently corrupt, inefficient and prone to collapse. Western historiography tends to present a dismal picture of the Ottoman Army at war. This volume hopes to provide a more balanced look.

The historiography in English of World War I in the Middle East that has evolved over the past 90 years is wide ranging, but tends to be focused on particular campaigns, leaders or units. There are few books that put together a single unitary picture of the entire Middle Eastern theatre, and those that do tend to focus on military, political or cultural matters. Moreover, even today the history of this theatre remains deeply rooted in English and German sources. This situation, of course, was directly caused by the lack of availability of Ottoman or Turkish sources. In fact, in the most widely regarded definitive

Supporters of the Young Turks in Jerusalem, 1909. Much of the early leadership of the Young Turk movement evolved in provincial cities like Salonika and Damascus, where its members could gather in secret and in safety. By 1909 these had become hotbeds of revolutionary activity.

work on the Turkish fronts, written by the French commandant Maurice Larcher in 1926, only a quarter of the cited sources were Ottoman. The resultant historiography, in turn, tends to tell the story from an overwhelmingly European perspective, which in many ways reflected what the Europeans saw or perceived, rather than reflecting what actually occurred. Today, this situation is rapidly changing, as historians take a fresh look at the events of 1914–18 through the lens of the Ottoman archives and Turkish narratives.

As a result of the way the history of World War I in the Middle East has evolved, there are many popular ideas about the war in this theatre that are largely untrue. For example, one is that the Turks often had large numerical superiorities of men (in most cases they were outnumbered). Another is that German

Although many of those in the Young Turk movement were military officers, some were civilians and government officials. All shared a desire to westernize and modernize both the Ottoman state and society.

generals provided most of the competent leadership and professional staff work for the Turks. There is also the idea that the Ottoman Army was incapable of modern military operations due to corruption and inefficiency. Finally, many histories present the idea that the Turks suffered unusually high numbers of casualties in campaigns against the Allies. For example, in the Gallipoli campaign, a commonly cited figure by British authors suggests that half a million Turks became casualties, whereas the actual number of Ottoman casualties was about 220,000. Finally, there is a pervasive myth that Arab soldiers serving in the Ottoman Army were unreliable and prone to collapse. None of these ideas are true, and in general Western historiography presents a dismal picture of the Ottoman Army at war, in which Turkish successes are largely attributed to Allied mistakes, the activities of German generals or inhospitable terrain and conditions. With these ideas in mind, this volume hopes to provide a balanced look at the Turkish fronts in the Middle East during World War I.

THE HISTORICAL BACKGROUND

The Ottoman Empire reached its zenith of power in the seventeenth century, after which it suffered a gradual decline characterized by a loss of competitiveness with the emerging European nation states. In the eighteenth century, the Ottomans lost territory in Hungary and the Balkans to Austria. Similarly, the Russians under Peter and Catherine took back the Black Sea coasts and the Crimea. The Mamluks took control in Egypt, and along the North African coast gained autonomy. The early nineteenth century saw the independence of Greece and Serbia, while Russia seized most of the Caucasus. The Ottoman sultan attempted a programme of reform, called the Tanzimat, which attempted to strengthen the government and the military. European advisers were hired, and attempts were made to create model structures. The Crimean War (1853–56) overtook these efforts and the Turks were set farther behind.

By the 1870s the English press had dubbed the Ottoman state 'the sick man of Europe', and it seemed destined to fragment piece by piece as the European

A scene from the Russo-Turkish War of 1877–78. Although ultimately defeated in the war, the Ottoman Army successfully defended the city of Plevna against greatly superior Russian forces using field entrenchments. The siege of Plevna foretold the kind of fighting that would characterize much of World War I.

powers took its land and its own ethnic minorities gained independence. From this notion grew the 'Eastern Question', which attempted to frame what the future Middle East might look like politically when the Ottoman Empire finally collapsed. Three of the Great Powers concerned themselves with the Eastern Question: Great Britain, France and Russia. The British interests lay in the security of the Suez Canal and the security of India. The French were interested in spreading influence in the Levant and eastern Mediterranean. The Russians wanted access to the Mediterranean through control of the Bosporus and the Dardanelles, as well as acquiring territory in the Caucasus and Trans-Caspian region. In a nutshell, Britain supported the continuation of the Ottoman state while the Russians wanted to destroy it.

The 1870s brought significant growth to the nationalist ambitions of many of the ethnic minorities within the Ottoman Empire, particularly the Bulgarians, Albanians, Macedonians and the Armenians. Firebrands within these communities formed revolutionary groups dedicated to independence by force of arms. In Bulgaria in 1876, a nationalist insurgency resulted in a violent Ottoman campaign of repression and massacres. These 'Bulgarian horrors' as they were termed led to the Russo-Turkish War of 1877–78. In truth, Russia and many Europeans supported and encouraged the Bulgarians to rise against the Turks. In any case, the Tsar unleashed his armies on the Ottoman provinces in the Balkans and in the Caucasus. The Russians quickly pinned the Turks in several fortresses and drove them back to the outskirts of Constantinople while taking Batum and Kars in the east. They forced the Turks to sign the Treaty of Santo Stefano, which created a Greater Bulgaria under the wing of the

11

Enver Pasha (1881–1922)

Enver Pasha was commissioned as a lieutenant in 1899 and went shortly thereafter to the Ottoman War Academy, graduating in 1903. He served in Salonika and then in 1909 as an attaché in Berlin. In the Balkan Wars he participated in the amphibious invasion of Sarkoy as X Corps chief of staff and was hailed as the liberator of Edirne (Adrianople) in 1913. Enver was appointed as Minister of War in January 1914. He was aggressively nationalistic and was prone to making reckless decisions with incomplete information. After the war he fled to Russia and was killed leading a cavalry charge in the Caspian region.

Enver Pasha (pictured at centre with the moustache) was charismatic, reckless and flamboyant. He would die as he lived, in a forlorn hope.

here that the Europeans, including the British and French, maintained an iron grip on the Ottoman economy by the imposition of capitulations dating back to the late 1700s. These capitulations granted the Europeans favourable trade privileges that were largely tax free and were a festering wound in European–Ottoman relations.

As the twentieth century approached, many young Turkish army officers and civil servants grew disenchanted with the pace of modernization and formed a secret group called the Committee of Union and Progress (CUP). They were popularly known in the West as the Young Turks. The CUP was dedicated to the overthrow of the sultanate and the establishment of a Western-style parliamentary democracy. The first among equals of the CUP was the Salonika Group, centred on officers of the Ottoman Third Army. On 23 July 1908, the Young Turks forced the sultan to abdicate peacefully. However, a counter-revolution in April 1909 pushed the Young Turks briefly out of power, until the Action Army marched on Constantinople to depose the sultan on 27 April 1909. Many of the future leaders of the Ottoman Government and the later Turkish republic were prominent members of the CUP at this time, including Enver, Taalat, Cemal and Mustafa Kemal.

The new government was, at first, democratically inclined and open to the idea of minority participation. However, over the next several years CUP ideology hardened and the rights of the minority communities were decreased. Naturally, this generated much unhappiness and led to the revival of the revolutionary committees. In turn, fresh insurgencies and violence broke out in Albania, Macedonia, Yemen and parts of the eastern provinces inhabited by Armenians and Kurds. In 1911, Italy invaded Libya, the last Ottoman province in North Africa. The war ended in 1912 with the loss of Libya and the Dodecanese islands. While this scarcely damaged the empire, it affected the prestige of the government.

Sensing weakness, the Balkan Christian states formed an alliance in the autumn of 1912 and attacked the rump Ottoman provinces in the Balkans. Epirus and Thessaly, including Salonika, quickly fell to

Russians. The new Greater Bulgarian state had access to the Mediterranean Sea and was regarded as a puppet of the Russians.

The treaty so destabilized the balance of power in Europe that Bismarck convened the Congress of Berlin in 1878. Supported by the British and the Austrians, Bismarck managed to dismantle the Santo Stefano Treaty and restore to the Turks much of what they had lost. In the end Bulgaria survived, but with a much reduced area. The Treaty of Berlin in 1878 was a reprieve for the Turks that allowed them to resume modernization and Westernization. It should be noted

the Greeks. The Serbs took the province of Novi Bazar and split Macedonia between themselves and the Bulgarians. The Bulgarian main army besieged Edirne (Adrianople) and marched to the Catalca Lines (just to the west of Santo Stefano), which was a suburb of Constantinople. A brief armistice was called in December 1912, and negotiations started in London. At the London Conference the Ottoman Government was forced to concede a position that gave away the Balkan provinces in their entirety, as well as Edirne and the Aegean islands.

When the terms of the pending agreement were made known, the government appeared as weak, hesitant and unpatriotic. There was much resistance from the army and from the hard-core ideologues within the CUP, and these men determined to act. On 23 January 1913, an aggressive triumvirate composed of the CUP members Enver, Cemal and Taalat seized power in the famous Raid on the Sublime Porte. In what amounted to a coup d'état, they murdered the Minister of War and forced the Grand Vizier, Kamil Pasha, to resign at gunpoint. They quickly installed one of their own, Mahmut Sevket Pasha, as the new Grand Vizier and vowed to continue the war. The armistice then broke down in February 1913. The new government, however, was unable to conduct the war any better than its predecessor, and the Ottomans continued to lose ground and personnel. The First Balkan War finally came to an end with the Treaty of London in June 1913. A Second Balkan War broke out shortly thereafter between the former Christian allies, during which Romania, Montenegro, Serbia and Greece attacked Bulgaria. The Turks stood aside, except for the peaceful reoccupation of Edirne.

The 1878 Congress of Berlin. The German Chancellor Otto von Bismarck, disturbed by the Russian creation of a Greater Bulgaria after the Russo-Turkish War of 1877–78, orchestrated a cancellation of the Tsar's war gains. In doing so, Bismarck prolonged the life of the Ottoman Empire into the twentieth century.

Cemal Pasha (1872–1922)

Cemal Pasha was an army officer who rose because of his connections with the CUP (Young Turks). He served in the Balkan Wars and in January 1913 was appointed as Minister of the Marine (the navy). At the outbreak of the war, Cemal took command of the Fourth Army in Syria and presided over operations in Palestine. Because of his lacklustre performance, he was marginalized in 1918 and replaced as a front-line combat commander. Because of his role in the Armenian deportations and massacres, Armenians tracked him down and killed him in Tiflis in 1922.

Cemal Pasha photographed at the Dead Sea, 3 May 1915. Political intrigue was his strong suit, and he was prone to leaving military decisions to others.

Ottoman casualties in the Balkan Wars of 1912–13 totalled about a quarter of a million men. Moreover, it lost its most productive and wealthy provinces, and millions of Muslim inhabitants from those provinces streamed into the empire. This created great hardship as the government struggled to absorb the influx of refugees. Militarily, the Ottoman Army lost an entire field army of 12 divisions, including its equipment, artillery and munitions. Politically, the Balkan Wars brought to power the triumvirate composed of Enver, Cemal and Taalat and it solidified their grip on the government. To the Ottoman public these men appeared as heroes who had overturned the Treaty of London and restored the historic city of Edirne to the empire. In the main, they (and their associates) were Western in their orientation, secular and were graduates of the Ottoman Military Academy or universities. All three were ambitious and had a common agenda of rebuilding Ottoman society on a Western model based on a constructed Turkish national identity. Importantly, their success gave them confidence and seemed to confirm a sense that their own destinies were conflated with that of the nation. In particular, Enver Pasha, the new Minister of War,

Turkish cannon destroyed by Bulgarian forces, in the Balkan Wars of 1912–13. The defeat and rout of the Ottoman Eastern Army by the Bulgarians in 1912 appeared to demonstrate that the Turks were inept and careless soldiers. This misappraisal caused the Allies to severely underestimate the potential of the Ottoman Army in 1914.

ABOVE The Italian cruiser *Morosini* discharging her 305mm guns on 24 April 1912 at the Dardanelles, during the Italian–Turkish War of 1911–12. The Italian fleet was unable to blockade the Dardanelles effectively, but was instrumental in the seizure of Rhodes and the Dodecanese from the Turks.

BELOW Asia Minor and the Middle East in 1914. Although greatly reduced in size after the Russo-Turkish and Balkan wars, the Ottoman Empire still extended over 2.4 million square kilometres and was inhabited by an estimated 22 million people.

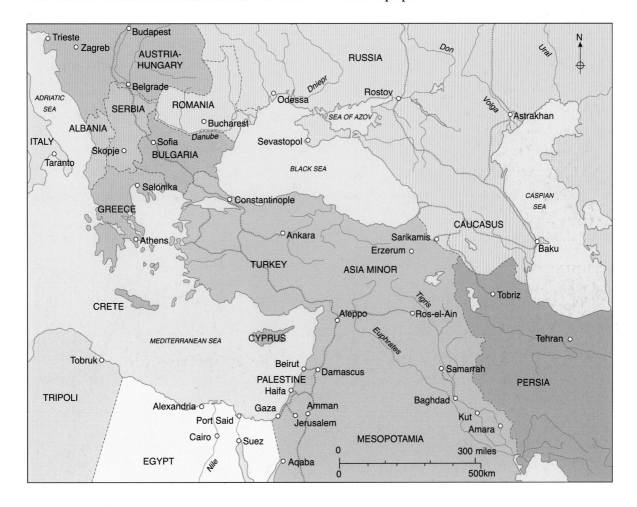

became imbued with a reckless sense of self-assurance, which would prove deadly to the people of the Middle East in the coming years.

THE OTTOMAN EMPIRE AND ITS OPPONENTS

By 1914, the Ottoman Empire was beset by hostile foreign interests and internal decay caused by nationalism and resistance to modernity. During the Balkan Wars of 1912–13, it lost almost all of its European provinces and the 'sick man of Europe' seemed about to expire. The Ottoman Empire was a geographically widespread, multi-national and multi-ethnic empire, whose predominately Muslim population was composed mostly of uneducated peasants in rural communities. About 22 million people lived in the empire, of which about 11 million were ethnic Turks, the remainder being Arab, Armenian, Greek, Kurd or one of dozens of tribal entities that peppered its territory. Many of the ethnic minorities had interests overtly hostile to the continued existence of the empire. Although the correct term for the empire and its people was 'Ottoman', the Europeans continued to refer to them collectively as the Turks (these terms will be used interchangeably in this book). Industrialization was almost non-existent, and the empire's chief products were agricultural. The empire produced no steel, and its coal production was less than Italy's or about 1/300th of Great Britain's. Communications within the empire were poor and commerce was dominated by foreigners, who operated under favourable trade concessions known as the capitulations. In particular, the railroad network was built piecemeal by foreigners to accommodate their own commercial interests, rather than to accommodate the military interests of the empire.

In contrast, the soon-to-be enemies of the empire were heavily industrialized Britain, France and Russia. Britain and France were world-class colonial powers that could call on the human and natural resources of vast empires – 45 million people lived in the British Isles alone. The Russians were industrialized to a lesser extent, but enjoyed an almost limitless population. There was historical enmity between the Ottomans and Russians and they had fought three major wars in the nineteenth century. Even in 1914, the Tsars still coveted the Bosporus and the Dardanelles. On the other hand, Britain and France maintained historically friendly ties with the Ottoman Empire, mainly to counterbalance the growing power of Russia. Because of this, when war broke out, the Turks were both intellectually and physically unready to wage war against Britain or France.

OPPOSING ARMIES

The Ottoman Army was torn apart by its defeat at the hands of the Balkan League. This seemed to validate European notions that the army was inefficient, corrupt and incapable of effective combat operations. However, the Young Turks recognized the need for reform and began a sweeping series of changes that restored much of, and actually improved, the Ottoman Army's capabilities.

The army had 36 combat infantry divisions in 1914, which were manned partially at a cadre level, giving a peacetime strength of about 200,000 men and 8000 officers. There were no organized cavalry divisions, but the Turks were able to mobilize their mountain tribesmen into an irregular cavalry corps on the outbreak of war. The active army was composed largely of illiterate peasants, who were called to the colours for a period of three years. There was also a reserve system, but in 1913, as a result of the dismal performance of reserve units in the Balkan Wars, the general staff entirely eliminated its organized reserve combat divisions and corps. They replaced them with a depot regiment structure designed to bring the units of the active army up to strength. Thus, when the army

> 'The Turkish Army is not a serious modern army … It is ill commanded, ill officered and in rags'
>
> Colonel Henry Wilson, Director of Military Operations, October 1913

entered the war – and in contrast to the European powers, who mobilized scores of reserve divisions and corps – the Ottoman Army did not immediately increase the number of its combat divisions. To make matters worse, weapons and equipment – especially machine guns, cannons, munitions, medical supplies and communications gear – were in short supply.

The army was blessed, however, with three important advantages that would enable it to endure through a multi-front war for four years. The first was the existence of a body of general staff officers whose selection and training were based on the extraordinarily successful Prussian model. These officers were young, but were combat seasoned and professional. The second advantage was a unique, combat-tested, triangular infantry division instituted in 1910. Each division contained three infantry regiments of three battalions each, a model that was ideally suited to trench warfare and which would soon be adopted by the European powers. This organizational structure was flexible, and enabled the Ottoman Empire to build an expansible army of some

Reki Bey, military commander of Jerusalem, and his staff during manoeuvres south of Jerusalem before the Turkish declaration of war. The Ottoman Army conscripted men locally into regimental depots for training. Consequently, the soldiers in Ottoman Army units in the Damascus and Jerusalem areas were mostly Arabs, who neither spoke nor read Ottoman Turkish.

60 effective divisions as the war progressed. Finally, the Ottomans had a remarkably resilient soldier in its average *asker*, who although illiterate was tough, well trained and generally brave (the Turks called their soldiers *Mehmetcik* or Mehmets). In truth, the strength of the Ottoman Army lay at the extreme ends of its structure – a solid base of soldiery and a proficient high command.

In the year prior to the outbreak of World War I, the army undertook a massive retraining and reconstitution effort to rebuild its shattered forces. Its garrisons were located in the major cities, and it was organized for peacetime in a system of army inspectorates. The Minister of War, Enver Pasha, wrote and implemented dynamic training guidelines, which were based on lessons learned from the recent wars. These guidelines stressed mobility, combined-arms operations and the importance of fire superiority. They also included instructions for digging trenches and immediate counterattacks. These tactical hallmarks would characterize the Ottoman Army in World War I and would make it a deadly opponent when fighting on anything near equal terms.

In December 1913, following a request from the sultan, the German general Otto Liman von Sanders arrived to head the German Military Mission. The latter initially comprised 40 highly trained officers tasked with helping the Turks rebuild their army. The German officers would assist mainly as high-level staff officers, but some would actually command Ottoman combat units. None of them spoke Ottoman Turkish, nor were they familiar with the new organizational structure; all of them held the Turks in very low

professional regard. These officers began arriving in the spring of 1914, although many did not actually arrive at their duty stations until the summer. Such help was not new: Germans had helped the Ottoman Army since before the Crimean War, and these men followed in the footsteps of illustrious officers including Graf von Moltke and Colmar von der Goltz.

The Allies' contemptuous opinion of the Ottoman Army was reinforced by the reports from the British Army attaché Lieutenant-Colonel Cunliffe-Owen, resident in Constantinople between 1913 and 1914. He viewed the Ottoman attempt to rebuild the army as feeble and clumsy. Other British opinions appeared to confirm this: the director of military operations characterized the Ottoman Army as 'ill-commanded, ill-officered and in rags'. As late as autumn 1914, reports from the field to London contained phrases like 'very much afraid of the enemy's bayonet' and 'inferior physique, nervous and excitable'. The French and the Russians formed similar opinions.

The British Army was small and based on an unusual model of professional long-service volunteer

The German Maxim Maschinengewehr '08. The Ottoman Army mostly used German machine guns during World War I. In 1914, such weapons were in short supply. Resupply from Germany post 1916 helped alleviate this situation.

soldiers. It also possessed the finest non-commissioned officer (NCO) corps in the world, although it still drew the bulk of its officers from the privileged classes. There was a regular army of six infantry divisions, but a further half a dozen could be mustered by bringing together the various battalions on foreign stations. This was backed by a reserve force called the Territorials, which could mobilize another 14 divisions for war. At the level of the individual soldier, the British had no equal in the world; however, their army was tightly compartmentalized, and the individuality of the different arms – infantry, cavalry and artillery – contributed to an overall inability to combine arms in combat. Another significant weakness in the army was the relative newness of the general staff and a general absence of modern doctrines of command and control. In 1914, instead of distributing the regulars among the reserves and the new 'Kitchener armies', the British concentrated their professionals in the British Expeditionary Force in France, where large numbers were slaughtered. This, of course, hurt the newly raised armies, which numbered 62 divisions by 1917, by leaving them largely without trained leaders.

The Russians, at the other end of the spectrum, used a mass continental army model that employed huge numbers of conscripted men. The army was famous for its inefficiency and for its lack of a professional NCO corps. It also lacked equipment, but was undergoing a modernization of its artillery force in 1914. At higher levels the Russians had a professional general staff whose officers were seasoned veterans of the Russo-Japanese War (1904–05). Like the Ottoman Army, the soldiers of the Russian Army were mostly illiterate peasants from agricultural villages scattered throughout the empire. Moreover, the Russian Empire was also a multi-ethnic one, and many of the conscripts spoke no Russian and had national interests overtly hostile to the Tsar's government. Nevertheless, the army was famous for its

numerical strength and its ability to endure and persevere in difficult conditions.

The French Army was a highly professional force composed of active and reserve divisions and corps that trained together on a regular basis. Every healthy Frenchman served in the military for three years, and then remained in the reserves thereafter. The French staff was well trained and the army well equipped. In large numbers, the French would only fight the Turks at Gallipoli, although a small number participated in the Palestine campaign late in the war.

THE YOUNG TURKS: RELUCTANT PARTICIPANTS
The assassination of the Archduke Franz Ferdinand in Sarajevo provoked the July Crisis of 1914 during which Austria-Hungary and Serbia spiralled into war. Diplomacy failed and ultimatums were followed by

The British Maxim .45 Mk 1. Like its Ottoman opponent, the British Army in the Middle East was underequipped with machine guns. Indian Army units in particular suffered from chronic shortages until late 1918.

German Military Influence

Although individual German officers had served in the Ottoman Empire it was not until 1882 that a formal German Military Mission was established under General von Kaehler. He died the following year, but the work was continued by Lieutenant-Colonel Colmar von der Goltz, a trained general staff officer who was already well-known as the author of *The Nation in Arms* (*Das Volk in Waffen*). Goltz would remain in the empire until 1896 and established the German staff curriculum in the Ottoman War Academy. This curriculum included doctrines and concepts about mass continental armies, conscription and mobilization, and battles of encirclement and annihilation. He returned in 1909 to assist the Turks in reorganizing their army into a modern army corps configuration. When Liman von Sanders arrived in 1913 to re-establish the moribund mission, German ideas were already well in place in the Ottoman Army. Goltz himself returned to command the Ottoman Army in Mesopotamia, where he died in 1916.

A German station at Abou Augeileh.

maintained their neutral posture. The alliance partners, for their part, attempted to woo or bully the Turks into a commitment to support them in the event of war. In addition to the German Military Mission, there was a British Naval Mission, and a French Mission that was training the substantial forces of the Ottoman Gendarmerie. The Russians, for their part, spied on the Ottomans and supported the activities of the Armenian Revolutionary Committee, which sought autonomy or independence. These competing concerns, as well as the diplomatic activities of the embassies in Constantinople, pressured the Ottoman Government, which in turn led to the emergence of interests and factions among the Young Turks.

It is clear today that all of the European powers had defined war objectives, which served to strengthen the will to wage war. The French, for example, wanted to recover Alsace-Lorraine, while the Austro-Hungarians wanted to stop the rising Serbian hegemony in the Balkans. In contrast, the Ottoman Empire, in the wake of its Balkan defeat, had no definable war goals in the summer of 1914, neither did it have any sort of offensive mobilization scheme or war plan. Indeed, the priority of its military was the rebuilding of the army and it was unprepared for war. In truth, the Turks had almost nothing to gain from entering a general European war, and the ruling Young Turks made overtures to both alliances as the Balkan crisis progressed. However, powerful personalities, in the form of the German ambassador Hans von Wangenheim and the pro-German Ottoman Minister of War Enver Pasha, seized the moment and propelled the empire towards provocative action.

Wangenheim and Enver conducted detailed conversations on 27 July, leading to the drawing up of the famous Secret Treaty of Alliance between Germany and the Ottoman Empire. The treaty was not a formal alliance, but the parties pledged to support each other and, importantly, from the Ottoman perspective the agreement was defensive in nature. Only in the event of active military intervention by the Russians were the Turks obliged to enter the war. As these discussions evolved, World War

military mobilization of the partners of the Triple Alliance and the Triple Entente. The war-weary Turks watched these unfolding events at a distance, but because they were not in either alliance they

I broke out on 1 August 1914 and the next day the ambassador and the Minister of War signed the treaty. The clauses of the treaty were technically overcome by events, and made irrelevant by the German declaration of war without waiting for Russian intervention. The treaty itself did not bring the Turks into the war, but aligned them with the Germans and alienated them from the British and French.

The Young Turks were not a cohesive governing body and the Grand Vizier, Prince Sait Halim, who was also Prime Minister and Foreign Minister, was surprised to learn of the signing of the treaty. It is certain that he did not want war; indeed, some of the Young Turks were even pro-Allied, the Ottoman Empire having long-standing friendly ties with Britain and France. But within days the insistent demands of the aggressive German ambassador began to worry Sait Halim, who in turn now pressed the Germans for additional concessions, which included a promise to help end the capitulations, certain territorial clauses involving Ottoman irredentist claims in Caucasia

Troops of the Young Turks man an artillery piece in Pera, 1909. The Ottoman artillery was composed largely of German-manufactured weapons in the calibre range of 77mm to 105mm. Most of these weapons were flat trajectory guns. Howitzers (with high-angle trajectories) were comparatively few in number.

and the Aegean islands, and a war indemnity. Wangenheim, who was seeking a safe haven for the German Navy's Mediterranean Squadron, agreed to these proposals.

Over the next several days, a deeply disturbed and wavering Sait Halim met with his cabinet to thrash out exactly where Ottoman foreign policy was heading. On 9 August 1914, he directed that the Secret Treaty be examined for its legality, because he did not believe that it obliged the empire to enter the war. He also sought to conclude alliances with Bulgaria and Romania and to convince the Entente powers that the Ottoman Empire intended to remain neutral. It is evident today that Sait Halim did not want war and intended to buy as much time for his country as he

A cartoon commemorating Abdülhamid II's deposition on April 27, 1909. The Young Turk revolution swept away the archaic Hamidian regime, but it in turn was overthrown by a counter-revolution. However, in 1913 the Young Turks seized power once again in the 'Raid on the Sublime Porte'.

could. Unfortunately for the Ottoman Empire, and perhaps the world as well, Sait Halim proved to be a reluctant and hesitant leader, who was incapable of controlling the actions of his government.

THE FLIGHT OF THE *GOEBEN* AND WAR

The events of the summer of 1914 conspired to overcome the concerns of the Ottoman Government, and served to bring the Turks into the war. One of the most famous episodes of the war was the flight of the *Goeben*, a heavily armed German battlecruiser that

was the flagship of Rear Admiral Wilhelm Souchon's Mediterranean Squadron, and the light cruiser *Breslau*. The outbreak of war found the German squadron trapped inside the Mediterranean Sea and hunted by superior British naval forces. Souchon, who was ordered to interfere with French forces coming from North Africa, eluded his pursuers, and instead of sailing for the friendly ports of Germany's ally Austria-Hungary, sailed for the eastern Mediterranean. Ambassador Wangenheim, alerted to the situation, persuaded the Young Turks to allow Souchon's squadron to enter the Dardanelles and find safety. On

The flight of the *Goeben* and *Breslau* across the Mediterranean in August 1914. This was one of the key episodes that drew the Ottomans into World War I on the side of the Central Powers.

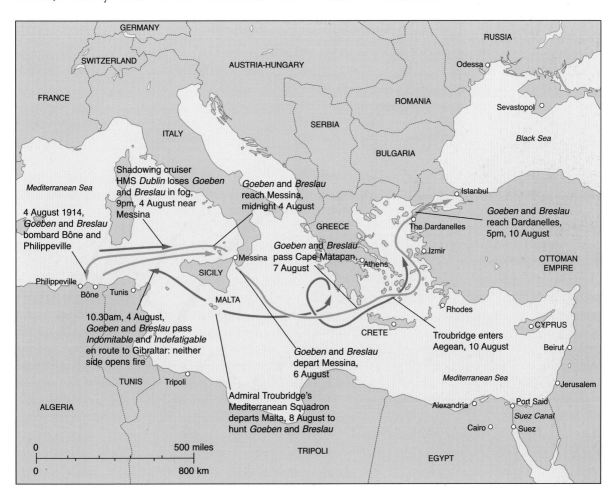

HMS _Erin_ was a Royal Navy battleship of the _King George V_ class originaly built for Turkish Navy as the _Reshadiye_. However, following the declaration of war against the Ottoman Empire, she was ordered to be seized by the British Government, and was retained for Royal Navy service.

10 August, the ships passed through the straits and anchored off Constantinople the following day. The resourceful admiral's escape deeply embarrassed the Royal Navy. Britain was in turn partially to blame for the Turkish decision to harbour Souchon, when she seized two Turkish battleships (paid for by public subscription) under construction in British yards on the outbreak of war.

The arrival of the German squadron destabilized the delicate political balance in the Ottoman capital. To avoid internment, and capitalizing on a wave of Anglophobic hysteria caused by the seizure of the Turkish ships, the Turks 'purchased' the German ships and reflagged them, with the German sailors famously appearing on the decks wearing the Turkish fez. Souchon was appointed as an admiral in the Ottoman Navy and was given command of the Ottoman fleet, thus maintaining control of the Kaiser's ships. The charade fooled nobody, and instead drove the British to begin planning for war against the Turks. Meanwhile, Otto Liman von Sanders, whom some of the Young Turks mistrusted, was sidelined as a player in the diplomatic processes by being put in command of the Ottoman First Army. Unlike Liman von Sanders, Souchon remained in command of an instrument of war that Germany could wield independently.

Throughout the autumn of 1914, Enver wrestled with the reluctant Sait Halim over the prospect of entering the war. Left to their own devices the Young Turks might not have entered the war, but the collaboration of the determined Souchon and the aggressive Wangenheim sealed their fate. Although Sait Halim was nominally the commander of all Ottoman forces, in reality Enver controlled them, and, working with the Germans, the latter was manoeuvring the empire into war. In September 1914, Souchon began taking the _Goeben_ (now renamed the

Yavuz) and her consorts out into the Black Sea, on what were termed 'training cruises'. In reality, he was hoping for a chance to confront the Russian Black Sea Fleet, as such an action would be considered a *casus belli* and would bring the Turks into the war. Sait Halim saw through this, and prohibited Souchon from exercising in the Black Sea, although Souchon continued sailing. The Russians, however, refused to take the bait.

Enver now took matters into his own hands, as well as several million Turkish pounds of gold from the Germans, and orchestrated the entry of his country into the war by encouraging Souchon to continue his sorties. In violation of Sait Halim's directives, Souchon took his ships and most of the Ottoman fleet to sea on 28 October 1914. It is possible that neither Enver nor his clique of interventionists knew Souchon's true intentions, thinking only that a high-seas engagement with the Russians would result. Early the next

morning, however, four task forces of Ottoman ships began to bombard Russian Black Sea ports, including Sevastopol, Odessa and Yalta. Unlike the Japanese surprise attack on the Russian fleet at Port Arthur in 1904, these widely dispersed attacks were not designed to cripple Russian sea power, rather they were designed merely to provoke the Russians, making them a political and not a military act. Sait Halim and the advocates of restraint had been outmanoeuvred by Enver and the Germans, who had stage-managed the whole provocative incident. On 2 November 1914, Russia declared war on the Ottoman Empire, swiftly followed by Britain and France.

Both Winston Churchill, the British First Lord of the Admiralty, and Henry Morgenthau, the American

SMS *Goeben* was a *Moltke*-class battlecruiser armed with 11in guns. She was fast, well armed and heavily armoured. At the outbreak of war, she was more than a match for any combination of Allied ships that might engage her.

ambassador in Constantinople, thought that the passage of Souchon's squadron through the Dardanelles made the Ottoman entry into the war inevitable. This is largely true, but it was more a combination of the strong personalities of Enver, Wangenheim and Souchon that brought this about. Unfortunately for the Ottomans, even at this late date, their empire was quite unready for a major conflict against the Allies.

OTTOMAN MOBILIZATION AND EARLY OPERATIONS

Although not at war, the Turks mobilized their army on 2 August 1914, mainly as a precaution against their Russian and Christian Balkan neighbours. Unlike the Great Powers, they had no immediate offensive plans

and their single war plan, which was rewritten in April 1914, brought the bulk of the army to Thrace against Bulgaria and Greece. The process of mobilization, which comprises bringing an active army and its reserves to a readiness posture enabling it to fight wars, had been perfected by the European armies, with timetable precision, so that it took about 10 days (for the Russians it took longer). Following this, armies concentrated on the frontiers by railway and then executed their war plan. The most complex and famous example of this system was the German Schlieffen Plan.

Unfortunately for the Ottomans, they were in the middle of a massive effort to restore their shattered armies and were quite unready for mobilization. General staff planners thought that it would take about 21 days but, in many cases, mobilization took between 30 and 45 days. Although the army's regiments and divisions had sufficient manpower, they lacked artillery, machine guns, and supplies of all sorts. To make things worse, the empire's inefficient railway system was in an abysmal condition and

Recruitment for the sultan's jihad (holy war) near Tiberias. Although the sultan called for a jihad against the Christian allies in the autumn of 1914, it failed to attract many followers. The Turks and Germans had hoped to rouse the Islamic peoples of Egypt, India and Caucasia against their British and Russian masters.

serviced the economic interests of foreign entrepreneurs rather than the needs of the military. Significantly, except in Thrace, the railways did not extend to the frontiers, making the concentration of forces problematic.

In September the army began the process of moving its units from their garrison cities to their war stations in Thrace, Caucasia and Palestine. In a terrible strategic error, no forces were sent to Mesopotamia, which was actually denuded of two of the four infantry divisions stationed there. Concentration took over 60 days and some units marched on foot over hundreds of kilometres to reach the frontiers. European military attachés observed the slowly unfolding mobilization and concentration, which appeared to confirm conventional negative opinions regarding the efficiency and capability of the Turks. British observers characterized the Ottoman Army as 'not a serious modern army' and its soldiers as clumsy, dull witted and 'very much afraid of the enemy's bayonet'. These opinions would be proved wrong in the coming year.

As the empire was not yet at war, this slow concentration of forces gave the general staff more time to consider the strategic situation and alter its defensive plans. In early September, under the direction of the capable German colonel Fritz Bronsart von Schellendorf, the staff began work on new plans for offensive operations in the Caucasus and Palestine. Germany certainly pushed its Ottoman partner into operations that its army was unprepared for. However, the relentlessly aggressive but inexperienced Enver Pasha, who was now in charge of the war effort, enthusiastically endorsed the German ideas. The result, contrary to military doctrine, threw nine divisions against the Russians in the Caucasian winter and four divisions against the British across the waterless Sinai Desert, while 18 of the army's best divisions sat idle in Thrace.

Throughout the autumn of 1914, the Ottoman Army relentlessly trained its soldiers in the battlefield skills necessary for survival and success in combat. This process was characterized by rigorous physical training and long marches through difficult terrain. As

Turkish troop columns marching out to drill. The Ottoman Army conducted large-scale peacetime maneuvers in the years leading up to the outbreak of World War I. The empire's soldiers were well trained, hardy, and inured to harsh condition. They were also highly mobile and capable of executing fast and difficult marches.

the proficiency of the men increased, the Turks conducted combined-arms training that linked infantry to artillery and stressed achieving fire superiority. When the soldiers were not marching, they were digging trenches. Such lessons had been learned in the Balkan Wars and the Turks took them to heart. By late October the army was very much improved, a condition that was noticed by the Western military attachés in Constantinople. Naturally, they attributed this to the presence of the German Military Mission, but in fact very few Germans were actually stationed with Ottoman troops.

Events soon overtook the Turks, as the Russian declaration of war took the uninformed general staff by surprise. In the meantime, both the Russians and

A holy carpet brought to Jerusalem by the Sharif of Medina. The Grand Mufti and Sharif are riding in the carriage. The Turks held the holy cities of Mecca and Medina throughout the entire war. Although not militarily significant, these centres of Islam had great spiritual and political value for the Ottoman Empire.

the British, anticipating that the Ottoman Empire would enter the war on the side of the Germans, had positioned forces for immediate offensive operations against them. On 3 November the British fleet cruising off the Dardanelles (hoping that its quarry the *Goeben* would sortie) shelled the Turkish forts at the entrance of the straits, which merely served to alert the Ottomans as to the weakness of their defences. In the Caucasus the Russians launched a powerful attack on 6 November against the Koprukoy lines northeast of the fortress city of Erzurum. The Turks were largely unprepared for this and lost thousands of men, before restoring the situation with a vigorous counterattack.

On the same day the well prepared British landed troops of the Indian Army in the Shatt al-Arab. There had been much discussion in the autumn between the Admiralty and the India Office over the need to protect British access to the oil fields owned by the Anglo-Persian Oil Company, on which the Royal Navy was rapidly developing dependence. As a result, Lieutenant-General Barrett's 6th Indian Division (the Poona Division) was designated as Force D and put on ships in the Persian Gulf to await developments. The mission of Force D was simply to secure the oil terminal and tanks at Abadan. The Ottoman military's failure to properly garrison Mesopotamia was probably its worst mistake of the war, and was the result of pre-war thinking that could not and did not envision its historic friend and protector, the British Empire, as a threat. Consequently, Mesopotamia was left almost entirely unguarded and its pre-war garrisons were sent elsewhere.

Barrett's Indians attacked the old Turkish fort at Fao, which was garrisoned by a mere 400 men, and easily took it. There were hardly any Ottoman soldiers in the area, and those present were either brushed aside or quickly surrendered. Encouraged by the terrible Ottoman showing and failure to mount effective opposition, the enthusiastic British commander, Brigadier W.S. Delamain, seized Basra on 20 November and advanced to Qurna two weeks later. By December the British had a secure foothold in lower Mesopotamia with an entire infantry division, and had begun to build up a river boat flotilla. This lodgement would prove irresistibly seductive for the Indian Army's high command, and would lead to problems within a year.

The outbreak of war was a disaster for the Ottoman economy. Almost everything made by machine was imported from Europe, as well as metals, coal and medical supplies. Moreover, the economy itself relied not on its weak internal lines of communications, but on a robust coastal trade to carry goods throughout the empire. In November 1914, the ever-present British Royal Navy clamped a rigorous blockade on Ottoman seaborne trade, which combined with the efforts of Russia, Serbia and the neutral Christian states of the Balkans effectively isolated the Turks. This situation continued for the first year of the war, until Germany crushed Serbia and re-established communications with the empire.

AN EFFECTIVE GERMAN VICTORY
The early campaigns of the war were disastrous for Ottoman arms. This was the result of not only poor planning, but poor political policy and inchoate war aims as well. The provocative Black Sea raids brought the Russians and British into the war, and they were able to attack the unready Turks immediately. The Turks were mauled by the Russians at Koprukoy and their dismal showing in Mesopotamia allowed the

Indian Army to gain an easy foothold at low cost. Mesopotamia would soon become a running sore for the Ottoman war effort.

Unlike the Europeans, whose diplomacy was closely tied to their war plans, the Turks lurched unsteadily into the war. There were points in the autumn of 1914 when it might have been possible for the Entente Powers to convince the Turks not to fight. Unfortunately, the Secret Treaty with Germany was not so secret by that time and the Allies, who did not know its terms, thought that it tied the Germans and Turks together in an offensive alliance. As a result, rather than actively pursuing diplomatic solutions, Entente leaders and planners assumed the worst and made preparations accordingly. Absent the presence of the *Goeben* and the powerful personalities conspiring in Constantinople, the Ottoman Empire might never have entered the war at all.

Unlike the Europeans in that dangerous and odd summer of 1914, who enthusiastically put on their uniforms and eagerly went off to war, the mass of Anatolian Turks were indifferent or even opposed to the war. In the Balkan Wars, many of the casualties were ethnic Turks, and a civilian population numbering in the millions was evicted from territory it had owned since the fifteenth century. Anatolia and Thrace suffered as a consequence, as the empire tried to assimilate millions of Muslim refuges from the Balkans. While a small part of the Ottoman elite welcomed the war, there were no spontaneous outbursts of patriotic fervour as there were in the European countries. Furthermore, about half of the empire's non-Turkish population had nationalistic interests overtly hostile to its continued existence, and welcomed the opportunity to throw off the yoke of Ottoman domination.

Overall, the entry of the Ottoman Empire into World War I was a significant strategic victory for the Germans. It cost them almost nothing and suddenly

> 'The imperative need of direct control of a reasonable proportion of the supply of oil fuel is required for naval purposes'
>
> Winston Churchill, First Lord of the Admiralty, memo to the Anglo-Persian Oil Company, 1914

opened up three land fronts with the Entente, as well as forcing the Royal Navy to conduct a blockade in three seas. Later, more Ottoman fronts would open up at Gallipoli, Salonika and even in Galicia and Persia. By the end of the war, the Germans would have committed some 50,000 men to the Ottoman fronts, while the British and Russians alone would commit over three million. Indeed, the Turks punched well above their weight and, over the next four years, absorbed massive amounts of Allied strength and resources. There were other problems for the Allies as well. Among the British there emerged two competing camps concerning the

strategic direction of the war: 'Westerners' (who believed in the primacy of the Western Front) and 'Easterners' (who believed that the war was best fought in peripheral theatres to knock out Germany's allies). For the Russians, the loss of access to the Mediterranean through the Turkish straits created an immediate and compelling problem with their grain exports and reciprocally with the importation of war *matériel*. While the Turks were not able to win the war for Germany, they were able to weaken significantly or divert the war efforts of two of Germany's three main opponents. This in turn would have a profound impact on the course of the war.

BELOW **Austrian artillery commanders entering Jerusalem. As the war progressed greater numbers of Germans and Austrians were sent to assist the Turks. Most of these soldiers went to Palestine. By 1918 up to 20,000 German and Austrian soldiers were serving in the Ottoman Empire.**

RIGHT **A soldier of the Indian Army. After Gallipoli, the Indian Army made up much of Britain's fighting strength in the Middle East. By 1918, Indian infantry in particular emerged as a potent force; indeed, the imperial armies that seized Mesopotamia, Palestine and Syria were mostly Indian.**

CHAPTER 1

Suez and the Caucasus

The assault on the town of Sarikamis, deep in the Caucasus Mountains, was the first major Ottoman offensive of the war, and sought to surround and annihilate the Russian forces present in the area. A further offensive aimed at severing the Suez Canal was launched, which sought to seriously damage the British Empire's commercial lifeline to its Eastern colonies. Both of these operations would end in failure.

A s the Ottoman Empire tumbled towards war in autumn 1914, there were bitter disputes in Constantinople between Bronsart von Schellendorf and his Ottoman counterpart Hafiz Hakki Bey over the strategic direction of the coming conflict. The Ottomans had never foreseen a multi-front war against a combination of Great Powers and, especially, against their long-time friend Great Britain. Consequently, the concentration plan, which had been written the previous April for a war against Bulgaria, stripped away forces from Palestine and Mesopotamia

Turkish troops muster on the Plain of Esdraelon in preparation for the attack on the Suez Canal. All Ottoman Army infantry divisions were permitted a military band. Under combat conditions the bandsmen performed duties as litter bearers and orderlies.

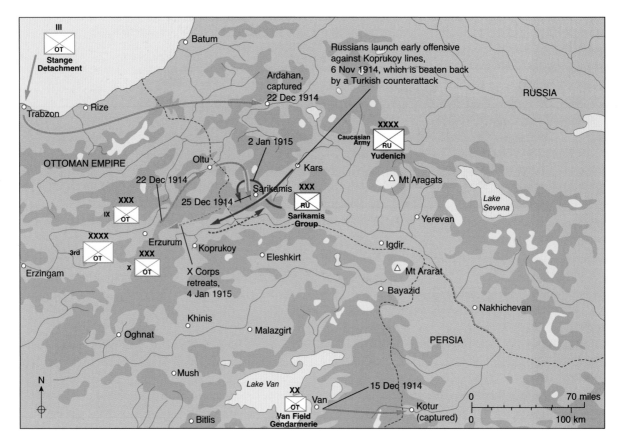

The Caucasus, November 1914–January 1915, including the Battle of Sarikamis. The Sarikamis encirclement was designed to create the conditions for an Ottoman version of Tannenberg and sought to annihilate the Russian Army.

and left the Caucasus devoid of reinforcements as well. In fact, the military deployment of the empire's armies did not align at all with the diplomatic situation as it developed. This situation vexed both men, who were aggressive professionals and, as both were trained general staff officers, recognized that wars are won by offensive action. Hafiz Hakki pushed for offensives in Caucasia, Palestine and even Persia while the Germans advocated an amphibious attack on the Russian Black Sea coastline.

In October, plans crystallized around offensives in the Caucasus and Palestine, and formal orders were sent to the respective armies. Liman von Sanders was offered command of the Ottoman Third Army, headquartered in the Anatolian city of Erzurum, but

wisely declined. Although the Third Army and the Fourth Army in Palestine remained in the hands of Ottoman commanders, they had German chiefs of staff, Colonel Guse and Colonel von Frankenberg respectively, to coordinate and assist in planning. Although short of equipment, both armies were at full strength in manpower, much of which had combat experience in the recent Balkan Wars.

THE SARIKAMIS CAMPAIGN

The first major Ottoman offensive of the war was aimed at the town of Sarikamis, deep in the Caucasus Mountains, and which in December 1914 was blanketed with snow and gripped by sub-zero temperatures. It was the brainchild of Enver Pasha, and contrary to the version of events in most histories, was not a massive effort designed to recover lands inhabited by fellow Turkish peoples. Moreover, to this day Enver's plan is almost universally seen as recklessly

Turkish troops muster in 1914. This is the famous 'Constantinople Fire Brigade', which performed ceremonial guard duties as well serving as the city's fire fighters. They are easily distinguished by their helmets.

ill conceived and doomed from the start. On the contrary, it was, in fact, carefully crafted and modelled on the German victory in September over the Russians at Tannenberg (in East Prussia); German operational reports from the latter indicated that when Russian units were surrounded, command and control collapsed and surrender soon followed. Enver envisioned a single envelopment of the over-extended Russian Army along the Ottoman northeast frontier, and thought that cutting their lines of communications at Sarikamis would force a collapse and surrender.

The actual planning guidance for offensive operations was sent from the general staff to the Ottoman Third Army in early September, when it became apparent that war against the Entente Powers was more likely than war against Bulgaria and Greece. There were two schools of thought within the staff concerning how this should be done: the first, from Colonel Bronsart von Schellendorf, envisioned a limited-scope offensive with the forces at hand, while the second, from Colonel Hafiz Hakki Bey, foresaw a

Ottoman Encirclement Operations

The Ottoman Army embraced the 'German way of war' as a result of the establishment of the German general staff system and German war academy curriculum. Part of this German legacy included campaign planning for battles of encirclement and annihilation. The German curriculum glorified Hannibal's battle at Cannae as the ultimate expression of the operational art, and the Schlieffen Plan would come to exemplify this concept. Over a period of several decades Ottoman commanders became wedded to this doctrine. In the Balkan Wars of 1912–13, Ottoman commanders consistently tried to encircle their enemies, notably at the battles of Kirkkilise, Kumanova, Bitola and Sarkoy. This doctrinal pattern of planning for encirclement operations continued into World War I, notably at Sarikamis, Kut al-Amara, the Caucasus in 1916 and First Gaza. Ottoman commanders failed in these ambitious attempts to execute the *ne plus ultra* of the military art. In 1922, however, Mustafa Kemal Ataturk would destroy the Greek Army in a dramatic battle of encirclement and annihilation known as the Great Offensive.

massive reinforcement of the Third Army, which would enable a large-scale offensive complete with an amphibious landing north of Batum on the Black Sea. For his part, General Liman von Sanders thought neither idea was sound, and advanced the idea that the Turks should maintain a defensive strategic posture. As autumn set in, the Tannenberg reports began to arrive and Enver sent Bronsart von Schellendorf and Hafiz Hakki Bey to Berlin in late October 1914 for strategic consultations. When they returned (after the outbreak of hostilities), planning for a Caucasian offensive resumed in earnest as all opposition to an offensive strategic posture was extinguished.

Russian troops in the trenches at Sarikamis. One of the lessons learned by the Russian Army in the Russo-Japanese War was to dig trenches quickly. A group of staff officers can be seen observing from the centre of the trench line.

On 8 November 1914, the Ottoman Navy cruiser *Mecidiye* brought Hafiz Hakki Bey to Trabzon on the Black Sea coast. His mission was to energize the offensive spirit of the Third Army, and he went directly to the headquarters at Erzurum. There Hafiz Hakki Bey delivered explicit guidance to the chief of staff, German Colonel Guse, to prepare an operational offensive against the Russians. Tannenberg was used as a model of how this might be accomplished, and Hafiz Hakki Bey hoped to use the oncoming winter weather for additional leverage against the Russians. He encountered immediate resistance from the commanders of the Third Army and the IX Corps, who opposed the ambitious plan. Enver summarily relieved the latter, and sent a message to the army by placing Hafiz Hakki Bey in command of the corps.

Planning now proceeded at an accelerated rate, and the Turks secretly massed six of their nine available divisions (which were organized into the IX and X corps) into a powerful attack force along the left flank of the Koprukoy lines. The attack force was to march northeast through Oltu and then pivot sharply to the southeast toward Sarikamis, which lay on the only paved road leading from the Russian supply base at Kars to the Russian frontline troops facing Koprukoy. Possession of the town of Sarikamis effectively cut off the Russians from their rear, isolating them in winter weather; if the Tannenberg paradigm held true, this would cause confusion and a collapse in morale.

The general staff was unable to send large reinforcements for the Third Army offensive due to time constraints and the distances involved, but it was able to send the 8th Infantry Regiment by sea to Trabzon as a limited reinforcement and to conduct a diversionary operation. This operation would shield the northern flank of the Third Army in the area south of Batum by advancing on the city of Ardahan, acting as a sort of matador's cloak to distract the Russians. To the south of the operational area, the Third Army thinned its lines to allow the concentration of effort, leaving mostly cavalry and gendarmes to watch the long southern front.

The Russian Caucasian Army had five infantry divisions, two Cossack divisions, and a handful of infantry brigades and cavalry regiments. Altogether in October 1914, it comprised about 100,000 infantry, 15,000 cavalry and 256 guns. The nominal commander was the regional viceroy, but the real work of planning and organizing the army lay in the hands of the chief of staff, General Yudenich. The Ottoman Third Army was slightly smaller with about 90,000 infantry and 250 guns. The Ottoman cavalry was organized into a regular cavalry division and four reserve cavalry divisions of irregulars, formerly known as the *Hamidiye* cavalry, whose value in combat was debatable. The Turks fielded 4000 regular cavalry and possibly as many as 10,000 tribal warriors. The Russians broke their army down into tactical groups, the largest of which, the Sarikamis Group, stood at the Koprukoy lines and was composed of about 65,000

infantry and 172 guns. For the attack the Turks massed 49,000 men in their enveloping wing and left 27,000 men, including their cavalry (which was of limited value in the rugged mountains northeast of Erzurum), on the line. This deployment gave the Turks a small numerical margin of superiority over the troops of the Sarikamis Group.

The attack began before dawn on 22 December in good weather. Together with his assistant chief of staff

Nikolai Yudenich (1862–1933)

Yudenich was, arguably, the most successful Russian commander of World War I. Born in 1862, Yudenich entered the Imperial Russian Army in 1879, graduating from the General Staff Academy eight years later, after which he served on the general staff until 1902. He served in the Russo-Japanese War of 1904–05 as a regimental commander and rose rapidly to general officer rank. Yudenich was appointed chief of staff of Russian forces in the Caucasian area in 1913 (having served as deputy chief of staff from 1907). He was instrumental in inflicting a series of defeats on the Turks, including that at Sarikamis in December 1914. In the following year he turned back Ottoman offensives, and captured Erzurum in February 1916 and Erzincan in July. In March 1917 Yudenich was forced to discontinue active operations in the Caucasus because of the ongoing revolution. The Provisional Government forcibly retired him and Yudenich fled to Finland during the October Revolution. He became a commander in the White armies and marched on Petrograd in the autumn of 1919, but was forced back into Estonia where the armies were disbanded. Fleeing for the second time, Yudenich went into exile in France, and died there in 1933.

Bronsart von Schellendorf, Enver Pasha had made the long journey to Erzurum and was on hand to watch the troops cross the frontier. The infantry of X Corps conducted a remarkable foot march advancing 75km (46 miles) through the mountains at Oltu to reach Sarikamis on 25 December. However, as they

Turkish riflemen en route to war. The Ottoman Empire had very few railroads. Those that existed were built by foreign entrepreneurs and seldom ran to the combat fronts. Ottoman soldiers usually deployed to their areas on foot.

progressed the weather turned colder. The adjacent IX Corps also came up, so that the Third Army had two corps in position to attack Sarikamis. But as they approached the city the Turks began to encounter resistance centred on the old town. Unlike the events of August in the dark forests of East Prussia, the Russians in Sarikamis fought hard for the town. Moreover, their command and control apparatus remained intact and they were able to take several regiments off the Koprukoy line and send them to reinforce the Sarikamis garrison. In spite of this, the Turks took most of the old town. Reacting to this, on 28 December the Ottoman X Corps seized blocking positions to the north along the Kars–Sarikamis road, aiming to further weaken Russian resolve. Enver now expected a rapid Russian collapse, but instead the aggressive General Yudenich kept his head and coolly orchestrated a counterattack using forces pulled off the line and fresh forces from Kars. Yudenich's effective actions now gave the Russians numerical superiority in the immediate vicinity of Sarikamis. To make matters worse, the weather turned against the outnumbered Turks, with temperatures dropping to minus 26 degrees centigrade; the Turks were unprepared and lacked winter kit, having expected a quick victory. The tempo of fighting slowed and the Russians used this time to plan an encirclement of their own.

On 2 January 1915, Yudenich unleashed a powerful counter-offensive that swiftly re-enveloped the Ottoman left wing around Sarikamis. Enver reacted by placing both Ottoman corps under a single commander – ironically, the general staff's strategic planner Hafiz Hakki Bey, who had argued for the Caucasian offensive earlier in the autumn. The battered Turks tried to form a perimeter, but the

> '‘There was one road out of the Turnagel Woods that night and only the X Corps returned – the IX Corps did not return.'
>
> Colonel Hafiz Hakki, Ottoman General Staff, 1915

Russians turned it into a noose. By 4 January 1915, Hafiz Hakki Bey was forced to choose between losing his entire force or leaving a rearguard to die while the others escaped. In the end, he left IX Corps in the Turnagel Woods to the northwest of Sarikamis in order to buy time for X Corps to retreat. IX Corps' three infantry divisions were destroyed and its commander Ali Insan Pasha was captured with his staff. The Turkish collapse and the subsequent rout lost them an entire army corps – a third of the Ottoman Third Army's combat strength.

The Sarikamis campaign ranks as one of the greatest military disasters of the twentieth century. It was neither badly planned nor badly conceived, rather it came up against unexpected and brilliantly effective Russian command and control in the form of General Yudenich. A humiliated Enver, who had come to the front to glory in his victory, crept back to Constantinople in early January 1915. Western estimates of 90,000 Turks killed are exaggerated, with the actual losses consisting of some 30,000 dead and 7000 taken prisoner. In scenes reminiscent of Napoleon's retreat from Moscow, many of the casualties froze to death or suffered serious frostbite. The shattered Ottoman Third Army returned to its defensive positions to begin rebuilding itself.

At the same time as the Sarikamis campaign, Ottoman military activity took place to the north and southeast. To occupy the Russians and divert their attention and reserves from the Sarikamis region, the Ottoman general staff sent an infantry regiment and artillery by ship to the Black Sea port of Trabzon. Command of the regiment (and some frontier forces) was given to German Major Stange, a Prussian artilleryman who had been assigned to the fortress at Erzurum; the entire force was named the Stange Detachment. Stange's mission was to advance and tie down the Russian Army near Batum. Instead, he attacked vigorously and seized the Russian town of

Friedrich Kress von Kressenstein (1870–1948)

Kressenstein (often called Kress von Kress, or von Kress) was a Bavarian artillery officer, and was assigned to the German Military Mission in January 1914. He was assigned to the Fourth Army in September as chief of staff. He planned the attack on the Suez Canal in January 1915. In March and April 1917 he planned the successful defence of Gaza during the Battles of Gaza and was awarded the Pour le Mérite. Kress's actions at Third Gaza in October 1917 led to the collapse of the Ottoman position and the loss of Jerusalem. He was given command of the Ottoman Eighth Army in defence of the coastal sector of the front until the summer of 1918, when he was transferred to command the German Military Mission in the Caucasus. He retired as a lieutenant-general in 1929.

Ardahan on 22 December 1914. There Stange found a number of loosely run, irregular bands of the Ottoman Special Organization (SO), who had been waging guerrilla warfare on the Russian Army and the local Armenian and Greek population. Stange's attack stalled, but together with the SO troops, he then held most of his ground through the winter.

Far to the southeast along the Ottoman–Persian frontier, Ottoman troops also attacked, in what is known as the First Invasion of Persia. This scheme was born of Enver's grand dreams of a pan-Turanian invasion, which would liberate and unite the Turkish peoples held in thrall by the Persians. While the Sarikamis operation is sometimes presented as a part of this scheme, it was, in fact, a separate and purely operational envelopment. However, the Persian invasion was the centrepiece of Enver's plan of pan-Turanic expansion. He hoped to invade Persia and then pivot northward into Azerbaijan, all the while raising rebellion among oppressed Turkic peoples. Unfortunately, the only force available for this ambitious undertaking was the Van Field Gendarmerie Division, a paramilitary force with few machine guns or artillery. Nevertheless, Enver ordered it forward and it crossed the frontier on 15 December to take the town of Kotur and a small corner of Persian territory. The local Turks failed to rally to the cause, and the poorly thought-out plan only served to provoke the Russians, who sent strong forces to occupy Tabriz and Tehran.

Recognizing that the ill equipped Gendarmerie would need reinforcement, Enver ordered the dispatch of two expeditionary forces from Constantinople to the distant front in Persia. These ad hoc units of divisional strength, under the command of lieutenant-colonels Kazim and Halil (Enver's uncle), began to depart by train on 11 December 1914. Enver's orders to them were to take Tabriz. However, the ageing and inefficient Ottoman transportation system failed to move them quickly, and by mid-January both expeditionary forces were only midway through Anatolia, where many of the men became infected with typhus. Finally, in mid-February 1915 they reached the front, but nowhere near the Persian frontier. In the aftermath of the Sarikamis disaster, the Ottoman general staff diverted them to the fortress city of Erzurum to shore up the battered Third Army. The unsupported Gendarmerie troops remained in Kotur until March 1915, when the Russians pushed them back to the frontier.

Also during the winter of 1914/15, the restive Armenian population began to stir under the agitation of the Armenian committees. The largest of these was the Armenian Revolutionary Federation or the Dashnaks, which had smuggled large quantities of arms and explosives into the six eastern provinces of the Ottoman Empire. Encouraged and aided by the Russians, the Armenian leadership now believed that a window of opportunity for rebellion had opened, with the Ottoman Empire at war with three of the Great Powers. Over the winter, terrorist incidents by Armenians mounted, and a part of the Armenian population prepared for insurrection against the Turks. There were also six highly motivated Armenian regiments, composed of émigré Ottoman Armenian subjects, fighting with the Russian Army and a highly organized 'fifth column' of Armenians began to lay the groundwork for outright rebellion in Van Province.

With minor exceptions, at the strategic and operational level Ottoman military performance in the Caucasus was very poor, and the strategic posture of the Third Army in early 1915 was worse than it was when the war began. For the most part, the Turks, and especially Enver Pasha, tried to do too much with too little and their wildly optimistic plans failed against the Russians, who had better railways and more soldiers. However, the Ottoman Army proved that it possessed an offensive spirit, and a remarkable ability to mass forces quickly and march long distances in harsh terrain and climates – an aspect significantly unremarked upon in Western historiography. This capability, based on good training and solid discipline, would serve the Turks well in the coming years.

THE FIRST SUEZ OFFENSIVE

In September 1914, Bronsart von Schellendorf and Hafiz Hakki Bey clashed in a major dispute over the strategic direction of the Ottoman Empire's war plans. While they disagreed about plans for the Caucasus, they agreed that the removal of Ottoman forces from Palestine needed to be reversed because war against Great Britain was almost inevitable. By the end of the month they were also in agreement that the Turks should launch an offensive aimed at severing the Suez Canal. This was thought to be a viable strategic option, which would in turn seriously damage the British Empire's commercial lifeline to its Eastern colonies. A new Fourth Army was formed and Cemal Pasha, the navy minister, took command of it on 18 November 1914. Several Germans were sent to assist him, including Lieutenant-Colonel Friedrich Kress von Kressenstein. The first-class infantry divisions were also ordered south to form the nucleus of Cemal's army, including 8th Division from III Corps and 10th Division from Smyrna. These were well trained formations composed of Anatolian Turks. The

Guarding the banks of the Suez Canal. The threat of an Ottoman strike cutting the Suez Canal forced the British to station a large garrison in Egypt until 1916. The Royal Navy deployed ships in the canal as well for gunnery support.

25th Division from Syria, an Arab unit that also contained a high percentage of ethnic Turks from the Syrian cities, was also sent south.

The evolving plan owed much to Kress, the new chief of staff, who envisioned marching an entire army corps across the Sinai Desert from Palestine. Once in position, the corps would launch a daring *coup de main* seizure of Ismailia using an infantry division. This would cut the canal at its mid-point, which the Turks thought might negate the tremendous firepower of the Royal Navy's ships. Kress planned to deploy a second division across the canal as well, and to secure the flanks with two additional infantry divisions. The plan was risky, but the Turks hoped that success might incite the Muslim population of Egypt into a revolt

The Turkish assault on the Suez Canal, January–February 1915. The Turks hoped not only to cut British communications through the Suez Canal, but also to raise a jihad amongst the Egyptian population against the British.

against their British masters. To this end, the sultan was persuaded to declare a jihad against the enemy, and agents of the Teskelati Mahsusa (the Ottoman Special Organization, or SO) were sent on into Egypt to stir up and organize the Egyptians. The general staff began to move the divisions of the Ottoman VIII Corps into southern Palestine near Gaza in readiness for the attack. Enver wanted to launch the attack in early December 1914, but chronic problems with the railway intervened. Palestine was particularly affected by two uncompleted stretches in the Ottoman railway system, one at Pozanti in the Taurus Mountains and a second at Osmaniye in the Amanus Mountains. At each location everything had to be unloaded and brought by animals over the (respectively) 55km (34-mile) and 35km (21.8-mile) gaps, and then everything was reloaded aboard trains. This meant that supplies going to Palestine might take as long as 60 days to arrive at the front.

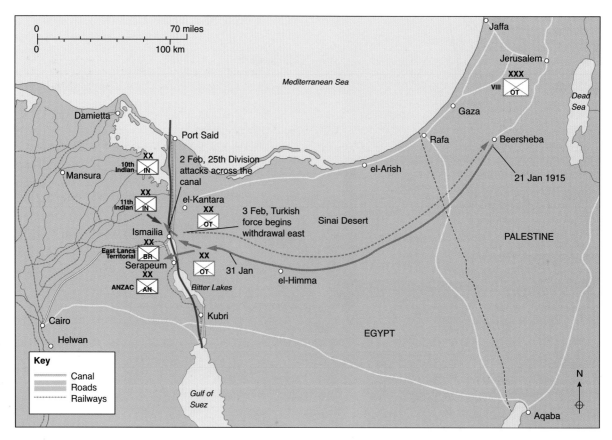

Logistics were thus a huge problem for the Turks, but their immediate tactical problem dealt with traversing the waterless Sinai Desert with an army of four divisions. In the end, they cut down their substantial force to a bare 13,000 men and eight artillery batteries, accompanied by about 1500 irregulars and Arabs, whom they planned to turn loose in Egypt to raise a revolt. Huge water tanks and storage depots were moved forward to support the troops, and for the actual movement through the desert the force used 1000 horses, 12,000 camels and 300 oxen. The oxen were needed to transport the heavy pontoons and boats necessary to cross the canal itself. The movement, organized into three tactical groups, began on 14 January 1915, and the Turks reached their assembly area on the last day of the month. It was a significant achievement and the British seemed unaware of the Ottoman presence on their doorstep. Morale in the Ottoman expeditionary force was high as it prepared to attack.

The pre-war British garrison in Egypt was small, merely a brigade, but in autumn 1914 two Indian Army infantry divisions were sent to Egypt as well as a

Turkish troops depart for the Suez Canal in late 1914. The first Ottoman offensive against the Suez canal in early 1915 failed. However, it highlighted the remarkable ability of the Turks to overcome geographic obstacles and the climate.

territorial division from England. Although the British had abandoned the Sinai, Major-General Sir John Maxwell established a strong defensive line along the western bank of the canal. By December Maxwell had 30,000 troops defending the length of the canal and a division of the ANZAC (Australian and New Zealand Army Corps) had arrived as well, for a total force that far outnumbered the Turks. Maxwell's army was a polyglot of territorial, Indian and colonial troops, but it was more than sufficient to defend Egypt. Importantly, the British enjoyed aerial reconnaissance and easily tracked the three major enemy groups across the desert; however, they remained uncertain as to the main objective. As the Turks neared the canal they began to move at night. Consequently, by 31 January 1915 the Turks lay in well concealed assembly areas about 10km (6 miles) east of Ismailia, leaving the British without a clear picture of exactly where the main body was located.

Turkish troops make use of camel transport in the desert. Throughout the war the Turks remained reliant on animal transport to sustain their armies. Some 210,000 animals were mobilized in 1914 to support the Ottoman war effort.

On the night of 2 February 1915, infantry of the 25th Division moved forward into assault positions on the eastern bank of the canal. There the division joined an assault force of two infantry battalions together with the pontoons and boats that the Ottoman engineers had laboriously brought across the desert. The flanking units prepared to conduct diversionary attacks, and eight batteries of light artillery were brought forward as well. However, as they loaded their boats and entered the water the Ottoman infantry were observed by the enemy, and although they actually achieved local surprise, a small British observation post opened fire almost immediately. This greatly disturbed the crossing troops, who had had very little practice in actual amphibious operations. Many panicked under fire and jumped out of the boats, but about two companies of infantry made it to the far side. They

secured a tiny bridgehead and began to dig in. The Turks supported their men with artillery fire and brought up another division to reinforce the crossing, but effective gunfire from Royal Navy ships in the canal made this impossible. In the meantime, the well orchestrated British defenders brought up an Indian Army counterattack force, which launched assaults throughout the following day. As the strength of the British force became apparent, Cemal ordered the abandonment of the attack at 4pm on 3 February. He was unable, however, to bring back his assault force, and most of his soldiers on the west bank were captured or killed as the main body withdrew into the desert. All the pontoons and boats, which had so laboriously been transported across the Sinai, were abandoned. Casualties were light on both sides. Many of the Ottoman troops involved in the crossing operation were ethnic Arabs, and some surrendered with little resistance. The ill conceived plan for a pan-Islamic insurrection in Egypt met with little enthusiasm, and many of the agents were rounded up.

The offensive ended as rapidly as it began, as Cemal

moved his forces back to the Gaza–Beersheba line. For their part, the British were content to let the Turks withdraw unchallenged, largely because they had few units trained in pursuit operations as well as an immediate lack of camels to carry water. The British were cheered by this victory, which appeared to confirm their experience in Mesopotamia that the Turks were, indeed, a sad excuse for a modern army.

OTHER THEATRES

In Mesopotamia the Ottoman strategic situation was rapidly unravelling, as the ill equipped 38th Infantry Division, which had been employed in piecemeal fashion, was destroyed by the advancing Indian Army. To restore the situation, Enver sent a famous irregular commander from the Ottoman Special Organization named Suleyman Askeri, and also reversed the deployment of the 35th Infantry Division, which had left Mesopotamia earlier for the Caucasus. Suleyman Askeri set up one division at Nasiriya on the Euphrates River and his other division on the Tigris River, and set them to digging in. He also reinforced the 38th Division with new levies, thus restoring some measure of combat capability. While the Turks remained weak, Suleyman Askeri's efforts restored coherent direction

to the theatre. This brought the British to a halt as they waited for reinforcements.

The Ottoman Army at this time was also engaged in two other minor, but active, theatres of war. The larger of these involved a counter-insurgency campaign against rebellious Arab tribes in the Hedjaz along the pilgrimage railroad to Mecca and against rebellious tribes in Yemen. These campaigns tied up an entire army corps of four infantry divisions, but, while irritating, were not a great strain on the Ottoman war effort. There was also a tiny campaign of insurgency supporting the Sanussi tribesmen against the Italians in Libya, which was extended into British-controlled Egypt. In a sort of Lawrence of Arabia scheme in reverse, Ottoman officers carrying gold and arms were sent (most often by submarine or coastal tramp steamers) into the interior to assist the tribesmen. The targets of their raids and sorties were the coast road and isolated outposts. This effort was heavily publicized in the Islamic world, but added almost nothing to the war effort.

Kankalah' stretchers on camels bringing wounded out of the Suez Canal area. Ottoman medical services were primitive by western standards. Over 450,000 Ottoman soldiers died of diseases alone during the war.

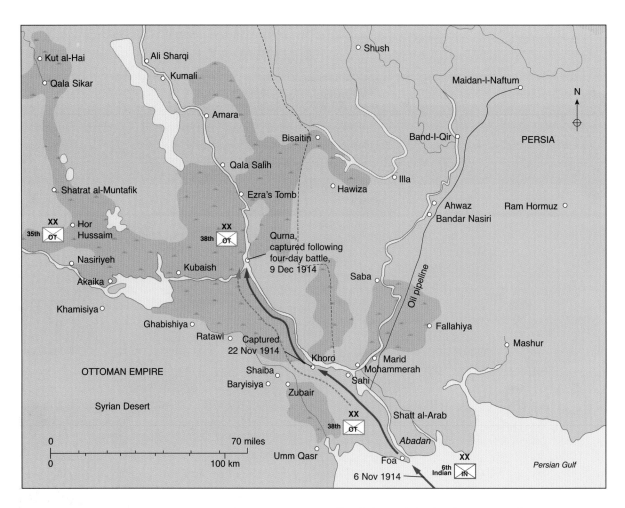

Lower Mesopotamia, November–December 1914. The occupation of Abadan and the push up the Shatt al-Arab was deceptively easy. The lure of Baghdad proved irresistible to British commanders.

MISAPPRAISALS

The initial campaigns against the Turks were apparently hugely successful at low cost to the Allies. The Turkish actions at Sarikamis, in particular, were seen as amateurish and doomed from the start, and the failed Suez Canal operation appeared as a minor, clumsy version of it. Compounding this picture was the successful occupation of lower Mesopotamia; moreover, Royal Navy raids near Alexandretta over the winter found a population that appeared to be apathetic to the war effort. Famously, Ottoman

officials hosted the landing parties from HMS *Doris* and actually helped the Royal Navy sailors blow up strategic railway bridges! The war against the Turks had almost a comic opera atmosphere and their army appeared inept.

All of this was seen by eager Allied leaders and planners as evidence that the 'sick man of Europe' was about to collapse. Easy victories over small portions of the Ottoman Army or over poorly trained troops was also seen as proof that pre-war observations concerning the low capability of the Turks were correct. In fact, none of this was at all true. The Sarikamis campaign failed because of faulty assumptions about Russian command and control. In that campaign the Turks secretly massed two-thirds of the Ottoman Third Army's combat strength and launched it over snow-covered mountains to seize objectives 75km (46 miles) distant, almost succeeding in doing so. In Palestine, the Ottoman Fourth Army moved a large force rapidly across a waterless desert and mounted an amphibious assault crossing of a major water obstacle. In both cases, the Turks displayed considerable staff proficiency in planning complex operations in harsh climates and difficult terrain. Moreover, Ottoman soldiers proved resilient and showed high levels of mobility and march discipline. The fact that the Turks were aggressive and possessed these kinds of strengths was lost on the Allies. Defeat disguised the real capability of the Ottoman Army.

The poor showing in Mesopotamia showed the Turks in the worst light of all, because there, many of the conscripts were untrained Arab tribesmen, who vanished at the first shots. In truth, the cream of the Ottoman Army, its best leaders and its best fighting formations had been sent to Thrace, where they idled waiting for a Bulgarian attack that never came. In particular, the best-trained and finest fighting formation in the army, the Ottoman III Corps, garrisoned the Gallipoli Peninsula, where it fortified its positions and prepared for war.

This misappraisal of the Ottoman Army was the product of European ethnocentrism and a result of Social Darwinism, which cast the Turks as uneducated peasants incapable of competing on even terms with Europeans. Ottoman performance in the first months of the war exaggerated these ideas, and appeared to confirm European notions. Even the Turks' German allies tended to think of them in terms of their weaknesses rather than their strengths. The British, in particular, badly underestimated their Ottoman adversary, which would haunt them in the coming year in their clashes with the Ottomans at Gallipoli and in the siege of Kut al-Amara.

Sudanese deserters serving as Ottoman guides. The Ottoman invasion force included contingents of Sinai Bedouins, Druses, Syrian Circassians, and Sanussi refugees from Libya.

CHAPTER 2

The Dardanelles

The relatively brief operations in the Dardanelles form one of the most famous episodes of the entire war. From the point of view of the Allies, the attempt to secure access to Constantinople and the Black Sea via the Dardanelles Straits and the Sea of Marmara was shown to be over ambitious and poorly planned, while the Ottoman forces proved themselves to be stubborn and courageous in their defence.

One historian claims today that 'there are more books written about Gallipoli in the English-speaking world than on any other campaign in World War I'. This high level of interest almost certainly derives from the fact that the Gallipoli campaign had the most wide-ranging implications and possibilities of any single effort in that war, which in a sense gives it the greatest 'What if…?' appeal as well. The campaign was singularly unique, in that it was the only large-scale amphibious operation of the war and it involved land, sea and air forces. It was also

The Ottoman coastal defences at the Dardanelles comprised forts containing 82 heavy guns. This photo shows a heavy coastal gun stationed at the Narrows. Eventually the Turks would augment these defences with an additional 230 artillery pieces including heavy howitzers.

a combined operation involving multi-national forces on land and sea. Moreover, it was fought over a landscape that was pockmarked with history and war; from the battlefield itself, it was even possible to see the ruins of Troy. As a result, today there are many levels of modern historical interest, among both professionals and amateurs, the focus of which ranges from political and diplomatic history down to the activities of individual soldiers in trenches. There are thousands of families in Europe, the Middle East, the Indian subcontinent and the Antipodes whose forefathers fought there, and who maintain an active interest in these events.

The Western view of the campaign dwells on the 'What if…?' factor, and tends to focus on the mistakes of the Allied commanders – for, in truth, it is regarded

as a battle that should have been won. The accepted thinking on the campaign maintains that an Allied naval victory was possible in March 1915 and a land victory was possible later in April. This view also maintains that a final possibility for victory was offered to the Allies in August 1915. However, in each case it is thought that disconnected and timid admirals and generals threw away victory when boldness would have succeeded. Most books in the English-speaking world take the approach that the British lost the battle rather than advance the idea that the Turks won it – that a combination of mistakes fatally disabled British plans and that the Turks won because they were brave and stubbornly held on to their ground. In addition to becoming the graveyard of 100,000 men, Gallipoli became the graveyard of reputations, both military and political.

In many ways, the Western historiography of the Gallipoli campaign is similar to that of the American Civil War battle at Gettysburg (1–3 July 1863), which

A Turkish fort in the Dardanelles viewed from the air. Many of the defences of the straits were built on the sites of older fortifications. The photo shows a fifteenth-century Ottoman castle with nineteenth-century gun emplacement additions.

By 1914, forts such as this one in the Dardanelles were a tactical liability for their Ottoman defenders because they attracted enemy artillery fire. They offered little protection against enemy shells.

broadly posits that General Robert E. Lee should have won the battle and threw away his chance for a decisive victory. Little is written about why the Union commander, General George G. Meade, actually won the battle. The Gallipoli story is most often told in a similar fashion.

The straits of the Dardanelles are about 65km (40 miles) in length and are dominated by the heights of the Gallipoli Peninsula, where high hills in the centre provide commanding terrain. North of these hills, the peninsula narrows to a tiny waist only a little over 1.6km (one mile) in width before merging into the mainland. The Dardanelles themselves are only 1462m (1599 yards) wide at the part known as the Narrows and the current from the Black Sea runs swift and deep. Ownership of the strategic straits has been contested since ancient times. More recently, Admiral Duckworth took a British fleet to Constantinople in 1807, and Florence Nightingale's mid-nineteenth-century hospital at Scutari looked out on the Bosporus.

OTTOMAN PLANS

In peacetime, the defence of the Dardanelles was organized as the Chanak Kale Fortified Area Command. The fortress command controlled 19 forts and a brigade of three heavy and medium artillery regiments, armed with coastal guns with calibres of up to 35.56cm (14in). The forts were grouped in two areas, at the mouth of the straits and at the Narrows, and, in times of peace, were lightly manned. Few regular troops were stationed on the peninsula, but to the north the Ottoman III Corps garrisoned the cities of western Thrace. The III Corps had the 7th, 8th and 9th Infantry divisions assigned to its rolls, and also the 9th Field Artillery Regiment, 3rd Cavalry Brigade and support troops as well. This corps was the most famous one in the army and had a hard-earned fighting reputation from the Balkan Wars of 1912–13, from which it emerged intact – the only Ottoman corps to do so.

In July 1914, during the Sarajevo crisis, the Ottoman Army was unready for war and the empire remained outside the general European scheme of military alliances. However, as Europe tumbled towards conflict, the general staff ordered military mobilization as a precautionary measure, even though the empire was not yet at war. The high command mobilized its army on 2 August and III Corps, in Thrace, received the orders at 1am the next morning. The corps commander was Esat Pasha, who got out of bed to read the orders. Esat was vigorous and professional, and had emerged from the Balkan Wars as one the empire's few genuine military heroes. During the war, his defence of the fortress of Janinna in Greece showed that Esat understood the dynamics of modern trench warfare. That he roused himself out of bed in the middle of the night to personally read the mobilization order offers a snapshot of him and his concern for his mission. Esat began immediate preparations for war at dawn, which was the first numbered day of mobilization. Like all Ottoman corps, III Corps had only about 15,000 men out of the 40,000 it was authorized under its war establishment and many of the soldiers were recently conscripted.

Turkish troops in the Dardanelles in 1915. The Ottoman III Corps conducted numerous training exercises prior to the attack of 25 April. These exercises tested the deployment and positioning of the Ottoman defensive plans. Here Turkish soldiers overwatch a landing beach.

As the war progressed soldiers from the various ethnic groups in the Ottoman Empire were thrown together under combat conditions. In this photo Arab and Turkish soldiers appear in the same formation.

Fortunately for Esat Pasha, the available force pool of the reserves programmed to fill the ranks consisted almost entirely of recently discharged combat veterans of the Balkan Wars, who were themselves veterans of III Corps.

Upon mobilization, the 9th Infantry Division was ordered to the straits fortress as a mobile reserve. Technically, it remained part of III Corps, but fell under the control of the fortress commander so that troops were available to defend the rear of the forts and the peninsula itself. Whilst the mobilization proceeded slowly for the other army corps, III Corps was the only one to meet its mobilization timetable of 22 days. Its strength had swelled to over 30,000 men (and some 7000 animals) and its infantry divisions filled to their full strengths of over 12,000 men. The fortress had a more difficult time, but on 17 August its commander had his heavy coastal artillery regiments

The Ottoman trench systems at Gallipoli became more robust as the campaign progressed. Many Turkish soldiers lived in bunkers equipped with such relative luxuries as beds, lamps and furniture.

ready for war. By late August, the commanders of III Corps and the fortress had detailed plans for the deployment of the 9th Division to the peninsula. The division moved there in September, followed by the 7th Division in October, and Esat's headquarters moved to Gallipoli itself in November. His 8th Division was diverted to Palestine, but III Corps would raise a replacement division over the winter.

The Gallipoli Peninsula was the most heavily defended point in the Ottoman Empire, with defensive works dating back hundreds of years. Construction of the modern defences began during the 1880s, and focused on defending against a naval attack on the Dardanelles Straits. Consequently, the

defences until 1912 were primarily composed of coast defence guns, underwater minefields and searchlights. In 1912, under the threat of a Greek amphibious invasion, the Ottoman general staff ordered the fortification of the Gallipoli Peninsula itself. During the First Balkan War, a corps-level command was created on the peninsula to construct and occupy the defensive works that would guard against an enemy landing. It is generally unknown that the Dardanelles defences were given a thorough workout during the First Balkan War (1912–13) and it was during this war that the Ottomans put together the basic defensive plans and concepts used to defend the peninsula in 1915. The Dardanelles Straits and the peninsula fell under the command of the Straits Forces and Fortification Command in 1912. The fortress command had an active infantry division, a provisional infantry division and three reserve infantry divisions. Altogether, for the defence of the peninsula the Turks had 40,000 men armed with 27,000 rifles, 38 machine guns and 102 cannons (not counting coastal artillery). The peninsula was defended by stationing two of the three reserve infantry divisions in beach defence roles, placing the active division at Bulair (the isthmus), and keeping one reserve division as a general reserve at Eceabat. A divisional detachment defended the Asiatic shore. Thus, by the end of the year, the general configuration and strength of the Turkish defence was established, and after the war the plan was retained for future use.

The pre-war Dardanelles fortress remained weak, because many of its cannons were obsolete, ammunition was in short supply and because the fortifications themselves were out of date. To help rectify this situation, the Germans sent an admiral, who was an expert in coastal defences, with about 500 German specialists in coast artillery, engineering and naval mines. At the same time Germany sent limited quantities of war *matériel* (including shells and underwater mines) to the Ottoman Empire through the neutral countries of Romania and Bulgaria. On 3 November 1914, ships of the Royal Navy briefly bombarded the forts at the entrance of the straits. This attack achieved nothing of value, and only served to alert the Turks to the vulnerability of the straits. Moreover, the bombardment thoroughly alarmed the high command and provided it with reasons to accelerate its defensive preparations.

Esat Pasha began a vigorous training programme on 8 November that focused on combined-arms training, detailed rehearsals of battle plans and anti-invasion drills. These were lessons he had learned from his experiences in the Balkan Wars. He also began to improve the seaward defences and constructed roads and interior lines of communication. Importantly, the infantry and artillery began to plan the coordination of fire on each of the likely landing beaches. By February 1915, the fortress (including the 9th Division) had 34,500 soldiers and 263 cannon on the peninsula. Esat's III Corps, the mobile reserve which now included only the 7th Infantry Division, had 15,000 soldiers and 50 cannon. However, a new division, the 19th, was hurriedly garrisoned; it came under the command of the young Lieutenant-Colonel Mustafa Kemal.

BRITISH PLANS

A full-blown assault on the Dardanelles was never part of Britain's pre-war strategic thinking; indeed, the best of its army went to France, and the pride of its navy monitored the North Sea. However, as early as August 1914 the British tried (and failed) to coax the Greeks into landing on the peninsula. When war broke out, Britain had no forces in place with which to mount a serious attack on the straits. Things might then have remained as they were, but for the presence of a uniquely dynamic group of aggressive personalities in London.

By chance, fate had brought Winston Churchill to the position of First Lord of the Admiralty in 1911. Churchill was ambitious, headstrong, sometimes reckless and was often possessed with the rightness of his own thinking. Upon the outbreak of war, Churchill in turn brought Admiral John Arbuthnot Fisher (known to all Britain as 'Jacky') out of retirement as his First Sea Lord. Fisher was relentlessly eccentric, prone to exaggerated and hyperbolic statements and possessed of a vivid imagination. He was undeniably brilliant and aggressive to an extreme. Churchill and Fisher often clashed over who ran the navy and its deployments, but both were fighters and took every opportunity to bring the war to the enemy. They were intolerant of inactivity and shared the view that Britain must wield its sea power offensively. In

> 'I do not consider that the Dardanelles can be rushed. They might be forced by extended operations with large numbers of ships.'
>
> Vice Admiral Sir Sackville Carden, January 1915

THE
DARDANELLES

An Admiralty chart of the Dardanelles. One of the most glaring errors of the British Army in the opening stages of the campaign was its failure to provide accurate maps to its troops. The absence of grid lines and comprehensive terrain features on this example highlights the problem.

December 1914, these men ordered British submarines through the straits. At the same time, General Herbert Horatio Kitchener returned to London from Egypt to serve as Secretary of State for War. Kitchener was a genuine British hero, whose main concern was raising the new armies required for sustained continental war. He was more cautious than his naval counterparts, but was a formidable administrator. The Committee of Imperial Defence, led by Prime Minister H.H. Asquith, included Churchill, Fisher and Kitchener, as well as David Lloyd George, Edward Grey and Lord Haldane.

WESTERN FRONT IMPASSE

By December 1914, operations on the Western Front had degenerated into stalemate, while in the east the hard-pressed Russians suffered a great defeat in East Prussia, and began to feel the pinch of isolation. Operations against the Turks, however, had proved thus far to be reassuringly easy. Intelligence reports also continued to pour in about the dismal state of readiness in the Ottoman Army. These were

seemingly reinforced by the comic opera Turkish response to Captain Larkin's raids sailing in HMS *Doris* around the Gulf of Alexandretta. Some in Britain began to question whether the war could be won on either of the main fronts, particularly the Secretary of the War Council, Maurice Hankey, who wrote a memorandum on Boxing Day suggesting that Turkey or Austria might be easily knocked out of the war. As the New Year approached, Churchill, Fisher and even Lloyd George began to advance similar theories, including amphibious operations in the Baltic.

In early January 1915 during the Sarikamis campaign, the Russians asked Britain for help; Kitchener informed them that none was available, and asked Churchill for a naval demonstration off the straits instead. Working relentlessly on a Sunday, Jackie Fisher swung toward this idea, but provocatively changed the 'demonstration' to 'forcing the Dardanelles', advocating an immediate attack using outdated pre-Dreadnought battleships. Churchill opposed the idea initially, as did the admiral commanding the Mediterranean Fleet. This generated much debate in the War Council; the army did not like the idea and instead stressed the importance of the Western Front, but the enthusiastic Churchill (now a convert to the idea) put the concept on the table on 13 January 1915. For the next two weeks, debate raged, and Fisher threw in the brand-new 15in-gunned battleship HMS *Queen Elizabeth* like a poker chip to sway the council. Kitchener and Balfour moved to support the operation and the War Council finally endorsed the scheme on 28 January. Moreover, having defeated the Turks on the Suez Canal, the mass of imperial troops in Egypt now seemed redundant there, and the general staff began preparations to support the fleet with the ANZAC and regulars from home. Britain was now committed to attacking the Dardanelles.

The first naval assault on the straits began on 19 February under the command of Vice Admiral Sackville Carden, who led a polyglot fleet of elderly ships that were not needed in the North Sea. Carden, himself, was a reflection of his ships and was considered by Churchill as 'second rate'. Nevertheless, Carden's staff drew up a three-phased plan to force the straits, central to which was the clearing of the underwater minefields laid in the channel.

THE NAVAL ATTACKS AND THEIR EFFECTS

The fortifications of the Dardanelles consisted of three layers: the outer defences, the intermediate defences and the inner defences. The outer defences comprised two very old forts at Kum Kale on the Asiatic side and two more at Sedd el Bahr (Seddelbahir to the Turks) on the peninsula. These forts had a dozen heavy guns, but were unprotected by minefields. The intermediate defences were positioned inside the straits to protect the interior minefields, and fielded medium and quick-firing guns; their purpose was to prevent enemy minesweeping activities within the straits. The inner defences were very powerful, composed of some 70 heavy coastal guns; however, many were antiquated and ammunition was scarce. After the 3 November bombardment of the outer defences, it was very clear to the Turks that the fortress complex required significant augmentation.

Over the winter, many reinforcements poured into the area. By mid-February 1915, the British were facing a significantly more powerful defensive force. In particular, the 8th Artillery Regiment commanded by the German Colonel Wehrle, equipped with 150mm howitzers, came to the peninsula. The howitzers of this regiment were capable of firing from behind protective terrain and delivering deadly plunging fire on the weakly armoured decks of enemy ships. Wehrle had 32 howitzers that he positioned on both sides of the straits, between the outer and the intermediate defences. The Turks had also been busy over the winter and had laid additional minefields, one of which was located inshore on the Asiatic side and parallel to the coastline (as well as parallel to the direction of the enemy fleet's advance). Nine previously laid belts of mines were positioned perpendicularly across the channel at its narrowest point. The unorthodox parallel line of mines lay directly under the guns of the 8th Artillery Regiment.

Admiral Sir John Fisher was one of the proponents of the naval and subsequent land assault on the Dardanelles. However, the second-class fleet that he sent against the Turks proved inadequate for the task.

On 19 February, Vice Admiral Sir Sackville Carden began the Allied attack, which went on sporadically ('utterly without vigour', according to Churchill) for the next several weeks. Some minesweepers were lost and Carden landed Royal Marines at the Kum Kale and Sedd el Bahr forts, which had been abandoned by the Turks under heavy British fire. The Royal Marines destroyed the guns in these old forts and withdrew. This action alarmed the Turks and only provoked them to work harder in preparing their defences with additional guns.

There were now three cornerstones in the defensive concept. First, groups of mobile howitzers would deliver plunging fire on the fleet entering the straits. This would keep the British from deploying their unarmoured and vulnerable minesweepers ahead of the oncoming fleet. Second, underwater mines and anti-submarine nets were laid in successive belts within the constricted narrows and heavily covered by

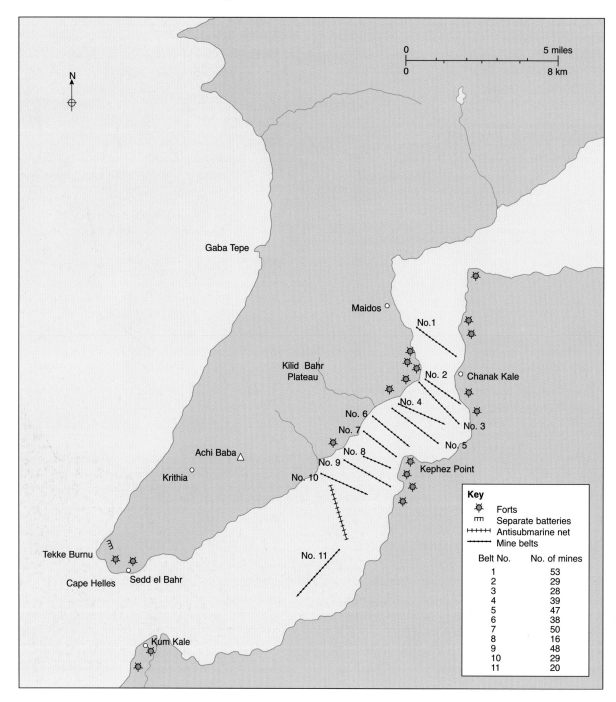

Key
- ☼ Forts
- ⌐ Separate batteries
- +++++ Antisubmarine net
- — — — Mine belts

Belt No.	No. of mines
1	53
2	29
3	28
4	39
5	47
6	38
7	50
8	16
9	48
10	29
11	20

fire. Finally, the inner defences (comprising heavy coastal defence guns) were ready to blast any ships that managed to break through the mine belts. Altogether, the Turks had 82 heavy guns in the fixed defences and an additional 230 guns posted along the shores. Ammunition availability remained a problem for the Turks, but was sufficient to withstand a number of determined attacks. The 150mm howitzers of the 8th Artillery Regiment divided the area between the entrance of the straits and the Narrows into sectors and registered pre-planned fire on the straits.

Carden's last attack took place on the night of 13/14 March 1915, against a thoroughly alert Ottoman defence; it too failed. By this point, he himself was

LEFT **The Dardanelles defences. By March 1915, the defences of the straits comprised over 300 guns and howitzers as well as hundreds of underwater mines. Moreover, two well-trained Ottoman infantry divisions garrisoned the peninsula.**

BELOW **Interior of fort of Sedd el Bahr following the bombardment. The forts at Sedd el Bahr and Kum Kale were exposed to direct naval gunfire and were deceptively easy to knock out. The inner defences proved more difficult to destroy.**

Admiral Sir John Michael de Robeck (1862–1928)

Admiral Sir John Michael de Robeck entered the Navy in 1875 and had reached the rank of rear admiral three years before war broke out. With the declaration of war, de Robeck was given command of a cruiser squadron. After the resignation of Admiral Carden, de Robeck took command of the Allied fleet at the Dardanelles. His vigorous attack of 18 March 1915 on the straits was a disaster and resulted in his recommendation of an amphibious attack on the Gallipoli Peninsula. He survived the Gallipoli campaign with his reputation intact and was promoted to serve with the Grand Fleet. From 1919 to 1920 he served as High Commissioner at Constantinople, and from 1922 to 1924 he was commander of the Atlantic Fleet.

thoroughly demoralized and close to nervous break-down. Two days later he relieved himself of command, which passed to Rear Admiral John de Robeck.

On 18 March, the Allies made a determined attempt to break through the Dardanelles into the Sea of Marmara. De Robeck's combined Anglo-French fleet attempted to force the straits, but unlike the cautious Carden, de Robeck planned to send his battleships directly into the straits to suppress the forts with heavy fire, clearing the way for minesweepers to create lanes through the mine belts through which the larger battleships might then pass. By noon his warships had silenced most of the forts; however, plunging fire from the howitzers of 8th Artillery Regiment remained heavy. Disaster struck around 2pm as the French squadron turned away to allow the

Sir Ian Standish Monteith Hamilton (1853–1947)

Sir Ian Standish Monteith Hamilton was born on Corfu and began his military career in 1873. He served in South Africa, where he was wounded and lost an arm. He was Kitchener's chief of staff during the Boer War. He was commander-in-chief of British forces in the Mediterranean in 1910. Hamilton also commanded forces at home. He was well qualified and a logical choice for command of the expeditionary force assembled in 1915 for the invasion of Gallipoli. In the end, Hamilton's failure made him a scapegoat for the lack of success of the operation and he was recalled on 16 October 1915. Although his active career was over, he was subsequently appointed Lieutenant of the Tower from 1918 to 1920. His testimony before the Gallipoli Commission revealed that the expedition he had commanded was riddled with problems. He published a diary of his experiences in 1920.

minesweepers access to the mine belts. In quick succession the *Bouvet* blew up and the *Gaulois* and *Suffren* were seriously damaged. De Robeck continued his attack, sending in minesweepers and more battleships. Around 4pm HMS *Inflexible* (a modern battlecruiser) and HMS *Irresistible* hit mines, receiving serious damage. *Inflexible* escaped, but when HMS *Ocean* went in to tow *Irresistible* she was also mined. Both of these ships sank during the night. The Turks had ambushed de Robeck by the unorthodox positioning of the parallel minefield. Encouraged by their success, the Turks rushed from their bunkers and returned fire. Reluctantly, de Robeck called off the attack, but was determined to renew it the next day. However, he changed his mind and announced on 22 March that the navy could not carry the straits alone, and that it required the help of the army. Ottoman losses were slight, while the Allies had three battleships sunk and two damaged, and a battlecruiser damaged.

This was a terrific defeat for the Royal Navy and led to even worse unforeseen consequences. Churchill claimed later that the Turks had expended most of their available shells during the day-long battle and that 'one more push' was all that was needed to force the Dardanelles. While the distribution of the remaining shells was a problem with some of the guns, the Turks in fact had enough ammunition left to withstand several attacks of similar scale. Ottoman morale soared when it became apparent that the Allies had quit the attack. In the meantime, the Allies began serious preparations for an amphibious landing intended to seize and hold the Gallipoli Peninsula; the capture of the high ground would dominate the straits and render the Ottoman defences useless.

In mid-February, the War Council agreed to make the ANZAC, then in Egypt, and the last remaining division of the regular army, 29th Division, available for operations in the Aegean. There was much confusion about what was to be done and who would be in command. Shortly thereafter, the Royal Naval Division and a French corps were added to the mix. On 12 March, General Sir Ian Hamilton was summoned to Kitchener's office and was offered command of what would come to be called the

Mediterranean Expeditionary Force (MEF). Hamilton was a hero of the wars in South Africa and had lost the use of one arm as a result of being wounded. He was highly intelligent, well qualified and widely regarded as the right choice for such an operation. Hamilton rushed off to the Aegean, only to find that his army had no accurate intelligence regarding the enemy defences, inaccurate maps, little field artillery and few fully trained soldiers. Indeed, Hamilton's ad hoc force was in every way a military counterpart of de Robeck's piecemeal fleet of cast-off ships.

Ottoman intelligence was keenly aware of the impending Allied operation. Famously, many of the officers of the Royal Naval Division, public school men like the poet Rupert Brooke and Prime Minister Asquith's son Arthur, told their friends to post letters to 'MEF, Constantinople'. On 20 February 1915, Enver Pasha directed the general staff to examine the defensive plans against an amphibious attack of 70,000 men (the Turks were well aware of the forces arrayed against them). The Ottoman staffs were also aware of Allied plans to coordinate a landing on Gallipoli with a Russian Black Sea fleet landing on the Bosporus. This led Enver to move two army corps closer to Constantinople to repel the expected Russian amphibious invasion. Liman von Sanders protested

Lieutenant-Commander E.G. Robinson, Royal Navy lays a charge to destroy a Turkish 4in gun, 26 February 1915: he was awarded the VC for his gallantry. Royal Marines and Royal Navy personnel landed at Sedd el Bahr and Kum Kale to ensure the destruction of the forts. The Turks never reoccupied them during the conduct of the campaign.

Otto Liman von Sanders (1855–1929)

Liman von Sanders was born in Pomerania, and began his military career in 1874 He was unpopular, but rose to the rank of lieutenant-general and divisional commander before being appointed commander of the German Military Mission to the Ottoman Empire in 1913. His portfolio brought a storm of protest from the Entente Powers. Prior to the outbreak of war in August 1914, Liman worked to improve the Turkish Army's fighting capabilities. He was nevertheless highly uncomfortable in finding himself in the dual role of diplomat and soldier. His influence upon Turkish affairs was further notably diminished by his self-evident inclination to pursue German interests at every opportunity. He took command of the First Army in the autumn of 1914, but assumed command of the new Fifth Army in March 1915. He consistently advocated a rational defensive strategy for the empire. In February 1918 Liman von Sanders took command of the Yildirim Army in Palestine. At the armistice he returned to Constantinople to oversee the repatriation of German forces. He was briefly arrested by the British on suspicion of war crimes in February 1919 but released in August, at which point he announced his retirement.

against this deployment: these troops were the closest reserves to the Dardanelles and he felt that they would be needed to assist in fighting off the Allies. However, the Allied attempt of 18 March to force the Dardanelles fully alerted Enver to the danger, and he decided to form a new army, which would be directly responsible for the defence of the southern straits. On 24 March 1915, the new Ottoman Fifth Army was activated and Enver asked General Liman von Sanders

to relinquish command of the First Army and take command (which he did on 25 March). Liman von Sanders left the capital taking Lieutenant-Colonel Kiazim Bey as his chief of staff and his two German aides – captains Muhlmann and Prigge. The recently arrived Field Marshal Freiherr von der Goltz took over the German Military Mission and the First Army, and Liman von Sanders arrived by sea at the port of Gallipoli the next day.

THE OPPOSING FORCES

Hamilton's MEF was a mixed bag of improvised units brought together for the purpose of assaulting the peninsula. It had five divisions and, on paper and in the minds of men like Kitchener and Churchill, was very powerful. In truth, though, it suffered from many deficiencies. The ANZAC was composed of an Australian division and a composite Australian–New Zealand division, and was commanded by Lieutenant-General Sir William Birdwood. Neither division had many regular officers, and over half the men had enlisted the previous summer. The divisions were very short of artillery and machine guns and, more importantly, while garrisoned in Egypt had done no combined-arms training or divisional exercises whatsoever. The men were sometimes undisciplined and resentful of authority, but were enthusiastic and in superb physical condition. The 29th Division, although composed of 11 regular infantry battalions and one Scottish territorial battalion, was put together in March from units brought separately to the UK from India. While the officers and men were sound professionals, likewise this division conducted no collective or combined-arms training prior to embarkation for the Aegean. The Royal Naval Division was composed of sailors for whom there was no room on board ships, and Royal Marines. Its first action of the war, at Antwerp in October 1914, was a disaster and over 2,000 of its members were interned in

The 25 April landings on the Gallipoli Peninsula. Simultaneous landings at five points on the peninsula's tip and in Asia confused the Ottoman tactical commanders as to the exact location of the main effort. This delayed the Ottoman response.

neutral Holland. Many of its junior officers were already well known or affluent young men, including Brooke, Asquith, Johnny Dodge, Patrick Shaw-Stewart, and a soon to be well known New Zealander named Bernard Freyberg. Likewise, the French Corps

Expéditionnaire d'Orient initially was composed of a single division that was cobbled together hastily from Senegalese, Zouave and regular troops. Although it was well led and had powerful artillery, it too had never trained together as a division.

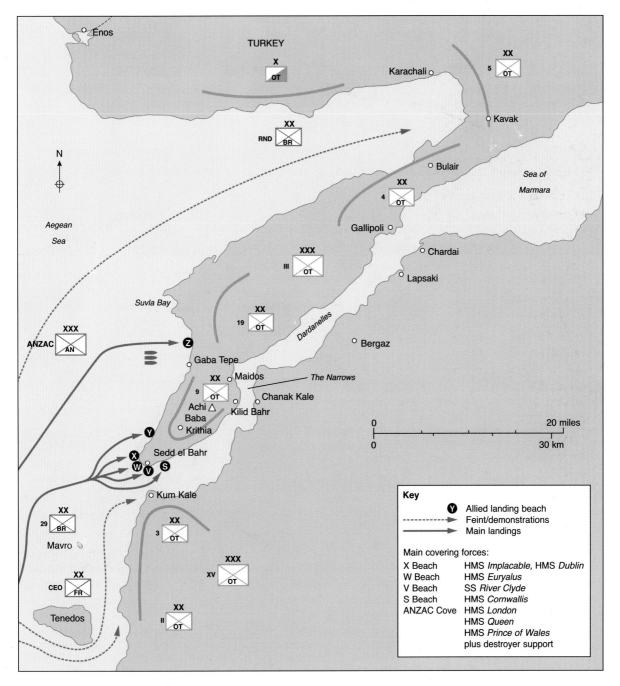

ABOVE **French troops preparing to embark for the Dardanelles from Mudros, Lemnos. The French expeditionary force sent to the Dardanelles was something of an afterthought. It was composed of lashed-together divisions of colonials and Foreign Legion regiments. In spite of this, it fought well.**

RIGHT **Australians en route to Gallipoli. In the era before specialized amphibious landing craft, soldiers had to debark into lighters from a merchantman or warship. The lighters were then towed to the shore by cutters, which were often commanded by teenage midshipmen.**

Nevertheless, the Imperial general staff and the Admiralty began to put its forces together to conduct a joint (involving more than one service) and combined (multi-national) amphibious landing on a strongly held enemy shore (considered by many to be the most complex of all military–naval operations). In less than two months, the British and French staffs organized, loaded and carried over 70,000 soldiers and their horses, artillery and equipment to the harbour of Mudros on the Greek island of Lemnos, located some 80km (50 miles) to the west of the entrance to the Dardanelles. Naturally, mistakes were made, notably in the loading of the merchant ships contracted to carry the MEF: in some instances artillery pieces would be placed in one ship while the ammunition would be in another. All manner of problems had to be planned for, such as building water carriers for 70,000 men, as water was scarce on the peninsula. Naval gunfire support, aerial reconnaissance and assault landing techniques were in their infancy, and tactics and procedures had to be created from scratch. Remarkably, by 24 April 1915, a readied landing force was anchored in Mudros Harbour. This remarkable feat performed by the Allied military and naval staff is a model example of creative staff work, ingenuity and sheer determination, a fact that is often overshadowed by subsequent defeat.

The British Army as a whole in 1914 was unprepared for modern war. Although the overseas deployment of the British Army went well, its immediate performance in combat in France was below that of the German and French armies. As a result, the BEF narrowly escaped disaster several times, and was unable to execute effectively offensive operations. Such success as it enjoyed resulted mainly from the heroic performance of its officers and men at regimental level and below. The British Army's initial performance against the Ottomans in 1914 and early 1915 appeared more positive when it came into contact under locally favourable operational conditions. However, many of the problems that had appeared in France would surface again against the battle-ready units of the Ottoman Army.

The newly formed Ottoman Fifth Army was a powerful force, and had as its main components III Corps, XV Corps, the 5th Infantry Division and an independent cavalry brigade. III Corps was composed of the 7th, 9th, and 19th Infantry divisions, while XV Corps commanded the 3rd and 11th Infantry divisions. The 5th Division and the Cavalry Brigade remained as army reserves, while the Chanak Kale Fortified Area Command (the Dardanelles forts) continued as a separate operational command. Under this arrangement, III Corps defended the Gallipoli Peninsula itself, with the 7th and 9th Infantry divisions watching the beaches and the 19th Division

Turkish sailors from the *Hamidieh*, photographed in 1915. The Ottoman cruiser became famous during the Balkan Wars of 1912–13 as a surface raider. In World War I it operated mainly in the Black Sea.

Mustafa Kemal, or Ataturk (1881–1938)

Kemal was born in Salonika, and was commissioned in 1902. He graduated from the Ottoman War Academy in 1905 and served in important staff positions in the Third Army, where he was swept up in the politics of the Young Turk revolution. He fought the Italians in Libya and served as chief of operations of the Gallipoli Army in 1913. He was a competitor to the CUP leadership and marginalized in 1914 as an attaché in Bulgaria. During the Gallipoli campaign he rapidly rose from division to corps command. He commanded armies in the Caucasus in 1916 and in Palestine in 1917–18. Kemal was the best general produced by the Ottomans in the war. After the war, he led the Turkish nationalists to victory over the Greeks solidifying his reputation as one of the twentieth century's greatest commanders. He was the first president of the Republic of Turkey. Kemal was brilliant, ambitious and committed to the westernization and modernization of his country.

effectiveness of their army. In fact, by the spring of 1915 the divisions of III Corps were very well trained and had achieved high levels of combat effectiveness as indicated by their training programmes, which showed a consistent pattern of tough and realistic battle training. For example, the 9th Infantry Division reported its battalions at war strength on 12 August 1914. Four days later its troops were ordered to occupy coastal observation posts and to prepare defensive positions. Later in October, the division's regiments developed fire plans from Achi Baba (or Alchi Tepe, as the Turks called it) overlooking Cape Helles and from Kavak Tepe overlooking what would become known as Anzac Beach. Beginning in November 1914, the division conducted combined-arms training with artillery and infantry in the reserve area.

Lieutenant-Colonel Mustafa Kemal's subsequently famous 19th Infantry Division was activated on 1 January 1915. However, two of its regiments were sent to join VI Corps, and the division was reorganized on 9 February by adding the 72nd and 77th Infantry regiments. On 6 April 1915, the division was assigned to the new Fifth Army. Several of the regiments were composed of 'Arabs', and this made portions of the 19th Division unsteady. Kemal's 57th Infantry Regiment was activated on 1 February 1915 and comprised experienced ethnic Turks led by highly trained officers; it was regarded by Mustafa Kemal as his most solid regiment. The regiment spent the next two months in 'very intensive training undergoing frequent field exercises'. The 77th Infantry Regiment was mobilized in Aleppo, Syria, and in September it was assigned to the Second Army and began intensive field training and manoeuvres. It came under Lieutenant-Colonel Mustafa Kemal's command in February 1915, and was provided with intelligence that the British would attempt to land during the hours of darkness.

A torpedo crew on board the *Muavenet* in 1915. The *Muavenet* was a typical Dreadnought-era torpedo boat destroyer. The Ottoman Navy rarely used this type of ship beyond the confines of the Black Sea. *Muavenet* sank the pre-Dreadnought battleship HMS *Goliath* on 13 May 1915.

held in corps reserve near Eceabat. XV Corps held the Asiatic coast, with the 3rd and 11th Infantry divisions defending the vulnerable flat beaches. XV Corps' headquarters was located at Calvert's Farm near Ciplak, the site of Heinrich Schliemann's archaeological excavation of ancient Troy. In the north, the 5th Division guarded the critical and narrow isthmus, and the independent Cavalry Brigade screened the long beaches of the Gulf of Saros. Liman von Sanders's Fifth Army headquarters was based in the town of Gallipoli.

A case can be made that the Ottoman Army at Gallipoli was not as efficient as the German or British armies, but the efficiency of the Turks belied the

Other regiments had similar experiences to those of the 9th and 19th Infantry Divisions. The 7th Division mobilized at war establishment and moved to Gallipoli in early November, where it continued field exercises and manoeuvres. The experience of the 11th Division reflected a pattern typical of Ottoman divisions. It reached war strength on 8 August 1914, and began to deploy the following week. On 8 October the division started its training regime near Bandirma. This included very intensive battalion and regiment training, division and corps manoeuvres, hard road marches and (unusually) the on and off loading of ships. On 14 October, the division participated in First Army field manoeuvres. Training went on throughout the winter, and by 3 March 1915 the division was conducting frequent night march training. Twenty days later the division was deployed to positions near Calvert's Farm where it was informed that 80,000 Allied troops (including 50,000 Australians) were expected to invade Gallipoli. Thus by April 1915, the fighting formations of the newly formed Ottoman Fifth Army were ready to receive the Allies.

In the weeks following the 18 March attack, Liman von Sanders worked tirelessly to improve the tactical situation in his new army area. He concentrated on realistic preparations that were within Turkish capabilities, such as improving the road network, camouflaging troop concentrations and artillery batteries, and improving the fortifications along the likely landing beaches. He commandeered tools and barbed-wire fences from the local farmers in order to fortify even more areas. He worked to improve the existing hospital situation and in between the gruelling periods of building fortifications, at night, and in inclement weather, the troops were subjected to anti-invasion drills. Although ammunition for some of the larger calibres of artillery was in short supply, morale in the Fifth Army was high.

British troops en route to the Dardanelles. The British and ANZAC forces were deployed to Mudros harbour several weeks before the invasion of 25 April 1915. The enlisted men remained on board ship while the officers toured the island of Lemnos.

In 1912, the Ottoman general staff identified three vulnerable areas on the peninsula: the isthmus of Bulair and the Gulf of Saros, the coast of Asia near Kum Kale, and the southern part of the Gallipoli Peninsula. The Fifth Army was organized into three operational groups corresponding to these areas. Colonel von Sodenstern with 5th Division and the independent Cavalry Brigade was assigned the Gulf of Saros sector. Colonel Weber was given XV Corps to defend the Asiatic shore. The critical Gallipoli Peninsula itself remained under the operational command of Major-General Esat Pasha's III Corps.

Esat deployed the 7th Division along the vulnerable isthmus of Bulair, 9th Division along the southern tip of the peninsula and maintained the new, but well trained, 19th Division as a reserve.

At the strategic level, the Fifth Army knew that the Allies had embarked and were about to launch a large multi-divisional Anglo-French expeditionary force somewhere either in European Thrace or in the Asian Troad. However, it did not know exactly where the main effort would be, and the dispositions of the Fifth Army reflected this weakness in intelligence at the operational level. Nevertheless by mid- to late April 1915, an almost continuous series of alarms and invasion scares had raised Turkish troop readiness to a very high level.

Tactically, as in 1912, the Fifth Army employed a light infantry screen in outposts sited on the dominating terrain overlooking potential landing beaches. These forces were usually in platoon strength and were well dug in behind wire in prepared trenches. The Turks did not intend to stop the Allies on the beaches with these troops. Instead, regiment-sized forces were positioned three to five kilometres (three miles) behind the beaches in protected ground. As the outposts slowed the enemy landing and channelled their advance, these larger forces would counterattack the enemy. It was hoped that these counterattacks, conducted immediately or as soon as possible, would throw the unwary invaders back into the sea. At all levels the Turkish commanders rehearsed these counterattacks in detail.

Hamilton's final plan likewise consisted of three components mirroring the vulnerable areas. Recognizing that he had lost the element of surprise, Hamilton planned to land at multiple locations and conduct feints as diversions. In this way, the Turks would be uncertain of his intentions and unable to respond coherently. Hamilton's main effort employed Birdwood's ANZAC landing mid-peninsula to seize the high Maltepe plateau overlooking Eceabat (Maidos). This would cut the peninsula in half and

isolate the western coastal forts. Major-General Aylmer Hunter-Weston's 29th Division was assigned to land on the very tip of the peninsula. At the same time, the French were to land in force at Kum Kale, divert the enemy, and then withdraw several days later, having tied down enemy reserves. To the north, in the Gulf of Saros, the Royal Naval Division was to conduct a very visible demonstration to convince the Turks that Hamilton intended to land there as well. Although this plan dispersed Hamilton's army, the Allies believed that at the 'man-to-man level' Europeans would easily beat the Turks.

THE 25 APRIL LANDINGS AT ANZAC BEACH

The long-awaited landings began early on 25 April 1915, as Hamilton's soldiers landed at six points on the peninsula and across the straits at Kum Kale. The alert Turks defending the beaches immediately sent word up the chain of command to Liman von Sanders,

Both sides made use of submarines in the Gallipoli campaign. Despite the formidable defences of the straits several Allied submarines managed to break through and reach the Sea of Marmara, notably *E11* and *E14* of the Royal Navy, causing havoc to Turkish shipping there.

describing large landings well supported by intense naval gunfire. In the Gulf of Saros, Fifth Army reported what appeared to be an impending landing there (although this was a deception operation).

Men from the Ottoman 27th Infantry Regiment defended what the Allies called Z Beach, or Anzac Beach as it came to be known, in well dug-in and recently improved positions. Their commander was Major Halis, who had taken command of the battalion in September 1914. Halis was a combat veteran of the Libyan War and the Balkan Wars, and had established his command post in the Gaba Tepe strongpoint. Two battalions of the regiment, under the personal command of Lieutenant-Colonel Mehmet Shefik, lay several kilometres behind in the 9th Division's reserve area. His attached artillery and cavalry had been under his command for almost nine months. Just to the north, in army reserve, lay Mustafa Kemal's 19th

The ANZAC beachhead, 25 April 1915. The planned landing at Z Beach would have brought the ANZAC troops on to a beach more heavily defended than V Beach. It is debatable whether the corps would have managed to get ashore in the face of such a strong defence.

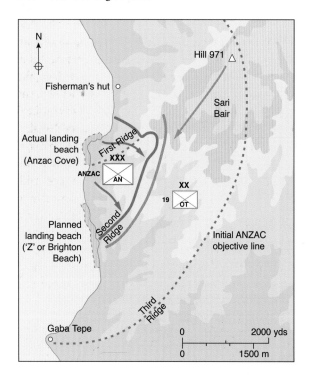

Division. These units had been alerted to the acute danger of an imminent Allied invasion, and since late February there had been continuous coordination between the regiment and Mustafa Kemal's division.

The Turks considered the most likely landing beach to be just north of Gaba Tepe (the area later known by the Australians as Brighton Beach). In fact, it was here that the Australians intended to storm ashore, but a misjudged landing instead cast them ashore in the narrow shelf-like cove at Ari Burnu. The long-standing British view is that this was a serious error, which upset the landings. However, had the Anzacs landed in the designated site, they would have found themselves immediately under the guns of the enemy (and in similarly dire circumstances to the troops on W and V beaches at Cape Helles).

Despite Allied attempts to remain unseen and unheard, 9th Division was alerted at 2.30am that the British were preparing to land. This news sped up the Turkish chain of command and 50 minutes later III Corps notified the Fifth Army that landings were imminent. By 4.30am rifle and artillery fire was engaging the incoming boats. The Australians began to land about 5am, and their location was immediately passed up to III Corps' headquarters. Although his soldiers were tired from night training, Lieutenant-Colonel Shefik immediately ordered his infantry and artillery to begin operations. Based on Shefik's reports, at around 6am the division commander, Colonel Halil Sami, issued orders to drive the enemy into the sea and relayed copies to III Corps and also to Kemal's 19th Division.

Some of the first troops ashore were from the Australian 3rd Brigade, and they quickly found that their maps were inaccurate. Nevertheless, they had landed in a spot protected from direct Turkish fire and, led by their officers, they pressed uphill to the east into the deeply cut terrain. Consolidated resistance began to be felt at about 9am as they met the Turks, who took positions above them. Conscious of growing enemy forces on the right flank, Brigadier Sinclair MacLagan, the senior man in the beachhead, brought the follow-on elements of his division into this area, changing the focal point of the attack. Because of the

difficult terrain, he also directed his soldiers to leave their packs and spades on the beach.

By 8am Shefik's two battalions, as well as his artillery, were moving along parallel routes toward Kavak Tepe, more or less in the centre of the Anzac beachhead. These were not the only Turkish forces preparing to engage the Australians. Earlier, at 5.30am, Mustafa Kemal alerted his 19th Division to prepare for action and ordered his cavalry forward to conduct route reconnaissance of the roads to Kocachimen Tepe (north of Kavak Tepe). By 7am, although he had received no orders, the impatient Kemal sent his 57th Infantry Regiment with artillery to Kocachimen Tepe. He then sent a situation report to III Corps outlining his intentions, and his troops began their march within the hour.

There were now two separate forces moving against the Anzacs. The 9th Division commander reacted quickly, and issued new orders at 8.25am to Shefik that revised and clarified the chain of command. These orders alerted him that Kemal's 57th Infantry Regiment was operating at Kocachimen and ordered him to coordinate his operations with Kemal in the Kavak Tepe area. About 9am, Shefik's leading elements were nearing Kavak Tepe and met the men of his 2nd Battalion who were conducting a fighting retreat up from the beaches. They brought with them captured enemy soldiers of the '3rd Australian'. At 10.30am, the 27th Infantry Regiment was firmly in contact with the enemy; however, Shefik's planned attack was now held up by the orders to coordinate with Mustafa Kemal.

Meanwhile, Mustafa Kemal had reached Conkbayri and prepared a short attack order specifying that two battalions (of the 57th Infantry) would attack, with the other held in reserve. Shefik's plan was brought to him at 11am, to which he wrote a reply outlining his own plan, thus effectively achieving tactical coordination; copies of these orders were sent to III Corps. The essence of Kemal's plan was that he would attack the enemy's left wing with his regiment and

The Australian infantry earned a reputation for independence and resistance to military discipline. The men were all volunteers and man for man were physically the most impressive force fielded in the Middle East.

ABOVE **The Australian beachhead at Gaba Tepe. This photo dramatically illustrates the narrowness of the tiny beach at Anzac Cove. It was not the intended landing spot, but it was protected from direct Turkish observation and fire.**

LEFT **Anzac Beach. The ANZAC perimeter was packed full of men, animals, supplies, ammunition and water containers. Turkish artillery rounds fired into the perimeter invariably hit something in the densely packed beachhead.**

artillery, but would wait to begin the attack until Shefik's regiment attacked. Shefik replied directly to Kemal half an hour later outlining the scope of the enemy's dispositions and stating his intent to attack toward Ari Burnu on the coast. Final orders were issued at noon, and Shefik weighted his right flank, which lay nearest to Kemal's regiment.

Sometime between noon and 1pm, Shefik's skirmishers went forward, followed by waves of infantry with bayonets fixed, at the same time that

Kemal's men advanced. They were supported by three batteries of artillery; Kemal also took the time to order his 77th Infantry Regiment forward to reinforce the left flank of Shefik's regiment, and his remaining 72nd Infantry Regiment to reinforce his own right flank. This attack rocked the Australians and brought their advance to a halt. Their subsequent staunch resistance stopped the determined but badly outnumbered Turkish assault – four Turkish battalions were attacking over eight Australian ones.

Although the Turks had delayed their counterattack by several hours from its optimum time of around 10am, they achieved considerable advantages by waiting until coordination was complete. Neither Shefik nor Kemal launched reckless, premature and unsupported attacks; instead, they executed a combined attack fully supported by artillery and machine guns. By releasing control of Shefik's regiment to Mustafa Kemal, Colonel Halil Sami had effectively and informally cross-attached what might be termed a regimental combat team to the 19th Division, thus ensuring that the senior man on the spot enjoyed unity of command. Descriptions of the severity of the Turkish attack speak of highly effective Turkish shrapnel fire and sniping. The continuous shelling and the subsequent Turkish bayonet attack initiated a disintegration of morale and effectiveness among the Anzacs, which would gather momentum as the day passed. As early as 1pm, messages began to arrive at Australian headquarters declaring that its men could not stand against the Turks without artillery support.

By 3.30pm two battalions of the 77th Infantry Regiment were in position, and Kemal launched a second powerful counterattack in concert with the five battalions in contact. This attack was supported by artillery fire from the area now known as Kemalyeri (Kemal's Place). An hour later, the three battalions of the 72nd Infantry Regiment, now in position, also attacked. Kemal now had 10 battalions in action against the Allies' 18. Fortunately for him, the Allied battalions were poorly deployed against the Turks. This was a result of MacLagan's aggressive push inland toward the sound of the guns rather than towards the

high ground. As a result, the Australians were weak at the point of Mustafa Kemal's attack. Moreover, MacLagan's decision to leave packs and shovels on the beach meant his men were now unable to dig in.

Meanwhile, at Esat Pasha's III Corps field headquarters on Maltepe it was apparent that it was necessary to revise the command arrangements to reflect the on-the-ground realities of the battle. From a purely technical perspective, Mustafa Kemal was fighting in the 9th Division's sector. Reacting swiftly to reorganize his corps, Esat designated Kemal as the Ari Burnu Front commander and attached the 27th Infantry Regiment to him. In effect, this transferred the coastline sector from 9th Division to Kemal's 19th Division. Esat now had Mustafa Kemal focused on the Anzacs at Ari Burnu and Halil Sami focused on the British at Cape Helles.

Six VCs before Breakfast

One of the most memorable displays of heroism in the war occurred as the men of the 1st Battalion, Lancashire Fusiliers came ashore at W Beach on 25 April 1915. The battalion was a regular army unit from the town of Bury and had served in India before the war. Deadly fire poured into the boats carrying the battalion onto the heavily wired beach. Once ashore, the men had to fight their way through heavy Turkish fire and scale a cliff to take the defenders' positions. Despite naval gunfire support from HMS *Euryalus* and *Implacable*, the fusiliers were pinned on the beach and the fighting resolved itself into a soldiers' battle. After a bitter day-long struggle, the battalion finally broke through to seize the cliff-like enemy positions on Hill 138. At day's end, out of over a thousand men, the Lancashire Fusiliers reported 11 officers and 399 men fit for duty. The Victoria Cross was awarded to Captain C. Bromley, Captain R.R. Willis, Sergeant A. Richards, Lance-Sergeant F.E. Stubbs, Corporal J.E. Grimshaw and Private W. Keneally.

The landings at Cape Helles encountered strong Turkish resistance. Here British soldiers watch from cover as a shell from 'Asiatic Annie', one of the Turkish guns from across the Dardanelles Straits, explodes in the sea.

The Turks had their share of coordination problems. Nevertheless, as darkness fell on the battlefield, it was the Australians who were notably demoralized. Mustafa Kemal now issued his famous order: 'I do not expect you to attack, I order you to die! In the time which passes until we die, other troops and commanders can take our place!' It was inspired and heroic leadership, and the final result of the battle probably rested on this single dramatic action. Encouraged by his success in pushing the enemy back during the afternoon, Kemal ordered his regiments to continue with night bayonet assaults. These attacks were unsuccessful, but served to keep pressure on the embattled Australians and New Zealanders. Remarkably, and despite having landed 20,000 out of 24,000 troops, both ANZAC division commanders

The Cape Helles beachhead and breakout, 25–28 April 1915. Ottoman resistance solidified as reinforcements arrived on the peninsula. Within days of the landings trench warfare asserted itself in the Mediterranean.

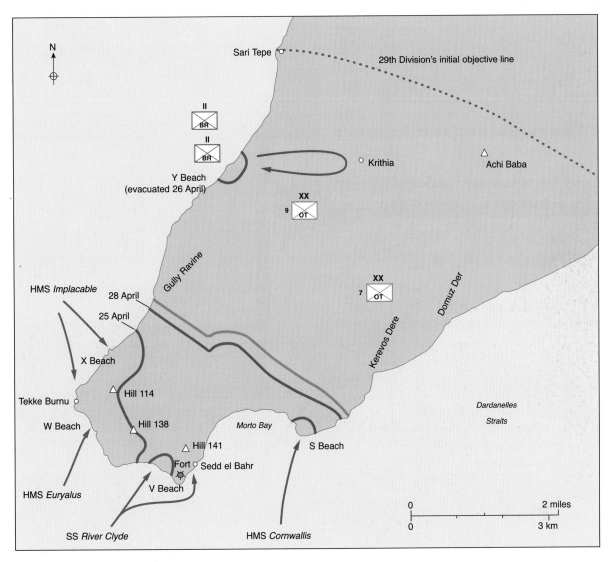

(Major-General W.T. Bridges and Major-General Sir Alexander Godley) became convinced that the Turks had the advantage and would overrun the corps at daybreak. Near midnight, they shocked Birdwood with a joint recommendation to evacuate the beachhead. Birdwood referred the decision to Hamilton, who issued no orders but famously advised the Anzacs to stay put and 'dig, dig, dig'. In truth, Hamilton did not set foot on dry ground that day (and nor did Birdwood until 10pm), instead relying on 'the man on the spot' to make tactical decisions. This pattern of disconnected leadership between the front and the high command would reappear later in the

The Cape Helles beachhead. In this image a lighter designed to ferry animals from ship to shore is shown in the lower portion of the photo. Most of the animals brought ashore were shot during the evacuation rather than attempting to bring them off.

campaign. Kemal would later note that the 57th Infantry Regiment was 'a famous regiment … because it was completely wiped out'.

THE 25 APRIL LANDINGS AT CAPE HELLES

The battles that raged on the southern tip of the Gallipoli Pensinula on 25 April 1915 were dramatically different to those at Anzac Beach, chiefly because they were fought mostly on the landing beaches themselves. The fighting revolved around the desperate struggle to get off the landing beaches and onto the high ground beyond.

The Ottoman defence of Cape Helles (or Sedd el Bahr to the Turks) was the responsibility of the 26th Infantry Regiment, which had occupied the area since August 1914. Troops of the regiment came under fire during the Allied naval attacks in February and March and, although bloodied, morale within the battalions

The Allied beachheads became huge logistical bases as the campaign progressed. Most of these stores at Cape Helles were destroyed during the evacuation rather than allowing them to fall into the hands of the Turks.

remained very high. As Ottoman reinforcements poured into the area in March and April, the 9th Division commander was able to place the entire regiment in the Cape Helles beach defences, and on the eve of the Allied invasion, it had been fully trained and was fully manned.

The regiment commander, Major Kadri, finalized the coordination of the defence and rapidly issued orders that would take effect on 24 April. Kadri's regimental order described in detail the occupation of the defensive works by his men and paid close attention to artillery support. As configured on the morning of 25 April, Kadri deployed a battalion in the Sedd el Bahr defences and another in the Kum Tepe defences. In the centre, he maintained three companies of his third battalion in regimental reserve, while positioning his last company on the western coast (thus linking the Sedd el Bahr and Kum Tepe

positions). Kadri's regimental command post and his regimental reserve lay in the village of Kirte (Krithia). Most of his artillery was positioned on the eastern slopes of the peninsula where it was partially protected from Allied naval gunfire, but the observers remained on the Achi Baba high ground. The division artillery was firmly connected to the troops and could call on additional fire support from the fortresses on the straits. Behind Kadri, the entire 25th Infantry Regiment waited in general reserve.

The fighting at Anzac Beach on 25 April comprised an intial engagement of forces followed by hasty Ottoman attacks, but the fighting at Cape Helles was characterized by direct British assaults on an enemy strongpoint system. It was more like the fighting then raging in France and, consequently, was far more violent and resulted in far more British casualties – as well as a large number of Victoria Crosses awarded for acts of gallantry. The British threw almost the entire strength of the regular 29th Division at the very tip of the Gallipoli Peninsula, with the objective of driving northwards to seize the high ground of Achi Baba (Alchi Tepe). Against this was Major Mahmut Sabri's single 3rd Battalion, 26th Infantry. This battalion had two companies in strongpoints (fortified with wire and trenches) on the low hills overlooking the landing beaches. Reserve platoons were positioned behind the hills. Mahmut Sabri's command post, two infantry companies, and his attached engineer company lay about a kilometre inland and he had an artillery battery southwest of Krithia for direct fire support.

FIVE LANDING SITES

The 29th Division was assigned five landing sites, designated as S, V, W, X and Y beaches, but its commanders were far from optimistic that the division would be able to take the high ground of Achi Baba. To assist in the assault, Royal Navy battleships lay close in to shore to provide fire support with their heavy 12in and 15in guns. The night of 24/25 April was quiet and moonlit, and in spite of the light breeze and waves, the Turkish sentries could hear enemy ships. At 4.30am the British naval bombardment began from three directions, fully alerting the Turkish defenders. About 6am the Turks observed over 40 boats in lines heading for W Beach and opened fire at 400m (437 yards) on the Lancashire Fusiliers. At the same time in nearby Sedd el Bahr (V Beach), the Turks, to their great amazement, watched a steamship (the converted collier *River Clyde*) heading inshore amidst the mass of smaller boats. Again, at 400m (437 yards) they engaged the enemy. Heavy fire kept the boats at bay, but the steamship continued on until it grounded out in the surf, at which point it became apparent to the Turks that it contained hundreds of enemy soldiers as well as numerous machine guns. The ship immediately became a magnet for heavy Turkish rifle and machine-gun fire.

The *River Clyde* was crammed full of Munster Fusiliers and men of the Hampshire Regiment, who were supposed to clamber over towed wooden lighters onto the shore. However, the lighters became lodged in the rocks and were taken under heavy fire. Commander Edward Unwin and Able Seaman Williams of the Royal Navy tried to salvage the situation, leaping into the surf to lash the lighters into a bridge. Both were awarded the Victoria Cross, Williams posthumously. The Fusiliers tried to run across, but were slaughtered by enemy fire. Some jumped into the sea and were carried to the bottom by their heavy packs. Out of communication with the battleships only 1500m (1640 yards) away, the *River Clyde* became a death trap. Mahmut Sabri judged that the *River Clyde* was a 'bankrupt operation', but felt that its presence confirmed that Sedd el Bahr was the enemy's main effort. He ordered his reserves forward.

Simultaneously, the British landed at S, W, X and Y beaches, the aim being to confuse the Turks, causing them to disperse and expose their reserves. At W Beach the Lancashires were able to land, but were immediately pinned down in the Ottoman wire. In conditions similar to the Western Front, the men struggled forward to reach the high plateau ahead of them. The battalion suffered 533 casualties (out of a total of 950) that day, but famously won 'six VCs before breakfast' as well as five lesser medals for heroism. The landings at S, X and Y beaches suffered fewer casualties because the Turks had not heavily fortified them. While it had been stopped at the tip of the peninsula, the 29th Division had troops on shore in flanking positions by mid-morning.

The battles for V and W beaches were bloody in the extreme. These actions brought the British main effort directly into the teeth of well prepared defences manned by fully trained men. Handfuls of Turks in strongpoints on the high ground held entire battalions of British on the beaches for most of the day. The conservatism of the British command and control ethos now came to the aid of the Turks. Exhibiting behaviour similar to that of Birdwood and Hamilton, Major-General Hunter-Weston was reluctant to over-supervise his subordinates and, more importantly, became fixated on W and X beaches, where the fighting raged heaviest. This institutional trait caused Hunter-Weston to miss a golden opportunity to exploit the favorable situation at Y Beach by ordering the troops there, the King's Own Scottish Borderers and a Royal Marine battalion, to drive on Krithia. Hamilton also failed to do this, and the men on Y Beach sat there throughout the day.

As the day progressed Hunter-Weston managed to bring in more boats loaded with troops to V Beach, and by mid-afternoon Irishmen were struggling uphill. The situation on the tip of peninsula grew steadily worse for the Turks. At 3pm, Mahmut Sabri reported that he had committed his entire command and that the situation on Ay Tepe was in doubt. At 5.40pm Ay Tepe strongpoint fell and the adjacent strongpoint on Gozcubaba Tepe came under direct attack. With all of the Turkish officers down, the defence fell to Sergeant Yahya, who found himself with five squads of infantry, and his position under assault by a large column of enemy infantry. He beat back several determined attacks on his hilltop position and personally led a bayonet attack that restored the situation. He survived to tell the story and his name is inscribed on a contemporary memorial at the site. Nonetheless, Yahya was pushed off Gozcubaba Tepe position that evening when the British were able to bring to bear heavy enfilading machine-gun fire on the hills. Written and telephone reports poured into 9th Divison's headquarters, and Colonel Halil Sami belatedly issued orders sending the remaining two battalions and the machine-gun detachment of 25th Infantry Regiment to Sedd el Bahr to close off the enemy landings by nightfall.

It is clear that Colonel Halil Sami was unsure exactly where the Allied main effort was, and

The fighting on the Gallipoli peninsula was never characterized by the intense artillery bombardments of the Western Front. Nevertheless, the armies constructed bomb proofs and bunkers to avoid casualties from indirect fire.

consequently felt compelled to disperse his scarce reserves to cover all of the landing beaches – a clear tactical success for the British multiple-landing plan. Halil Sami's apparent lack of situational awareness contrasts significantly with that of Mustafa Kemal, who realized that the ANZAC had conducted a single massive landing at Ari Burnu. Halil Sami had also previously detached 27th Infantry Regiment to Mustafa Kemal (about one third of his combat power), leaving 9th Division with only two infantry regiments to oppose the Cape Helles landings.

At 1am on 26 April the Turks crafted a plan to retake the lost high ground of Ay Tepe using fresh troops, which began about 3.30am. A night bayonet attack was met by a wall of British rifle fire and grenades that hit the advancing Turkish infantry. The battle seesawed back and forth; some parts of the British trenches were taken, but the attack collapsed. Similar night bayonet atacks simultaneously hit the British on Y Beach. The difficult first 24 hours of the battle then ended with the British lodged in their precarious beachheads.

ABOVE **Many of the opposing trenches, particularly at Anzac Beach, were as close as 20m (65ft) apart. Homemade periscopes fabricated from shaving mirrors were often used to avoid the risk of being shot in the head.**

RIGHT **The Australian troops earned their infamous nickname of 'Diggers' at Gallipoli when General Sir Ian Hamilton famously advised the Australian commanders to 'dig, dig, and dig'.**

Across the straits the French intended to land the 6th Colonial Regiment at Kum Kale early, but strong four-knot currents thwarted them until about 9.30am. Resistance was weak and they came ashore with few losses. The operation was, however, a diversionary one, and the French had no intention of either advancing inland or remaining on shore.

NAVAL DIVERSION

To the north, in Saros Bay, ships of the Royal Navy began bombarding the Turks at Bulair while almost the entire Royal Naval Division cruised off the coast. Hamilton did not intend to actually land the division, but a platoon was supposed to go ashore and light flares as a ruse. However, because of the danger, the officer in charge – Lieutenant Bernard Freyberg (a swimming champion from New Zealand) – swam alone to the shore with his flares and a revolver in a waterproof bag. Freyberg found only dummy positions, lit his flares and swam back in the frigid water. Freyberg spent hours alone in the water in darkness, an astonishing feat that earned him a DSO.

The demonstration at Bulair, using only ships and a few flares, was unconvincing at best, but Liman von Sanders personally rode to the threatened isthmus to gauge for himself the strength of the Allied effort. Later in the day, he consulted with Esat Pasha and became convinced that the Allied presence in the Gulf of Saros was merely a diversion. Liman von Sanders also endorsed Esat's contention that the Anzacs represented the gravest threat to the peninsula. He ordered the 7th Division to prepare to move south in response to Esat's plea for reinforcements. Additionally, he ordered the 5th Division to send troops south as well. Incoming reports from the Asian side of the straits indicated that the situation there was under control.

At dusk on 25 April, the tactical situation appeared threatening, but favourable to the Ottomans. The Allied landings had been contained to a handful of

Esat Pasha, commander of Ottoman III Corps, is shown talking to his troops in a well-camouflaged artillery position. Grandfatherly in appearance, Esat was arguably the finest Ottoman corps commander of the war.

small beachheads and the Turks held commanding positions over them. Reserves were deploying to reinforce the thin defensive lines holding the invaders. Although the Turks did not know it, not a single Allied objective had been reached.

THE FIRST WEEK ON THE PENINSULA

The next morning, even more convinced that he had correctly anticipated the Allied assaults, Liman von Sanders sent the regiments of the 5th and 7th divisions to the Sedd el Bahr front, and ordered an uncommitted regiment from the 11th Division in Asia to be brought to the Anzac beachhead. The reinforcements sent earlier were now on hand and were immediately pressed into the fight by Esat Pasha. In Asia, the situation had stabilized, with German Lieutenant-Colonel August Nicolai's 3rd Infantry Division inflicting heavy losses on the French, who withdrew on 29 April.

On 26 April Fifth Army sent an encrypted telegram to Enver Pasha at the Ministry of War outlining its intent to attack the enemy beachheads in the coming days. This telegram reflected Liman von Sanders's most important contribution to the decisive defeat inflicted on Hamilton's landing force. The Fifth Army commander had personally evaluated the diversionary operation at Saros Bay, and was not deceived by the manoeuvre. With this understanding clear in his mind he was able to commit his army entirely to the fighting at Anzac Beach and Cape Helles. In doing so, he stripped away the defenders from the Bulair isthmus and from the French front (itself a diversion) in Asia.

This decision indicates an unusually high degree of situational awareness at army level (by 1915 standards) and reflected the capability of Turkish units to transmit accurate and timely information. Overall, the Turks characterized 26 April as a quiet day, and that evening Kemal directed his formations to make preparations for renewing the attack and also to carefully coordinate their defences with flanking units. At higher levels, more reinforcements (in the shape of the Fifth Army units of XV Corps) were on the way by ferry to Maidos from Asia.

Kemal's attacks began on 27 April at 7.30am with determined bayonet assaults that spread panic in the Allied lines. These were repulsed, but the Turks attacked again later with reinforcements. Throughout the day further fitful attacks materialized, but the Turks were unable to synchronize their operations. Casualties began to mount and by 6.30pm losses amounted to between 30 and 40 per cent. At this point, Mustafa Kemal decided to call off the attacks and prepare for a night assault, which would mitigate the effects of Allied naval gunfire. He was also, by now, aware of the severe collapse of morale suffered by the Australians and New Zealanders on the previous night, and he hoped to capitalize on this with a force that now numbered 15 infantry battalions (organized into two tactical groups) and nine batteries of artillery.

The night attack began a little after 9pm, as Kemal's two-regiment northern group swept forward into the enemy's trenches. Intense fighting at close quarters ensued, but heavy Anzac fire drove the Turks back. Shortly thereafter, his southern group, comprising four regiments, launched its attack. Kemal committed every available man to this, leaving no reserve. Again the Turks broke into the enemy trenches, but the attacking regiments, exhausted and depleted from two days of combat, could not break through. Moreover, Turkish soldiers from various regiments became mixed up in the confusion of darkness. The night attack then degenerated into a series of small actions, and eventually collapsed. The tempo of battle slowed on the following day as each side sought to consolidate gains and stabilize their lines. The ANZAC had grown to 21 infantry battalions and now outnumbered the Turks in the battle area. Another regiment arrived, and Enver Pasha promised that Ottoman forces held in general reserve near Constantinople would soon be on the way to the front. Encouraged by this development, the Fifth Army ordered the renewal of the attack and ordered the remainder of 5th Division south to join the fight at Anzac Beach.

Mustafa Kemal now planned a decisive attack to drive the invaders into the sea. He decided to launch a three-pronged assault, supported by an artillery preparation, with his main effort in the centre. To accommodate this he organized a Right-Wing Column (of seven battalions from four regiments), a Centre Column (of the six battalions of the fresh 14th and 15th Infantry regiments) and a Left-Wing Column (of six battalions from four regiments). Kemal's artillery spent most of the day of 30 April repositioning their guns to support the attack. Essentially, Mustafa Kemal was launching a divisional-scale main attack of fresh men, supported by two simultaneous divisional-scale supplementary attacks, and he planned to throw over 18,000 men into the fight. The divisional orders reached the company officers in the frontline trenches in the early evening hours. He reckoned that morale among the Australians was almost broken, and that once his men broke into the enemy trenches his opponents would collapse. He was also convinced that his artillery would have an especially demoralizing effect. There were some lingering concerns over the reliability of the Arab soldiers of the 77th Infantry Regiment, but Kemal kept these troops on the right flank where a failure would not endanger the decisive main attack. That night the troops rested in anticipation of the events of the coming day.

At 5am on 1 May 1915, the Turkish artillery began to fire on the enemy trenches. Fifteen minutes later the centre and left columns went over the top on time, but the right column was somewhat delayed. The distance between the trenches (no man's land) was about 200m (219 yards) in the critical centre sector, and, unfortunately for the Turks, it was open ground. They were met by a wall of fire, suffering huge casualties, but small groups managed to reach the Australian lines, where hand-to-hand fighting using bayonets

These well equipped and fresh-looking Ottoman soldiers are probably reinforcements coming to the Gallipoli front from the Constantinople area. They are gathered in an assembly area and are awaiting orders.

and knives broke out. The Turkish attacks faltered and ground to a halt in the face of fierce resistance. Kemal committed his reserves at 10.30am in the centre. However, by noon all of his column commanders reported that the massive attack had failed, although some ground had been gained on the left flank and at certain points along the front a mere 10m (11 yards) separated the two armies. The fire of the Turkish artillery had died away to nothing because of ammunition shortages. Kemal was discouraged and was tempted to call off his offensive. But, in the early afternoon, he was cheered by an intercepted Australian radio transmission indicating that their tactical situation was critical. Kemal began immediate preparations for a night assault.

Kemal's attack was timed to begin at midnight, but unfortunately for the Turks, the Anzacs were alert and observing their fronts. Again, the Turks ran into a withering barrage of machine-gun and rifle fire. By 3am Kemal acknowledged failure and called off the attacks. The Allies estimated that as many as 10,000 Turks were killed, while the Turkish official history admits to 6000. The attacking regiments were shattered and with this battle the first phase of fighting at Anzac Beach ended.

At the southern tip of the peninsula, on the morning of 26 April, the 29th Division had its infantry ashore and was preparing to bring in its artillery. Some of the infantry battalions had suffered terrible casualties in the landings, but the division nevertheless intended to push inland toward its main objective of Achi Baba. At 9am British infantry units began to push off the high ground. The Turks were still under the control of Major Mahmut Sabri, who had the remnants of about three infantry battalions under his tactical command and was opposed by 14 weakened British infantry battalions. There were no other Turkish troops available in the lower peninsula to reinforce him. Throughout the day, he conducted a deliberate withdrawal to a new defensive line centred on the high ground of Achi Baba. Here the front stabilized. Ottoman reinforcements arrived around noon on 27 April and by evening the 9th Division now had a fresh regiment (over 3000 men) on the west side of the Gallipoli Peninsula and a composite regiment of equal strength on the east side.

Because of the relative calm on 27 April, the Turks decided to conduct a local attack with fresh troops before the Allies could consolidate their gains. There was considerable confusion concerning the orders: changes were made in the evening that resulted in the finalized attack order being considerably delayed. The attack began on time, but was poorly organized because of the haste with which the division had coodinated the operation. Predictably the attack failed to even give pause to a major Allied attack that began at 8am on 28 April.

Hunter-Weston had spent the day of 27 April preparing for a corps-level attack designed to seize the village of Krithia. Hunter-Weston now had 14 British infantry battalions and five French infantry battalions, and although he had scant field artillery ashore, he had the guns of the combined Allied fleet at his disposal. The Turkish 9th Division had 10 badly battered infantry battalions, but three fresh battalions

arrived from the north, giving them good odds against their enemy. Moreover, III Corps identified Mustafa Kemal's attempt to drive the Anzacs into the sea as the Ottoman main effort, relegating Halil Sami's fight to a secondary effort (although Esat Pasha intended to eliminate the Cape Helles beachhead after dispensing with the Anzacs). As a result, he received fewer reinforcements and less support than Kemal.

The multi-national attack was hastily coordinated and employed British regulars, Indians, Royal Naval Brigade infantry and the French. Moreover, field artillery support was lacking (only 28 field guns were ashore) and the troops had no time to rehearse. The 29th Division was ordered to push north to seize Krithia and the high ground, while the French attacked to shield the right flank. Once these objectives were in hand, Hunter-Weston intended to wheel east and seize Achi Baba. By the standards of the

The French initially landed at Kum Kale in Asia as a deception, but were quickly withdrawn and moved to the eastern sector of the Cape Helles front.

day, the plan was tactically complex and, moreover, required multi-national coordination. Over 10 battalions of British infantry stormed the Turkish forward trenches. In many locations, they broke through but were confronted immediately by locally positioned, platoon-sized Ottoman reserves. However, the local reserves were quickly decimated by Royal Navy gunfire, and Halil Sami committed his reserves at 10am. By noon, the Turks were in trouble and Halil Sami decided to authorize a withdrawal to the Achi

Baba–Yassi Tepe line. Orders to this effect were sent out to the regimental commanders, but many ignored them. In the east, the intrepid Mahmut Sabri was put in charge of a hastily gathered-together reserve force and tasked with launching a counterattack at 3pm. Simultaneously, delayed Ottoman reinforcements arrived and launched a timely bayonet attack to the right of Mahmut Sabri's men. These attacks were well supported by the Ottoman artillery. This counterattack sounded the death knell for Hunter-

meant that, potentially, III Corps was in danger of losing control of the battle. The safest way to keep this from happening was to form new operational groups under trusted commanders, who would control the battle on the spot. On 1 May 1915, Liman von Sanders created corps-level group headquarters to weld together these disparate formations into two ad hoc but coherent combat groups. He placed Colonel von Sodenstern in command of the Southern Group at Cape Helles, and Esat Pasha in command of the Northern Group on the Ari Burnu front (Anzac beachhead). The officers of XV Corps manned Sodenstern's headquarters.

Thus, a combination of prompt reactions by Turkish commanders at lower levels and carefully weighed decisions by the senior Turkish and German commanders enabled the Fifth Army to accomplish much in the decisive initial phase of what would become known as the Gallipoli campaign. Except at Anzac Beach, the well drilled Turks had stopped the Allies on the landing sites. By the end of the second day, the Fifth Army had five of its six infantry divisions in contact with the enemy. On the third day of battle, every Ottoman infantry division had regiments in action. By the end of the fourth day, only two infantry regiments remained in Asia and two infantry regiments remained at Bulair.

For the Allies, the operation was discouraging. Historians have universally criticized Hamilton for remaining on board ship and for not intervening directly at critical moments. Presumably his presence ashore might have added momentum or direction to the attacks. This is largely unjustified since Hamilton would have shared the experiences of those already ashore and, most probably, would have arrived at similar conclusions. In truth, Hamilton was as able and as well prepared as any senior general then serving in the British Army. He was, however, trapped inside the same antiquated command paradigm that afflicted the British Army until 1918, and was also a prisoner of

Weston's offensive, and the tired and disorganized Allies began to retreat and dig in. The battle became known as First Krithia.

According to the memoirs of Liman von Sanders, the confusion of the first several days of battle forced him to feed reinforcements into the fight without regard to formal command arrangements. Regiments from 5th and 11th divisions were fighting under 19th Division and regiments from the 3rd, 5th, 7th and 11th divisions were fighting under 9th Division. This

European society's Social Darwinism that held the Turks in contempt.

STALEMATE ON THE PENINSULA

Shocked by the violence of these encounters, the political will to prevail hardened in both London and Constantinople. At the end of April, Enver ordered the Ottoman V Corps, with the 13th, 14th and 15th divisions, to Gallipoli, together with the 4th Division. Simultaneously, Kitchener ordered the 42nd Division and 29th Indian Brigade to Gallipoli from Egypt, and Australian Light Horse brigades were also inbound. The French rallied to the cause and also dispatched a second composite division.

With the arrival of fresh reinforcements, Colonel von Sodenstern launched a massive 21st Battalion night attack on 1 May. Like Kemal's simultaneous attack, a short bombardment was followed by waves of thousands of men with bayonets fixed sweeping into the British lines. Sodenstern's attack also failed, as coordination and command broke down in the darkness. The Turks suffered some 3000 casualties. Undeterred, Sodenstern launched a smaller, eight-battalion night attack on the French lines on 3/4 May. Because of the scarcity of ammunition, the artillery barrage lasted only a few minutes and succeeded only in waking the French in their trenches. The attack was repulsed with heavy losses (perhaps 2000) to the Turkish divisions.

A frustrated Kitchener sent Hamilton a signal urging action, leading Hamilton to reorganize his forces to try once again to seize Krithia. The 29th Division broke up a brigade, but received the fresh 125th Brigade (42nd Division) and 29th Indian Brigade. The Royal Naval Division attached the 2nd Naval Brigade to the French, and in return received the 2nd Australian Brigade. While this appeared to balance the divisions, the Allies were totally unpractised in cross-attaching brigades in this

> 'The English officers were brave but inexperienced, and did not seem to know how to command or to lead their soldiers into battle.'
>
> Turkish officers to Captain R.H. Williams, American military attaché, 1915

manner. Altogether 25,000 Allied soldiers and 95 guns were assembled for an attack.

Hamilton wanted to attack at 5am, but due to severe shortages of officers Hunter-Weston convinced him to wait until full daylight. Hunter-Weston was in overall command, as Hamilton remained at sea, and his plan comprised a straightforward attack. At 11am on 6 May began what became known as the Second Battle of Krithia, with the launching of the Allied assault on the Turkish lines. Hundreds of men were killed attempting to cross no man's land, but some made it into the Turkish trenches. The battle raged for two days. Hamilton finally came ashore, but his presence made no difference as the Allies made their last attack on 8 May. Although the British were short of artillery shells the French had plenty, and the field artillery barrages were the heaviest yet seen on the peninsula. Unfortunately, the artillery was unable to knock out the Turkish machine gunners. Altogether, Hunter-Weston's men advanced 600m (656 yards) in some places but at a cost of over 6000 casualties.

In the meantime, Ottoman attacks were launched by the newly arrived 2nd Division. Esat Pasha launched a night attack again on 18 May; he was confident of success because he had numerical superiority at the point of attack using two fresh and highly regarded Turkish infantry divisions (the 3rd Division also participated). However, the Australians and the New Zealanders were warned by aerial reconnaissance, and by the observation of preparations in the enemy trenches. The Turks went over the top at 3am into withering fire, taking over 13,000 casualties, including 3000 killed; the 2nd Division alone lost over 9000 men. For the first and only time in the Gallipoli campaign, the local British commander asked for and received permission for a Red Cross-supervised truce in which to bury the ANZAC dead. Liman von Sanders agreed, and on 23 May both sides suspended hostilities.

On 24 May Hamilton organized his army at Cape Helles into VIII Corps, commanded by Hunter-Weston – a sound decision, given that Hunter-Weston had laboured under divisional and de facto corps command for almost a month. On 4 June the Allies again took to the offensive in the Third Battle of Krithia, sending in both the British and French corps, with a rifle strength of some 30,000 men. They repeated their frontal daylight attack, with some variants such as more artillery and an armoured car squadron. In the enemy trenches lay the Ottoman 9th and 12th divisions, which were well wired in and had constructed strongpoints for their machine guns. The attack began with a combined naval and artillery bombardment from 8am. The 20,000 men in the

Allied first wave attacked at 11.20am. Within 15 minutes the British were in the frontline enemy trenches. Most of the attacks penetrated 200–450m (218–492 yards) into the Turkish defences and the farthest advanced about a kilometre. Hamilton was ashore to watch the battle, and was later criticized for failing to prompt Hunter-Weston to commit his large reserve (18 battalions) at the decisive moment. This gave the Ottomans a momentary opportunity to launch counterattacks, which they did. These blunted the penetrations, and the attacking troops were held

These British soldiers have the look of veterans who have served on the front. Unlike in France, conditions at Gallipoli in the summer tended to be dry and hot. Water was a critical factor in planning operations in such an environment.

in check. Tired and disorganized, the Allies seemed to become bogged down. The Turks then began to wipe out any isolated pockets of Allied men. All Allied attacks were finally repulsed and the front stabilized about 8pm. The Turks estimated that the British suffered 4500 casualties and the French another 2000 on that day. Expecting the British attacks to continue, two Ottoman divisions moved into staging areas

The battles for control of Krithia. Determined to reach the high ground, the Allies mounted a joint British and French offensive. This failed in the face of well-entrenched and determined Ottoman defenders.

behind the lines in readiness for a massive counterattack in the event of an Allied breakthrough. At the day's end the survivors mostly returned to their trenches, leaving the front relatively unchanged.

The early phases of the fighting on the peninsula were intense, but were characterized on the Turkish side by massed rifle fire, bayonet assaults and sniping rather than by machine-gun fire or artillery attacks. Indeed, the Ottoman Army was very short of shells for all of its artillery (it had gone to war with stocks of about 500 shells per gun, while the Allies went to war with about three times that number). Moreover, shells for the most

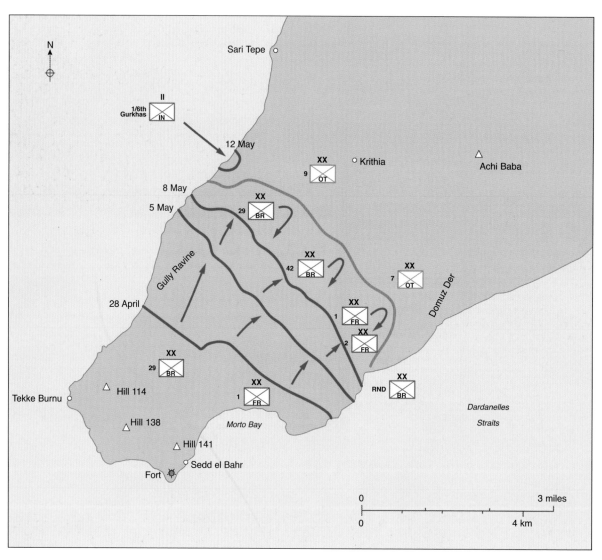

useful category of artillery used in trench warfare – howitzers and mortars (because of their high arcing trajectories) – were in critically short supply. In fact, in these two important categories the Turks only fired 30,000 shells in the first 30 days of fighting (a tiny fraction of a single day's shooting in France). The British and French also experienced shortages of shells, especially high-explosive ones, but could call on the guns of the Royal Navy for naval gunfire support.

Further attempts were made to break the deadlock, but neither side made any progress. The French conducted a well prepared attack on 21 June, lavishly expending some 30,000 artillery and mortar shells. It was locally successful, securing a piece of high ground that commanded their positions. While they lost several thousand men, the artillery fire was particularly devastating to the Turks, who suffered some 6000 casualties. Later in the month, the British attempted a similar offensive on 28 June using the newly arrived 52nd Division, aimed at seizing the enemy positions on Gully Spur; in the process they expended about 12,000 rounds of precious ammunition focused on the attack frontage. The fighting in Gully Ravine was bitter and lasted several days, after which the British attack eventually stalled. The Turks lost fewer men in this battle.

ABOVE **An Australian recruitment poster, May 1915.**

HMS *Majestic* **of the Royal Navy, sunk by the German submarine** *U21* **off the Dardanelles on 27 May 1915. For most of the campaign, the Royal Navy employed similar pre-Dreadnought battleships for naval gunfire support. Armed with four 12in guns, these ships were poorly protected and sank easily when torpedoed or mined.**

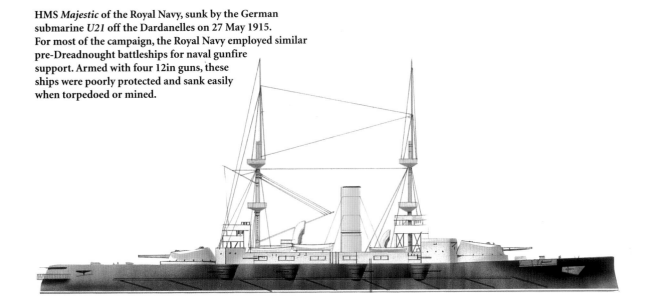

French artillery firing at Turkish positions. The French Corps at Gallipoli was more lavishly equipped with artillery than its British counterpart, and so were frequently called upon to reinforce the British with artillery support.

Neither the Allies nor the Turks were able to break the deadlock at the tactical level. In Constantinople, Enver continued to repeat his call for continued Turkish offensives against the two Allied beachheads. Many of the Fifth Army's infantry divisions had been depleted to regimental strength by months of continuous combat. As a result, the Ottoman Army sent a steady stream of replacements. The continuing battles absorbed large quantities of available Turkish resources, and Liman von Sanders now commanded a total of 16 Turkish infantry divisions. In addition to his original six divisions, the 12th, 15th and 16th divisions arrived in May, with the 1st, 4th and 6th divisions following in June, and V Corps with the 13th and 14th divisions and XIV Corps with the 8th and 10th divisions in July. At the end of July 1915, Liman von Sanders had about 250,000 men under his command (of which some 120,000 were infantrymen). However, the Turks had become aware of a second Allied landing force assembling on the island of Lemnos, preventing Fifth Army from employing all of these forces on the front lines.

Indeed, the British were building up their army in the Aegean as well. The 52nd Division arrived in June. This gave Hamilton a total of eight divisions (and some independent Indian brigades), which seemed to put him at a severe numerical disadvantage. However, British divisions contained 12 infantry battalions (the Royal Naval Division being a notable exception with nine), while the triangular Turkish divisions contained nine infantry battalions. Therefore, Hamilton's army contained the equivalent of 11 Turkish divisions. Moreover, Liman von Sanders had to guard the long, vulnerable coastlines of Asia and the Gulf of Saros, an effort that absorbed some five divisions. In fact, on the front lines at Anzac Beach and Helles the opposing armies were surprisingly well balanced.

AIR OPERATIONS

One aspect of study that is worthy of note is the evolution of aerial operations in the Middle East.

While both the Turks and the Allies deployed aircraft in the Caucasus, Mesopotamia and the Sinai in the first two years of the war, air operations in those locations were sporadic and contributed little to the overall ground war (in fact the Turks had used aircraft in military operations as early as 1912 in Libya against the Italians). The Gallipoli campaign, however, saw the beginning of effective Middle Eastern air operations.

The British air effort was two fold, involving military and naval air assets. Royal Flying Corps (RFC) squadrons, based on the islands at the mouth of the Dardanelles, flew reconnaissance and artillery spotting missions over the peninsula; in contrast to the Western Front, fighter and bomber operations were rare. The Royal Navy sent HMS *Ben-My-Chree,*

The air war over Gallipoli consisted mostly of reconnaissance and photographic missions, conducted by aircraft such as these Short seaplanes. As a result contact between fighter planes was minimal and no 'aces' emerged from the campaign.

a converted civilian steamer that carried half a dozen seaplanes, to the Mediterranean. Like the RFC squadrons, these aircraft were used primarily for reconnaissance and naval gunfire spotting. However, on 12 August 1915, Flight Commander C.H.K. Edmonds, flying a Short 184 seaplane, made the first successful aerial torpedo attack in aviation history – although it happened to be on a beached Turkish ship previously torpedoed by a British submarine.

The Turks also sent squadrons to the Gallipoli Peninsula. Of seven operational flying squadrons in the Ottoman air service in 1915, two (Nos. 1 and 6) flew in support of Liman von Sanders's Fifth Army. These aircraft performed reconnaissance missions but most importantly flew routine missions over the British bases on the islands of Lemnos and Imroz. This kept Liman von Sanders up to date on enemy preparations and concentrations. The Turks were short of trained military pilots and integrated German aviators and even Ottoman civilian pilots into their squadrons.

PLANNING TO BREAK THE DEADLOCK

In early June 1915, the British Government formed the Dardanelles Committee, composed of Asquith, Grey, Lloyd George, Churchill, Kitchener, Balfour, Lord Curzon and five other distinguished men. Their charge was to determine the future course of action that best suited Britain's war effort. Their options ranged from reinforcing Hamilton to abandoning the entire endeavour. The committee met amidst a level of great popular enthusiasm for the campaign, which had captured the public imagination in Great Britain and Australia. They decided to send large reinforcements in an attempt to settle the issue quickly. By 5 July, the Dardanelles Committee had assembled five additional divisions and a unique fleet of monitors and cruisers with special 'bulges' to support the additional land forces. The ships were perfect for the waters around the peninsula, being of shallow draft and heavily armoured; they had been designed for operations in the Baltic that had been cancelled. Further divisions of dismounted Australian light horsemen would be sent later.

In the meantime, the Allied high command learnt of a significant Ottoman weakness on the northern flank of the Anzac beachhead, via reconnaissance conducted in late May by New Zealanders who had nearly reached the summit of Chunuk Bair. Additionally, New Zealanders landed to the north and reported that the Salt Lake was passable and undefended. In turn, Birdwood, began to draw up plans for a major offensive that would swing to the north via Chunuk Bair and envelop the Turks. This would then break the deadlock and open the way to the straits. He asked Hamilton to consider the plan and to support it with reinforcements. Hamilton and his staff ignored this opportunity by reinforcing Hunter-Weston instead, who continued the fruitless attacks at Cape Helles in June. Thereafter, Hamilton moved to endorse the plan, which would be executed in July. However, when word arrived from the Dardanelles Committee that sizeable reinforcements were being sent, he decided to delay the operation until early August 1915. The immediate tactical problem became one of where to put the 60,000-plus

General Aylmer Hunter-Weston with staff officers in the communication trench approach to the Staff Headquarters in the Gallipoli Peninsula.

troops of the incoming divisions, as the Anzac beachhead was already packed with troops. With this in mind, Hamilton's staff began to explore options that ranged from more attacks at Helles to operations in Asia. In the end, conversations between Hamilton, de Robeck and Roger Keyes convinced Hamilton of the feasibility of landing an army corps in Suvla Bay. Planning now gathered a momentum of its own as the MEF began working on a major offensive that would redefine the entire campaign.

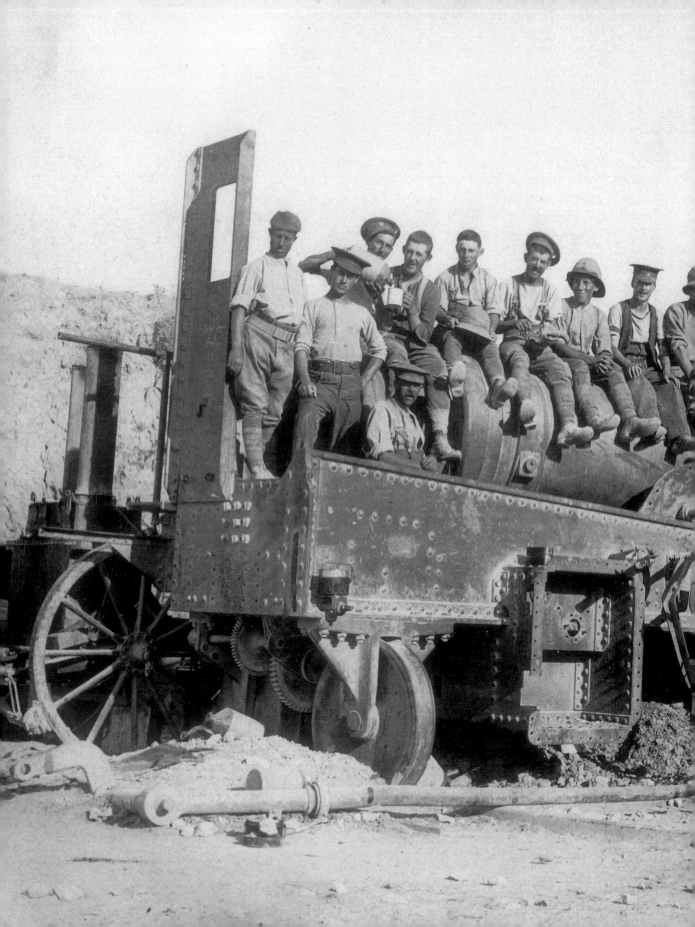

CHAPTER 3

Suvla Bay and the Caucasus

Concerned about their losses and their continuing inability to break through the Turkish lines at Gallipoli, the British had come to the belated conclusion that the small size of the Cape Helles and the Anzac beachheads negated the Allied manpower and reinforcement superiority. They therefore decided to conduct a second major amphibious operation in an attempt to outflank the Fifth Army.

Plans were set in motion to assemble a force that would conduct an invasion at Suvla Bay, immediately to the north of the Anzac beachhead, in conjunction with a large breakout by the ANZAC. The amphibious force would protect the left of the ANZAC as it outflanked Esat's defensive lines and thrust across the peninsula to the Narrows.

The British were confident, knowing the area to be lightly held by the Turks. In fact, aerial reconnaissance and patrols indicated that not only was the northern shoulder of the Anzac perimeter lightly fortified, but the Suvla Bay area appeared to be almost completely

British Tommies sitting on a Turkish gun at Cape Helles. The destroyed Turkish forts at Sedd al Bahr were never repaired during the campaign, but made great photo opportunities for the Allied troops on the peninsula.

unfortified and ungarrisoned. Moreover, in one of the driest years on record, the large Salt Lake (Tuz Golu) located just past the beaches was dry enough to support the weight of advancing troops.

BRITISH PLANS

Birdwood's original plan simply envisaged a breakout from the Anzac perimeter, but once it became clear that London was making an entire additional army corps available, Hamilton's staff began to re-examine the situation. The original architect of Birdwood's plan, Colonel Skeen, was set to work to revise the operation. In its final configuration the plan comprised a two-part operation in which the ANZAC would launch an attack through the northern part of its perimeter, followed almost immediately by an amphibious landing at Suvla Bay. Skeen thought the combined force might then be in a splendid position to outflank the Turks and seize the high ground, making their position untenable. It was aggressive thinking and was devised to break the deadlock.

Kitchener sent IX Corps out to assist Hamilton in this endeavour. The corps was commanded by Lieutenant-General the Hon. Sir Frederick Stopford, who was then 61 years old. Stopford was a 'dugout' – an officer recalled from retirement (in this case, five years). He was a guardsman and had been on staff during the Sudan campaign, the Ashanti expedition and the Boer War. Surprisingly, Stopford had never personally commanded men in battle, but he was well liked and an expert in ceremonial affairs and military history. Compton Mackenzie found him courteous and fatherly, but a poor choice for commander of an army corps 'that might change the whole course of the war in 24 hours'. Hamilton was dismayed when he found out that Stopford was coming out with IX Corps, and requested a more experienced and active commander, such as Byng or Rawlinson. Unfortunately, the tradition-bound system of seniority in the British Army made such a selection impossible and Stopford came anyway.

The principal formation available for the offensive was IX Corps, composed of the 10th (Irish), 11th (Northern) and 13th (Western) divisions, which were part of the first wave (K1) of Kitchener's all-volunteer New Armies. Although these formations were activated in late August 1914, many of their senior officers were recalled from retirement and most of the junior officers were directly commissioned without proper training. There were a few battalion and brigade commanders who were regulars (mostly men on home leave from India). The 10th Division, the first all-Irish division in the army, was thought to be especially keen and was commanded by one of the best men available, Sir Bryan Mahon.

Kitchener also made two more divisions available. The 53rd and 54th divisions were put on orders for the operations, although they were sent without their artillery. The reason for this was the ongoing shell shortage that affected the entire British Army, and also there was the fact that the tiny Allied beachheads were already packed full of men, animals, guns and supplies, leaving no space to emplace more guns. The 53rd and 54th divisions were first-line Territorial

Suvla Bay viewed from the sea; to the right is Chocolate Hill. Behind the wide flat beaches of Suvla Bay lay a large salt lake, which in the summer of 1915 was dry and hard. The width of the Suvla beaches made them almost indefensible.

The August landings at Suvla Bay and the breakout from Anzac Cove. The offensive toward Buyuk Anafarta by the ANZAC and the supplementary landing by IX Corps was an attempt to outflank the Turks. By doing so, Hamilton hoped to break the deadlock between the armies.

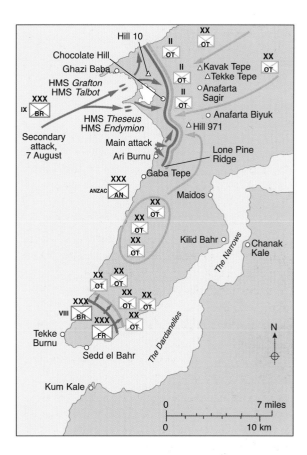

divisions, part of Britain's reserve force. Although these divisions were not as well trained as the regular army, they were commanded by regulars at brigade level and above, and contained a sprinkling of regular officers and NCOs throughout the battalions. A high percentage of the men were ex-regulars or serious reserve soldiers. These divisions had spent almost a year in training for war and were considered to be more ready for combat than the divisions of Kitchener's New Army.

There were three basic elements to Hamilton's revised offensive plan, which was scheduled to begin on 6 August. On that day, the troops at Cape Helles would start a demonstration attack with a view towards confusing the Turks as to Allied intentions, thus delaying their response and counterattacks. Simultaneously, Birdwood's ANZAC would swing around through the northern perimeter, conducting a 'left hook' towards the high ground. Finally, at dusk, IX Corps (minus the 13th Division) would execute an amphibious landing at Suvla Bay. To say that there was confusion regarding priority of effort understates the failure of Hamilton and his staff to communicate with clarity his intent to each of his subordinates. Many senior officers were not even briefed about the operation until 30 July; this of course, was a knee-jerk reaction to the scandalously ineffective operational security that had exposed the 25 April landings to the Turks.

Nevertheless, it was clearly a major flaw to exclude the men on the ground (who had to execute this difficult plan) from the staff work. Hamilton appears to have viewed the ANZAC breakout as the main effort and the Suvla and Helles operations as complementary. Certainly his directives to Stopford were ambiguous, causing Stopford to think that the establishment of Suvla Bay as a base for Hamilton's forces operating in the northern area was his principal objective. Further, Hamilton continued by explaining

that the role of Stopford's corps was to assist the officer commanding the ANZAC by advancing on Buyuk Anafarta.

Guarding the beaches in the Suvla Bay sector were two understrength infantry battalions, a Gendarmerie Regiment and four artillery batteries, under the Bavarian Major Willmer – a light force for such a critical area. Liman von Sanders (and Esat Pasha too) regarded the Gulf of Saros as a far more likely landing spot and stationed the entire 7th and 12th divisions in that location. Mustafa Kemal, in contrast, had pointed out the Suvla Bay vulnerabilities to Pasha in mid-summer, and he was also alert to the profound weakness of the northern flank of the perimeter.

THE AUGUST OFFENSIVE

The Allied offensive began with an attack at Cape Helles, which started with an artillery preparation at 2.20pm on 6 August 1915 (the afternoon was hot and

Sir Frederick Stopford (centre) at Crystal Palace, London, on Saint Patrick's Day. Stopford had little actual experience commanding soldiers in combat. Brought back from retirement for the expedition, he proved to be a poor choice.

the sky cloudless). The 29th Division came out of its trenches at 3.50pm, but effective Turkish artillery fire inflicted heavy casualties and the division failed to achieve its objectives. The next day, the 42nd Division attacked with similar results, losing 3500 men. The Turks were well dug in and the group commander, Vehip Pasha, was able to mass decisively his reserves to attain local fire superiority. The attacks failed to convince the unfazed Turks that they were the British main effort.

At Anzac Beach, the Australians had been shelling the Turks since 4 August, and by 6 August this had inflicted casualties and caused damage to their trench

systems. At 2pm, three large mines were detonated in no man's land. Then at 5.30pm the artillery bombardment ceased, and the Australians erupted from their trenches. Complete surprise was achieved, and the attacking infantry poured into the Turkish lines at Lone Pine. The Ottoman response was rapid: strong counterattacks stopped the Anzacs and fighting raged there for the next two days.

The ANZAC also staged an unprecedented night attack in two columns that would climb up the steep ravines (or *dere* in Ottoman Turkish). The right assault column was composed of New Zealanders, who went forward at 9.30pm with bayonets fixed. Surprise was complete and the enemy outposts were quickly overcome. As dawn broke the column was 915m (1000 yards) from the summit of Chunuk Bair. The left assault column was Australian and that night it became lost and overextended in the Aghyl Dere. As dawn broke it was nowhere near its objective. Reacting to imprecise reports, Esat Pasha ordered German Colonel Hans Kannengiesser to occupy Sari Bair Ridge, which was undefended. Kannengiesser arrived on Chunuk Bair about 6am on 7 August, and was stunned to see the full Allied fleet in Suvla Bay, as well as the assault columns threatening the empty high ground. Needless to say, by the time the New Zealanders continued the advance, the Turks had a firm hold on Chunuk Bair. The price of failure was high, as the New Zealanders were to form the northern arm of a pincer movement that would converge with a southern arm composed of Australian light horsemen, who began their attack on the Nek at 4.30am. After a heavy bombardment, the light horsemen went over the top and were obliterated by the alert Turks, who had no threat to their rear. This attack was made famous in the film *Gallipoli*.

In spite of accurate intelligence that the coast was undefended, except for several observation posts, the main landings at Suvla Bay began after dark at 9.30pm on 6 August. The 11th Division landed first and resistance was slight, but as the New Army battalions moved forward they encountered snipers and Ottoman Gendarmes. The darkness negated the British advantage of surprise, and as dawn broke 11th Division was two-thirds ashore and one-third afloat. The advance stalled as the division commander, Major-General Hammersley, lost his nerve and failed to push his men forward. Stopford did nothing.

Willmer's tiny force held the high ground but could not effectively guard the long sandy beaches, which

Australian gunners in action. Artillery did not play as decisive a role in the Gallipoli campaign as it did in France. The Turks had few guns and scant ammunition while the British had little ground on which to emplace their guns.

Bernard Freyberg (1899–1963)

One of the most dynamic personalities on the peninsula was Bernard Freyberg, who was born in Britain but raised in New Zealand. He was a talented athlete who received a commission in the New Zealand Territorials in 1912. In London when war broke out in 1914 Freyberg received a commission into the Hood Battalion of the Royal Naval Division. He served in the debacle at Antwerp in August 1914 and was a member of Rupert Brooke's burial party on Skyros the following spring. Freyberg swam to shore in the darkness on 25 April 1915 to light flares as part of the Bulair deception operation, earning himself a DSO. He was wounded numerous times and went to the Western Front after Gallipoli. Freyberg earned a Victoria Cross for refusing to leave the Hood Battalion in spite of suffering no fewer than four wounds in the space of 24 hours. He had earlier led his battalion's attack at Beaucourt which resulted in the capture of 500 prisoners. He was promoted to to brigadier-general in 1917, making him at 27 the youngest in the British Army. During the war Freyberg was wounded no fewer than nine times. In April 1941 Freyberg commanded during the withdrawal from Greece and the subsequent defeat on Crete. He served in Eighth Army as a corps commander and later with distinction in Italy. After the war he was appointed governor-general of New Zealand and died in 1963.

Bernard Freyberg, photographed near the town of Cassino, Italy, in January 1944.

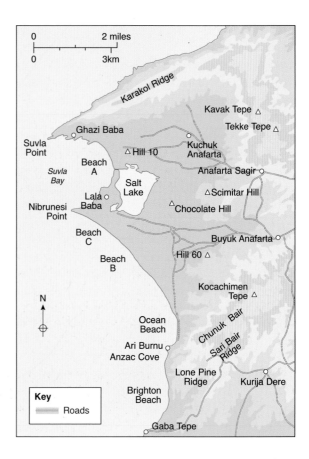

The key terrain features of the Suvla Bay area. The bed of the Salt Lake was completely dry in the summer of 1915. Stopford's IX Corps should have enjoyed a quick and easy advance from the undefended beaches.

were put under observation by individual posts. The British came ashore in force very quickly, but, inexplicably from the Turkish point of view, failed to rapidly seize the lightly held dominant terrain of the Kuchuk and Buyuk Anafarta ridgelines. Willmer sent accurate reports to Fifth Army, and reacting with his typical sense of urgency, Liman von Sanders put the 7th and 12th divisions of XVI Corps on the road south towards Suvla on 7 August. The nearby 9th Division was also ordered into action to assist Willmer's troops. That morning, the Irish 10th Division began to come ashore in piecemeal fashion. Its commander landed to find his brigades in the wrong places and observed 11th Division troops stationary and awaiting orders. The brigades of both divisions became intermingled

and a critical attack on Chocolate Hill failed. Willmer's detachment of about 1500 men had held up a British Army corps for 24 hours. Stopford seems to have suffered from a lack of urgency and remained onboard ship. When his reports indicating that his troops remained near the beaches reached the dismayed Hamilton, he likewise did nothing.

The following day, to the surprise of Liman von Sanders, the XVI Corps commander appeared early and reported that he had double-marched his corps southwards and that he was ready to join the fight a day earlier than expected. He was immediately ordered to bring his 7th and 12th divisions into line; however, due to the exhausted condition of his troops, he failed to execute this order in a timely manner. Liman von Sanders now determined that he needed to energize this critical sector and he gave command of the newly formed Anafarta Group to Colonel Mustafa Kemal, in whom the German commander had full confidence. The Anafarta Group controlled XVI Corps, the 9th Division and the Willmer Group. Liman von Sanders now had Esat Pasha's group

The Suvla Bay perimeter was larger and composed of less broken terrain than the corresponding Anzac and Helles perimeters.

focused on the ANZAC and Mustafa Kemal's group focused on Stopford's IX Corps.

Stopford spent another comfortable night onboard ship and on 8 August sent dispatches to his men congratulating them on their splendid achievement. By this time Hamilton was burning to know what was happening at Suvla Bay and sent Lieutenant-Colonel Aspinall to look over the situation. Aspinall went ashore and was stupefied to see men of 11th Division relaxing; some were even swimming. Aspinall went to the *Jonquil*, Stopford's floating command post, to query the IX Corps commander as to why his corps was simply sitting on the beaches. Stopford happily told him that his men had done splendidly. Aspinall frantically but unsuccessfully signalled Hamilton, who became increasingly agitated.

Finally, late in the day, Hamilton personally came to Suvla and directly ordered Stopford to advance and seize the high ground. Stopford demurred, saying that

11th Divison needed rest first. In fairness, water supplies had not landed in quantities sufficient to compensate for the torrid heat. An angry Hamilton then went ashore to find Hammersley (Stopford was invited to accompany him, but due to a wrenched knee remained on board the *Jonquil*). Hamilton tracked down Hammersley and ordered him to attack the next day. That night, in pitch-black conditions, the scalded 11th Division commander and his staff attempted to issue a coherent attack order.

UNSUITABLE COMMAND STYLE

It was Hamilton's inability to properly supervise Stopford that wrecked the reputations of both officers.

the 25 April landings, Hamilton's actions are difficult to understand. In the end, Hamilton's method of command mirrored command in the BEF in France, which suffered from a similar 'hands-off' approach. This institutional focus in the British Army of 1915 that trusted the man on the spot to demonstrate initiative and good judgement was unsuited to the twin demands of trench warfare and a mass continental army. Hamilton might have changed this dynamic had he given the Suvla Bay operation to the superb and seasoned 29th Division.

Unfortunately for the 11th Division, by the morning of 9 August the Turks had four infantry divisions from their reserve in line against the British. The results were predictable as 11th Division's poorly coordinated attacks foundered on the hastily dug Turkish trenches. A third British division, the 53rd, came ashore under heavy Turkish artillery fire. Again command and control were non-existent, as the incoming division was assigned neither a mission nor a sector of front. Finally, towards the end of the day its lead brigade received a hand-written scrap of paper from the division stating simply 'Attack the Turks.' Parts of the 159th Brigade were issued orders at 3am to attack three hours later. Again poor coordination ensured that the British were soundly thrashed at what would become known as the First Battle of Scimitar Hill. By 10 August IX Corps was disorganized and leaderless – even the energetic Mahon was demoralized at this point – and the Turks still held the high ground. There were some successes, notably when the troops from Suvla made contact with the troops from Anzac Beach, thus creating a sizeable two-corps beachhead.

While IX Corps was stumbling over itself at Suvla, the ANZAC main effort, commanded by Major-General Godley, was bogged down by the failure of the night attacks by columns. Futile attacks continued on 7 and 8 August. Godley had been reinforced by 29th Indian Brigade and 13th Division (from IX Corps), but

However, in the greater scheme of the overall plan, Stopford's mission was a complementary, limited operation supporting the main effort at Anzac Beach. Between 6 and 8 August, Hamilton was focused on the main effort and only became energized when he understood that IX Corps had stalled. However, after heavy criticism for failing to personally intervene in

was unable to achieve a decisive success, despite having heavy artillery and naval gunfire support. By 9 August the main effort had effectively disintegrated into a soldiers' battle for individual points such as No. 2 Outpost, Point 971 and Hill Q. Moreover, in addition to the large numbers of dead and wounded, many men (10,000 in the first week alone) were evacuated as seriously sick. Most historians believe that the failure to take Sari Bair Ridge and Chunuk Bair ended any real hope that Britain and her allies might have had to win the Gallipoli campaign.

> 'Driving power was required, and even a certain ruthlessness, to brush aside pleas for a respite for tired troops. The one fatal error was inertia. And inertia prevailed.'
>
> General Sir Ian Hamilton, Report on the Suvla Landings, 1915

RENEWING THE OFFENSIVE

On 10 August the 54th Division came ashore at Suvla; Hamilton, having learned of the dispersion of the 53rd Division, gave Stopford clear orders to keep the division together. The next day, Hamilton came to Suvla and lectured the hapless Stopford about the need for aggression, to which Stopford replied that the 53rd Division was poorly trained. Hamilton gave him 24 more hours and ordered the renewal of the attack on 13 August. This attack, also haphazardly planned, failed. One noteworthy incident involved an infantry company of the 5th Norfolks, which was recruited from the king's estate at Sandringham, led by Captain F.R. Beck. Captain Beck (who had been issued the wrong maps showing an entirely different part of the peninsula) veered off with his company and disappeared into the smoke of battle. Most were never seen again. Because of the connection of the men with the king, a post-war commission scoured the battlefield in 1919 for evidence of their fate. It appears that Beck and others were surrounded in a farmhouse, and fought to the last round. It also appears that some were captured and summarily executed by the Turks in violation of the laws of war.

Hamilton paid a further visit to Suvla on 13 August and again ordered Stopford to attack, but by now Stopford was ignoring his commander's direct orders. Belatedly, Hamilton recognized that he must make major changes in his command structure and he decided to start relieving subordinate commanders. The first to go was Egerton of the 52nd Division who was sent home earlier in August. Several brigade commanders were also relieved and sent home. Hamilton now decided to replace the unfortunate Stopford. With Kitchener's approval he gave command of IX Corps to Major-General Sir Beauvoir DeLisle, commander of 29th Division. Unfortunately, DeLisle was junior to Mahon of 10th Division, who immediately resigned in protest. Stopford was relieved on 15 August and sent home with his chief of staff Brigadier Reed. The next casualty was Major-General Lindley of the 53rd Division, who told Hamilton that he was not the man to pull the dispirited division back together. Finally, Hammersley of the 11th Division collapsed completely on 23 August and was invalided home.

Mustafa Kemal launched immediate counter-attacks, personally leading one himself on 10 August, which pushed the British back to within a kilometre of the landing beaches. Although the Turks were outnumbered in the new Anafarta sector, the British had committed every unit available to the fight. This allowed Liman von Sanders to bring in critical reinforcements from the Asiatic side.

While Hamilton considered DeLisle a tough fighter and a competent commander, he recognized that he was unpopular with the men of 29th Division, personally characterizing him as 'rude to everyone' and a 'brute'. Nevertheless, Hamilton resolved to continue the attacks, now making DeLisle's IX Corps carry the main effort. To add mass to DeLisle's demoralized force, Hamilton brought the veteran 29th Division from Helles as well as the incoming 2nd Mounted Division from Egypt to the Suvla perimeter.

The mounted division was composed of dismounted British yeomanry regiments – 'curious semi-feudal relics of the militia' recruited from the rural fox-hunting counties of England. This would be the final serious British offensive of the campaign. DeLisle demonstrated enthusiasm for his new assignment and developed a plan quickly, which in its final form threw the 29th Division at Chocolate Hill, 11th Division at the centre and a composite ANZAC brigade against Hill 60. The newly arrived yeomanry division was in immediate reserve. For his part, Hamilton, requested 75,000 reinforcements from Kitchener; the latter had had enough of the campaign and did not respond.

Final orders from DeLisle went out to his units on 20 August. The mid-afternoon attack (2.30pm) was strongly supported by artillery and by naval gunfire, but as the men left their trenches visibility deteriorated, as haze and low cloud obscured the battlefield – and thus the targets of the artillery observers. The Turks, on the other hand, were fully alert and were able to fire their pre-registered and pre-planned barrages onto the oncoming enemy. DeLisle's men were slaughtered, although the revitalized 11th Division was able to take the forward line of trenches. Under heavy shrapnel fire the 2nd Mounted Division was sent forward around 5pm. Its attack was poorly organized with no clear objective and, essentially, it moved forward into the haze and smoke towards the sound of the guns on Scimitar Hill, disappearing into the approaching darkness. Casualties were heavy and included Brigadier-General Kenna, VC, Colonel Sir John Milbanke, VC, and Brigadier-General Longford.

Lieutenant W.T. Forshaw, VC, exposes himself to enemy fire to launch bombs at the enemy in the Vineyard, 7–9 August 1915. Many of the battles at Gallipoli took place at the tip of the bayonet. The trenches were close together and the density of machine guns and barbed wire was much lower than in France.

By 9pm the attack had clearly failed, with that on Hill 60 faring no better. For their part, in spite of the large-scale British attacks, the well dug-in Turks in the Anafarta Group suffered relatively few casualties during this period.

Both sides were now exhausted, physically and psychologically. While hard fighting continued and attacks were maintained at the tactical level, the fighting on the Gallipoli Peninsula slowly atrophied into a dogged stalemate with no end in sight. The Fifth Army held the key terrain in every sector, which compensated for its lack of artillery, artillery ammunition and machine guns. The ever-changing Turkish command arrangements had now solidified into four operational groups of various sizes: the Anafarta Group under Colonel Mustafa Kemal, the Ari Burnu (ANZAC) Group under Esat Pasha, the Sedd el Bahr (Cape Helles) Group under Vehip Pasha, and the Asia Group under Mehmet Ali Pasha. During August further Turkish reinforcements had reached the

peninsula: VI Corps with the 24th and 26th divisions and XVII Corps with the 15th and 25th divisions.

It might be said that the British press quashed the nation's will to maintain the campaign. An influential British journalist named Ellis Ashmead-Bartlett was present during the disastrous final offensive. He had been also been present at the initial landings and had formed his own negative opinions about the campaign's prospects of success. His reports through the summer cast a pall on the enterprise. However, it

was 29-year-old Australian journalist Keith Arthur Murdoch who prepared a 'long and highly coloured' statement about the horrid conditons on the peninsula and the wasteful frontal attacks, which caught the attention of the Dardanelles Committee. Fuelling the fire, Major Guy Dawnay, a member of Hamilton's staff, returned to London in late August and began to talk to anyone in Whitehall who would hear him. Although he had been sent by Hamilton to plead for reinforcements, Dawnay felt that the truth should be known at home. Hamilton reinforced the uneasiness in London by asking for some 95,000 reinforcements and by maintaining that, if he had to evacuate the peninsula, he would lose half his army.

On 14 October, the Dardanelles Committee met and decided to replace Hamilton. A telegram was sent to him two days later. Hamilton appeared to take this in his stride, thanking all his subordinates and staff for their hard work while preparing to depart. His replacement was General Sir Charles Monro, fresh from the Western Front, who arrived on Imbros on 28 October. Monro was an ardent advocate of beating Germany in France in order to win the war. Nevertheless, he received intensive briefing on the situation in the Mediterranean and met four times with Kitchener. He was then sent off with instructions to evaluate the situation and recommend a course of action to London. Kitchener promised to support him with reinforcements if Monro thought the campaign could be won, and also promised full support if he thought the peninsula ought to be evacuated.

Monro arrived to find the divisions of the army reduced to less than half of their authorized bayonet strength. Moreover, sickness and disease, particularly dysentery, were talking a daily toll on the army. Monro immediately toured the fronts and, surprisingly, maintained an optimistic attitude. His initial report to London proposed the idea that it was too soon to consider an evacuation and he asked for priority in

ANZAC troops advancing with bayonets fixed. This well published photograph has come to characterize the Australian participation at Gallipoli. The men are athletic and fit, but are obviously an easy target, indicating that the photo was almost certainly posed.

resupplies of winter kit and fortification material. However, Monro followed this with a lengthy report at the end of October, carefully weighing up the poor condition of the men, the fact that the Turks dominated the high ground entirely and that the small beachheads were exposed to observation and offered no room to mass or achieve tactical surprise. Moreover, all intelligence indicated that Germany was about to reinforce the Ottoman Army massively. His conclusion was that an evacuation was the only feasible course of action.

In the late summer of 1915, Bulgaria had joined the Central Powers. This opened up an overland route for German material asistance to reach the Dardanelles, especially for much-needed artillery

The British howitzer shown here is in full recoil and was probably firing at maximum charge. The massive hydraulics needed to return the gun barrel to its firing position are clearly visible above the barrel.

ammunition and spare parts. In addition, vital reinforcements began to arrive in September, including a 150mm howitzer battery fom Germany and a 240mm howitzer battery from Austria-Hungary. Along with the artillery came German and Austrian technical specialists, as well as three German general staff officers. Although the tempo of the campaign was slowing down, the Ottoman general staff sent the 20th Division, stationed at Smyrna, to the peninsula, and the operations division of the staff alerted a cavalry brigade and two infantry regiments to prepare for deployment to the battlefront. This was in reponse to reports that the Italians were poised to invade the Asiatic coast in support of the British. Well into the autumn of 1915, Liman von Sanders remained convinced that the Allies might conduct further landings in Saros Bay or on the Asian side, and he maintained substantial forces there until the end of the campaign.

The long-awaited artillery ammunition began to arrive in November, along with several additional batteries of heavy Austrian howitzers. Encouraged by these reinforcements, Enver and the Ottoman general staff began to lobby for an all-out offensive to push the Allies back into the sea. However, as the winter season set in, they decided against such an operation.

EVACUATING THE PENINSULA

On 3 November Monro went to Cairo, from where he was abruptly sent to command the British forces then flowing into Salonika, Greece, to salvage what remained of the Serb Army and the Balkan situation. This left Birdwood in overall command on the ground at Gallipoli. Kitchener was initially opposed to an evacuation and came out to the peninsula on 9 November to evaluate the situation in person. He was taken aback by the harsh terrain and the cramped beachheads, but Birdwood maintained that the

Allied troops taking medication under supervision. The campaigns in the Middle East were characterized by high casualty rates from tropical endemic diseases. These soldiers are probably taking quinine, a preventative against malaria.

British ought to hang on to what they had gained. Kitchener went next to Salonika, finally signalïng to London on 22 November that the Gallipoli operation should be abandoned.

To make things worse for Birdwood, who now understood that he must evacuate his men, a terrific winter gale struck the peninsula, destroying piers and stores and filling the trenches with cold water. At Suvla, the winter storm had even refilled the dry Salt Lake and cases of frostbite began to appear. The Turks, for their part, settled down on the high ground and continued with small local attacks and constant shelling. It was apparent that they too had no desire to continue with major assaults in the muddy, harsh conditions.

Birdwood's staff began to craft one of the most remarkable operations of the war, which sought to withdraw his army intact. The first phase was an evacuation of the combined Suvla–Anzac beachhead, and its success turned on maintaining all routines so that the Turks would be unaware of the impending withdrawal. As preparations were made to pull out, there was no perceptible change in the British

Turkish infantrymen lined up besides railway wagons. The Ottoman railway system was inefficient and did not service the fighting fronts. As a result, the Turks were never able to shift large numbers of reserves as quickly as the European powers could.

position, but by December Birdwood was thinning his lines and pulling out men. This was a giant undertaking, as 85,000 men lay inside the perimeter, as well as 5000 animals and 200 guns. Movement and loading were done after dark, and by 18 December half the men had gone. The remainder took up the job of deceiving the Turks with great enthusiasm, fabricating numerous devices to maintain the charade. Self-firing rifles using weighted tins of water were set up to convince the Turks that men still inhabited the trenches, and food was left cooking on fires. In the meantime, the animals that could not be evacuated were killed and the huge dumps of supplies were

rigged for demolition. On the night of 19 December only 5000 men manned the perimeter; Birdwood thought that most of these would not make it onto the ships. The evacuation quietly continued, and by 10pm only a rear guard of 1500 picked men remained. The Turks remained silent, and at 1.30am on 20 December the final withdrawal began, reaching completion at 2.40am. The self-firing rifles and fires maintained the deception until about 4am, when the demolitions began to go off.

Within minutes of the detonations, Captain Ali Remzi was notified by field telephone from his forward outposts that the enemy trenches appeared empty. News was immediately relayed to the Fifth Army headquarters and the captain was ordered to investigate. He went forward and penetrated 150m (164 yards) into the British trench system, finding it empty and manned by dummy soldiers. At this point the Fifth Army staff awoke Liman von Sanders and told him the news. The entire enemy force, and most of the artillery, had withdrawn successfully, but not all of the demolitions went off as planned and large quantities of stores and supplies fell into Turkish hands. Overall, the evacuation was a remarkable operation.

Cape Helles remained a source of concern for the British, who were now convinced that the Turks were on to their evacuation plans and would make a final attempt to overwhelm the remaining beachhead. The 29th Division, pulled out of Suvla, was sent back to Helles to stiffen the defence. There were mixed opinions about whether the position should be held or abandoned. The navy wanted the army to retain the beachhead because it eased the burden of blockading the mouth of the Dardanelles.

As the New Year approached, it seemed certain that the Allies would evacuate the Cape Helles position as well. Despite intense Turkish observation and interest,

> 'The entire evacuation of the peninsula had now been completed. It demanded for its successful realization two important military essentials: good luck and skilled, disciplined organization.'
>
> Sir Charles Monro's first dispatch, 1916

the Allies repeated their successful deception efforts through a very aggressive tactical posture by General Davies's VIII Corps. The withdrawal of surplus supplies and guns took place during the hours of darkness, but incessant winter storms interfered with this process. By 7 January 1916, there were fewer than 17,000 Allied men on the peninsula. The divisions remaining until the end were the 13th, 29th, 52nd and the Royal Naval Division. The 29th Division, at full strength in August, had been reduced down to just over 4000 men. On the night of 8/9 January, the Allies again produced a remarkable feat of tactical deception and tricked the Turks into believing that the lines were strongly held. By 3.45am the final reaguards were safely away, and carefully laid charges destroyed the substantial abandoned stores. Thousands of mules, which could not be evacuated in time, were shot standing in their lines. Once again, large amounts of military supplies, horses, tents and rations fell into Turkish hands. Liman von Sanders noted that it took two years for the Turks to organize and carry away the material that they captured.

By 9am on 9 January 1916, Liman von Sanders was able to report to the Ottoman general staff that the British had abandoned the peninsula, and the Turks began moving their forces out of the area immediately thereafter. Within 10 days, 11 Ottoman divisions left the peninsula for garrison towns in Thrace. Liman von Sanders returned to Constantinople on 15 January 1916. The Fifth Army gradually reduced its strength to pre-invasion levels as its divisions were sent to active fronts. By the end of January 1916, the Fifth Army was composed of only VI Corps with the 24th and 26th divisions and XIV Corps with the 25th and 42nd divisions. The strength of the fortress command remained more or less the same. Later in the war, as the Gallipoli divisions recuperated and were brought

back to full fighting strength, they were sent to more active fronts.

The cream of the British divisions was sent to the Western Front, including the 29th Division and the Royal Naval Division, which was assimilated into the army as the 60th Division in 1916, and the ANZAC, which expanded into a small army in its own right. The Territorial and Kitchener divisions were sent to the newly formed Salonika bridgehead, to take on the Bulgarians and Germans. Most would find their way to Egypt in 1916 and 1917 for another round with the Turks. Ian Hamilton returned to London and was never offered an active command again. Of note, four future field marshals served on the peninsula: Birdwood, Slim, Harding and Blamey (an Australian). Politically, the campaign damaged Churchill, Kitchener and Asquith's government, leading the historian Alan Moorehead to characterize it as 'a mighty destroyer of reputations'.

A parliamentary commission was assembled to review the evidence of the campaign and to take testimony from those who had planned and fought it. The preliminary report found that errors in administration and logistics doomed the effort. However, the final report in 1919 apportioned blame to Hamilton and Stopford, and highlighted the ability of the Turks to mass forces effectively. Later, the official British account of the campaign drew attention to the dogged defensive qualities of the Ottoman soldiers and the brilliant leadership in the Fifth Army.

The campaign was, perhaps, the greatest 'What if...?' of the war. Although many histories credit the Allies with inflicting greater casualties on the Turks, in truth losses were about equal. The British (and colonials) lost about 205,000 men, including 43,000 killed or missing. The French lost 47,000 men of the 79,000 they sent to the peninsula. Liman von Sanders states the Turks lost 66,000 killed. Many histories, including the official British version, speculate that the

Private, Turkish Army, at Gallipoli in 1916. The Turks affectionately called their soldiers *Mehmetcik* or 'Mehmets', which corresponded to the British term 'Tommy'. The *Mehmetciks* were similarly hardy and rarely complained.

Turks lost over 350,000 men and suggest that because of careless Turkish record keeping, the exact number cannot be ascertained. In fact, Ottoman Army record keeping was very good, and the final total for the period 4 April 1915 through to 19 December 1915 was 56,643 killed, 97,007 wounded and 11,178 missing. Actual losses between Turks and Allies were, therefore, approximately the same.

The Allies sent about 490,000 men to the Dardanelles over the course of the campaign. Most Western historians and authors note that the Ottoman Army committed about 500,000 men to the campaign over the nine-month course of the battle. However, given the known dispositions of the Ottoman Army in 1915, this figure is, perhaps, on the high side, and disguises the Allied humiliation suffered at the hands of the Turks. From the Ottoman records and from Liman von Sanders's memoirs, it is doubtful whether the Turks ever had equal numbers of combat troops engaged during the campaign. In fact the opposite was probably the case: the Turks were outnumbered most of the time. The highest strength that the Turks had on the peninsula was in October 1915 when a total of

BELOW **Allied stretcher bearers evacuating casualties from the peninsula. The British evacuation process was slow and manpower intensive. The wounded had to be brought to the beaches, loaded onto lighters and then transported by ship to hospitals in Egypt.**

ABOVE **The British Royal Naval Division was one of the best Allied formations to fight on the peninsula. It was later sent to France where it was absorbed into the Army as the 61st Division. Here, two men of the RND are shown inside a cave position on the peninsula.**

Triangular Infantry Divisions

By 1917 the French and German armies had discarded their pre-war infantry division architecture of two brigades each of two regiments (totalling 12 infantry battalions). Both armies adopted the triangular three-regiment architecture (totalling nine battalions). In 1918 the British also reverted to a nine-battalion division. The new organizations were able to put two regiments in the trenches while keeping one in reserve. In fact, the Ottoman Army created what became known as the 'triangular division' in 1910 in a massive reorganization. The new Ottoman divisions contained three infantry regiments of three battalions supported by an artillery regiment of three battalions. This basic configuration was tested in combat during the Balkan Wars of 1912–13. Command and control was streamlined as the division commanders talked directly to regiment commanders without going through a brigadier. The new arrangement proved flexible and highly successful in the war. The Ottoman Army retained this architecture as the army mobilized in 1914. By the beginning of World War II the triangular division had become the world's standard.

Allied troops on a raft during the evacuation. Very little British equipment was taken off during the evacuations. Most of the inventory was blown up or burned. Nevertheless, the Turks captured huge quantities of abandoned supplies.

315,500 officers and men were assigned to the rolls of the Fifth Army.

The Gallipoli campaign produced a number of significant outcomes. Despite some favourable opportunities late in the war around Alexandretta, the British never attempted another amphibious attack on the Ottoman Empire. The campaign refocused the leadership in London on the idea that the war must be won on the Western Front while those advocating peripheral campaigns fell from power. From the Ottoman perspective, there were several other important outcomes, which were generally ignored by the world at large. The most significant outcome for the Ottoman Army was the emergence of a group of capable commanders of proven ability who were tested in combat. Many of these individuals would make important contributions to the empire's war effort as well as playing major roles in the War of Independence (1919–22). Another important outcome for the Ottoman Empire was that the Young Turk leadership drew renewed inspiration for the continuance of the war and the ultimate victory of the Central Powers. In 1916, Enver Pasha would send the Ottoman Army into battle on three additional fronts in Europe, reflecting his belief in victory. Finally, there emerged from the Gallipoli campaign a group of veteran Ottoman infantry divisions that quickly became an effective cadre around which Ottoman commanders built successful operations in subsequent campaigns.

1915 IN THE CAUCASUS

The Third Army commander, Brigadier-General Hafiz Hakki Bey, died in the spotted typhus epidemic in early February and was replaced by Mahmut Kamil Pasha. After the disastrous winter offensive, replacements were arriving monthly from the First and Second armies. The 36th Division arrived from Mesopotamia and took up positions along the southern flank of the Third Army near Lake Van. Moreover, the 3rd Logistics Inspectorate was able to restore much of the combat capability of the Third Army by mid-March 1915. Although their combat

strengths were scarcely that of normal infantry divisions, X and XI corps were in the line and fighting. Built around the surviving remnants of artillery and combat trains, a reconstituted IX Corps moved back to the front as well. The best reserve light cavalry regiments were consolidated into a single stronger division (3rd Reserve Cavalry Division). By April the strategic situation appeared to have stabilized along the frontier, although the Russians maintained control of a salient projecting into the Eliskirt Valley.

This stability enabled the Turks to maintain defensive lines and move the still shattered IX Corps to the rear near Erzurum for reconstitution and training. Only a thin screen of 2nd and 3rd Cavalry

Turkish troops captured by the Russians. The climate conditions experienced by Ottoman forces in the war were extreme, particularly in the high Caucasus regions, and caused considerable suffering.

Russian sharpshooters. This posed photograph shows an officer with binoculars fully exposed to enemy fire. The men appear well cared for and fit.

divisions held the long vulnerable front between Lake Van and Erzurum. The Van Gendarme Division and the 1st Expeditionary Force held the front to the south of Lake Van. The Russians launched a major offensive down the Tortum Valley towards Erzurum on 6 May. This offensive was beaten back and stalled later that month, but the Turks lost about 15km (nine miles) of ground. Determined to regain this territory, the Turks began a flanking attack on the Russian salient on 11 June and pushed the Russians all the way back to their starting positions.

The Turks had less success in the south. During May, their position on the southeastern frontier crumbled as the Russians took the city of Van on the 13th. To the north of Lake Van, the Turks lost Malazgirt two days earlier. In early June, the Russian Army swept around the north shore of Lake Van and threatened the approaches to Mus. Effectively, the Russians created a large salient in the southern sector of the Caucasian front. In part, these losses may be explained by the gathering logistical shortages that were beginning to affect the Third Army's combat effectiveness. Accelerating the deterioration of the Ottoman logistics situation was a growing Armenian insurgency, which threatened the lines of communications to the rear areas.

THE ARMENIAN REBELLION

The most contentious problem in the historiography of World War I in the Middle East revolves around the events relating to the destruction of the Armenian population of eastern Anatolia in 1915. Today, the Armenians, as well as most Western historians, assert that the Young Turks conducted a premeditated campaign of extermination (amounting to genocide)

War Continues in the Caucasus

The campaigns in the Caucasus region were fought by armies that appeared strong on paper, but which were actually very weak. In theory, the Russians had about 130,000 infantry, 35,000 cavalry and 340 cannon, but their actual strength was only around 70,000 infantrymen, 9000 cavalry and 130 cannon. Against this, the Turks fielded about 53,000 infantry and cavalry combined, accompanied by 131 guns. Because the Turks could not be strong everywhere along the 720km (447-mile) front, the Russians shifted their centre of gravity to the southeast for a concerted push, and began a major offensive. Unknown to the Russians, the Turks had sent the reconstructed IX Corps to the area as well as two expeditionary forces and the cavalry divisions. It was a skilful assembly of forces, conducted in secret under difficult circumstances, in an area where the Russians did not expect to see Turkish strength. By 16 July the Russian attacks had collapsed, and Turkish counterattacks forced the Russians back with heavy losses. The enthusiastic Turks continued their counter-offensive and liberated the city of Malazgirt; then, in early August, they attacked into the Eliskirt Valley. The Russians counterattacked and threatened to encircle the Turks, who called off the attack and retreated. Once again Malazgirt fell into Russian hands, but the front soon stabilized. Both sides suffered heavy casualties, which could not easily be made good, leading to a lull in campaigning until January 1916.

on the Armenians. The Turks claim that the Armenians, in active revolt during wartime, were a threat to national security and were relocated from the war zone, where many died of starvation.

There had been considerable recent conflict between the Armenians and the Ottoman Government dating back to the 1870s, which saw the creation of the Armenian revolutionary committees. These were modelled on the successful Macedonian and Bulgarian committees and were supported by many Europeans. In the immediate aftermath of the Young Turk revolution of 1908–09, Ottoman restrictions against minorities first relaxed and then tightened. The hopes of the minorities, especially the Armenians and the Greeks, who had thought that the ending of the sultanate and the establishment of a modern constitutional structure would lead to greater autonomy and political inclusion, were shattered. Disorder broke out throughout the empire amongst minorities disappointed by this development and by increased taxes and restrictions of civil rights. In particular, Armenians in Adana rose in revolt on 14 April 1909, and the army and the Gendarmerie killed many thousands in quelling the uprising.

In 1914, the Armenian population of the Ottoman Empire amounted to several million people, with those in eastern Anatolia totalling some 1.3 million. There had been numerous Armenian uprisings in the latter from the late 1700s and culminating in the infamous and widely reported massacres of the 1890s. While many of the Armenians were loyal and law-abiding citizens of the empire, subversive societies dedicated to the establishment of an autonomous Armenia had existed for many years. After 1909, internal dissent accelerated interest in these groups. In 1910, the Dashnaks (a revolutionary Armenian nationalist society) launched a campaign of terror in eastern Anatolia. Thousands of Turks and Armenians were killed before the army was able to restore order and the rule of law. In Albania, Kosovo and Macedonia similar patterns of killing evolved as other minorities became disaffected as well. The Balkan Wars of 1912–13 brought Ottoman control of its European provinces to an end, which effectively ended a substantial part of its minority problem. However, the Armenians remained in the Anatolian provinces of the empire. As World War I approached, well organized and effective Armenian revolutionary committees operated openly in Europe and in Russia. These committees were sponsored and supported by the Great Powers and advocated the establishment of an independent Armenia.

Inside the Ottoman Empire many Armenians were becoming alarmed by a new political philosophy

An Armenian volunteer. This photograph shows the signature kit of the Armenian nationalist committeeman: a modern military rifle, bayonet and several bandolier ammunition belts.

Gökalp's theories on their lives. Gökalp's advocacy of greater Turkic participation in the empire's economy was equally worrisome to the hard-working and industrious Armenians. By 1914 the Armenians had cause to believe that the Turks intended to consolidate their hold on the Anatolian heartland by sending Muslim refugees from the Balkans to live there, and that some kind of cultural and economic Turkification programme was about to be imposed on the empire's non-Muslim peoples.

By the spring of 1914, the activities of the Armenian committees had reached the point where formal offices opened in Tiflis and Paris, comprising a kind of government in exile. These expatriate groups were actively involved in smuggling weapons and explosives into the empire, and the Turks intercepted some shipments. In late July, the Armenian committees held the important eighth party congress under the leadership of the Dashnaks in Erzurum. The congress was conducted to peacefully advance Armenian concerns through legitimate political processes and the CUP even sent its own representatives. However, as Europe went to war in August 1914, the congress dissolved when some of the more important Armenian leaders departed for Europe and Russia. The Ottomans became convinced

known as Turanism, based on the pan-Turkic nationalist theories of Ziya Gökalp, who advocated the imposition of a Turkic identity, language and culture on the empire. It is certain today that some members of the Committee of Union and Progress, especially Enver Pasha and Talaat Pasha, were ardent enthusiasts for Gökalp's ideas. This new Turkic nationalism became intertwined with the modernity advocated by the CUP and found many adherents within the army as well. Gökalp's supporters even made contact with non-Ottoman Turks living in Russia's Trans-Caspian regions. Naturally, the Christian, linguistically and culturally different Armenians were very concerned about the impact of

Tens of thousands of helpless Armenian civilians were massacred in the brutal relocations of 1915. Even more died of starvation and neglect enroute to the deserts of Syria.

Armenian volunteers. The Armenian nationalist revolutionary committees were very well organized and heavily armed. They rose in revolt in many Eastern Anatolian cities in the spring of 1915.

thereafter that the congress led directly to agreements between the Armenians and the Russians aimed at the establishment of an independent Armenia in eastern Anatolia. In fact, immediately after the German declaration of war on Russia, many of the influential leaders went to Tiflis to begin raising the Druzhiny, or Armenian regiments.

In September, evidence of violent intent accumulated as Turkish authorities found bombs and weapons hidden in Armenian homes. By early October 1914 (prior to the commencement of hostilities), the Turks received reports of Armenians returning to Turkey with maps and money, and

aggressively nationalist Armenian meetings attended by thousands. Late in the month, Third Army cabled the capital that large numbers of Armenians with weapons were moving into the eastern frontier cities of the empire. Reports also arrived in the capital claiming that large numbers of Ottoman Armenian citizens were leaving their homes in the empire and travelling into Russian-held territory. Although the Ottoman Empire was still officially at peace with the Entente, many staff officers became convinced that Russia and France were actively conspiring to initiate an Armenian rebellion.

The situation worsened as war broke out in November 1914. Throughout the winter and into 1915 incidents of terrorism increased, particularly bombings and assassinations of civilians and local Turkish officials. In February, the general staff cabled

A monument to Ziya Gökalp. His nationalist writings were responsible for forging much of the modern Turkish identity. Many of the Young Turks were ardent advocates of Turanism, which was a form of pan-Turkism.

the armies noting increased activity by Armenian dissidents in the central Anatolian cities and along the Mediterranean coast; moreover, these reports identified Allied agents, influence and activities in these areas. As a result, all ethnic Armenian soldiers were removed from important Turkish headquarters. The Turks also learned that the Armenian Patriarchy in Constantinople was transmitting military secrets to the Russians. From February through to July 1915, a great many additional reports reinforced this pattern of Allied intelligence gathering.

A massive Russian offensive was expected following the spring thaw in 1915, and the Turks became convinced that an Armenian rebellion in the rear areas of the Ottoman Third Army was imminent. The main Armenian centres of population (and thus of potential armed resistance) lay directly astride the only two all-weather roads leading into the eastern front. These cities included substantial Armenian populations and some contained Armenian majorities. Moreover, Armenian activity in southern Anatolia interdicted the only railroad as well. Since the logistically poor Turks had only limited quantities of food, medicine and military stores to hand, interdiction of these key lines of communication spelled disaster. These concerns over security drove the army staffs as they planned their operations.

It is hard to pinpoint when the rebellions broke out first. Many historians have concluded that the Turks themselves deliberately instigated the revolts by massacring Armenians as early as December 1914, in order to provoke an Armenian reaction. The Turks deny this and claim that it was the Armenian committees, encouraged by the Russians, who began the violence.

As a matter of record, armed revolts by the Armenians broke out in April 1915, the most visible incident of which was a rebellion in the city of Van. Heavily armed committees seized most of the city and the Turks responded by rushing troops to besiege it. Simultaneously the Russian Army, led by Armenian Druzhiny, began its long-awaited offensive into the region. The situation around Van seemed so critical that the Turks sent regular army reinforcements to the city. In May the Russians broke the siege and relieved the Armenian defenders of the city. Other Armenian centres of population soon followed suit, and in the following months revolts broke out in many of the central Anatolian cities. These revolts were instigated by the Armenian nationalist committees.

Massacres of Armenians of all ages were widely reported by numerous neutral observers, many of whom claimed to know that local Ottoman officials had received secret orders to exterminate the entire Armenian population. Other witnesses, including neutral Americans and Germans with direct access to

'John Bull's Dilemma.' While the Allies were aware of the Armenian massacres and relocations of 1915, there was little they could do about it. They watched in helpless horror as the Ottomans erased the Armenian presence in eastern Anatolia.

Armenians to the Euphrates Valley, Urfa and Süleymaniye. Confirming the worst fears of the Armenians, the directive ominously specified that the goal was to create an eastern Anatolian demographic situation in which the ratio of Armenians would drop to 10 per cent of the local total of Turks and tribes. It would appear from this directive that the general staff intended this evacuation to be an orderly one.

April and May brought massive Allied offensives at Gallipoli and in Mesopotamia. The expected Russian offensive started in early May towards Erzurum, following close on the heels of the earlier attack on Van. The timing of the Allied attacks – all but simultaneous

the ruling elite, claimed to have been told about similar orders. Modern historians note that there is very little surviving documentary evidence to support these allegations. It should also be noted that the Armenians were heavily armed and that thousands of Muslim villagers were slaughtered in turn as a quasi-civil war erupted among the people of Anatolia.

In the late spring and summer of 1915, Turkish reaction to these armed rebellions escalated from localized to regional relocations. Unfortunately for both sides, the Turks, then heavily involved at Gallipoli, had few forces in place with which to suppress the insurrection. On 24 April, Enver Pasha wrote a directive noting that the Armenians posed a great danger to the war effort, particularly in eastern Anatolia, and outlined a plan to evacuate the Armenian population from the region. At the same time, he ordered the Armenian intelligentsia in the capital and major cities to be imprisoned. This directive specifically identified the six eastern Anatolian provinces as the operational area affected by the evacuation plan. The intent was to move the

Thousands of innocent Armenians were killed resisting relocation. Thousands more were wantonly massacred by their captors for their possessions.

on three widely separated fronts – indicated to the Turks cooperation on a level previously unseen. In the geographic centre of these attacks lay the heavily armed Armenians, who were in a position to throttle the Ottoman lifelines.

This caused a major shift in the government's policy towards the Armenians, with the Young Turks taking a different approach. Enver Pasha thought it necessary either to drive the Armenians then living around Lake Van into Russian territory, or to disperse them throughout the Ottoman Empire. Enver also wanted to resettle the area with Muslim refugees from abroad (Turkey had still not fully assimilated the millions of

An Armenian mother mourns over the body of her dead child. A number of Armenian relief societies were organized in the United States to alleviate the effects of suffering and starvation.

Turkish and Muslim refugees from the Balkan Wars). The military now began to press for a complete evacuation of the Armenian population from the area affected by the insurgency. This was a contemporary counter-insurgency strategy, evolved by the Spanish in Cuba and the British in South Africa (against the Boers), which sought to separate the people from the rebels. This would, in theory, buy time for the hard-pressed Ottoman Army to deal with the insurgents. A provisional law was passed on 27 May that established military responsibility for crushing Armenian resistance, but the law stated that direct action against Armenians would only be out of military necessity or in reply to hostile behaviour.

On 30 May 1915, the infamous regulation directing the relocation of the Armenians was promulgated in the Ministry of the Interior. The regulation was the basis

for the establishment of a series of concentration camps in the Syrian deserts along the Euphrates River. There is nothing in the record to indicate that the military, the Ministry of the Interior and local officials coordinated their efforts to alleviate the horrible conditions suffered by many of the deportees. Importantly, such a scheme wildly exceeded Turkish capabilities. Even if the Turks had been inclined to treat the Armenians kindly, they simply did not have the transportation and logistical means necessary with which to conduct population transfers on such a grand scale.

Making things worse, the continuing rebellion grew more intense as many Armenians, often loyal citizens who were anti-nationalists, now took up arms to defend their lives and homes. In some places the Armenians gained the upper hand, notably in Urfa, Kayseri and on Musa Dag. The hard-pressed Turks now mobilized the local Kurdish and Circassan population by arming irregular bands to combat the Armenians. This, in turn, led to a brutal series of

Armenian women and children. Atrocities against women and children began almost immediately and were well documented by neutral observers. Many of the survivors were forcibly converted to Islam.

massacres and atrocities. In the end, by the late autumn of 1915, most of the Armenians had been forcibly removed from eastern Anatolia. Hundreds of thousands had fled to Russian-controlled territory and tens of thousands more were massacred or starved. The Armenian population of Constantinople and the Aegean region was not relocated, and the army continued to use Armenian manpower in its labour battalions until the end of the war. Hundreds of thousands of Armenians died during the rebellion and deportation and a similar number of Muslim Turks also died in the revolts and during the Russian occupation. Controversy over responsibility continues today and affects contemporary political affairs between the Republic of Turkey and the West.

CHAPTER 4

Mesopotamia

In early 1915, skirmishing took place between the Turks and the Indian Army in Mesopotamia. The Turks began an operation to force Allied troops from the area, leading to General Charles Townshend's counteroperations. Despite a resounding victory at the First Battle of Kut, Townshend's force became encircled and was forced to surrender. Fighting would continue in the theatre until late 1918.

In February and March 1915, there were several small engagements between the Turks and the Indian Army in Mesopotamia, but each was too weak to secure decisive victory. Alarmed by the seemingly effortless seizure of the lower Tigris and Euphrates basin by the Indian Army, the Turks began to contemplate offensive operations designed to push them back down river. The Turkish area commander, Suleyman Askeri, decided to conduct a flanking attack on the British positions at Basra. In doing so, he hoped to avoid the main British positions at Qurna, and achieve local numerical superiority. A British cavalry

A Bavarian Artillery unit at Kut al-Amara. Most German troops sent to the Ottoman Empire served in Palestine, the Sinai and Syria. However, some specialized units, such as artillery and air detachments, reached the outer theatres.

Major George Godfrey Wheeler, VC, of the 7th Hariana Lancers leads his squadron in an attempt to capture a Turkish flag at Shaiba, Mesopotamia, 13 April 1915. In the early campaigns in Mesopotamia the British and Indians faced second-rate and poorly equipped Ottoman forces, and their easy victories drew them up river towards Baghdad.

brigade held the town of Shaiba – the key to the southern approach to the city. Suleyman Askeri began moving in early April 1915, but was detected by the British, who used their time to strengthen their defences. On the morning of 12 April the Turks attacked the fortified camp at Shaiba with a brief artillery bombardment from 12 field guns. Turkish infantry attacked shortly thereafter, but failed, and further attacks continued all day and the next as well. Suleyman Askeri called off his attacks when a British cavalry counterattack threatened his flanks. He lost a third of the 4000 men he started with, and was unable to prevent the remainder from fleeing north.

The British immediately advanced on the Turkish positions. They took the first line of Turkish trenches as many Arabs, who were drafted involuntarily into the Ottoman Army, surrendered en masse, but they failed to break through Suleyman's lines. Over a three-day period, the Turks suffered 6000 men killed or wounded, including 2000 Arab tribesmen, and lost over 700 prisoners, forcing them to withdraw to Khamisiya, 144km (89 miles) up river. There the unfortunate Suleyman Askeri, who had been wounded earlier in the campaign and was now semi-invalided on his camp bed, assembled his staff. He was something of a legend in the Ottoman Army and was a renowned guerrilla leader. Depressed by his defeat, he shot himself to avoid further humiliation. The official Turkish campaign history mentions his suicide, but it is not explained in great detail. It notes that he was concerned about the discipline and fighting spirit of his Arab levies as well as the high percentage of these men in his infantry regiment. It was a bleak day for the Turks, and interim command in Mesopotamia fell to Mehmed Fazil Pasha.

However, the Turkish forces in Mesopotamia were about to receive an injection of reinforcements that would restore their strength, as the general staff began to return forces to the region, such as the 35th Division. Although the latter was incomplete at that point, it would gain strength throughout the remainder of 1915.

Largely due to their unexpected success in Mesopotamia, the India Office and the Indian Army's general staff decided in late April 1915 to continue the advance up river to the port of Amara on the Euphrates and to Nasiriya on the Tigris. General Charles V.F. Townshend arrived in Qurna to command the small British army. Once there, and seeing the effects of the seasonal flooding, Townshend determined to make a single advance up the Tigris with his small force, and soon Amara was captured. The Turks contested the advance with a small fleet of armed river steamers. In June, after the seasonal flooding had ended, Townshend took Nasiriya as well. The Indian Army's 12th Division arrived to reinforce the expedition, but (save one brigade) Townshend was forced to employ it along the river to assist in bringing supplies forward. The political repercussions from the already failing Gallipoli campaign meant the British War Office and the India Office now began to view the successes in Mesopotamia with interest. Although aware of how short of soldiers Townshend was, London began to push for further advances towards Baghdad itself. With strong Ottoman forces entrenched on the Euphrates, Townshend began to make preparations for moving up the Tigris on the town of Kut al-Amara. Facing him at Kut al-Amara were the remnants of the 38th Division, a poorly armed group of about five infantry battalions.

Corporal Trice of the 6th Ammunition Column, Royal Field Artillery lands a machine gun from a barge under enemy fire near Nassiriyah, Mesopotamia, on 24 July 1915. Trice was later awarded the Distinguished Conduct Medal for his actions. In the absence of railways in Mesopotamia, the Tigris River became an important British transportation artery. However, the meandering of the river tripled the distance British forces had to cover moving between Basra and Baghdad.

The weak Ottoman position in Mesopotamia quickly changed for the better when a new and aggressive commander, Nurettin Pasha (or Nur ud Din Pasha in the British histories), arrived to re-energize the defence. Moreover, well trained reinforcements were slowly finding their way to Mesopotamia. In November 1915, the 45th Division began to arrive and the 51st Division, formed in Constantinople in the late autumn of 1914 from First Army assets as an expeditionary force, was ordered to Mesopotamia from the Caucasus. Its sister, the 52nd Division, would shortly follow. In Baghdad, Nurettin

An illustration commemorating the alliance of the Central Powers, although only the Ottoman crescent is shown. Cooperation between the Turks and Germans was excellent throughout the war. German staff officers and technicians provided great assistance to the Ottoman Empire, especially in logistics, transportation and communications.

augmented the 45th Division with 5000 Gendarmes and frontier guards, bringing it up to full strength. However, these forces would not be combat ready for months, and in the meantime, Nurettin had to rely on the 35th Division and the remnants of the 38th Division, both of which comprised fewer than 4000 infantry. Nurettin had a total effective strength of about 7000 men, supported by a tiny amount of cavalry and artillery, available to deal with the renewed British attack.

As the autumn campaigning season of mild and dry weather set in, Townshend began his move on 1 September 1915. By 26 September, he was closing on the river port of Kut al-Amara. As the Turks were unsure where he would strike, they positioned the 35th Division on the right bank of the river and the 38th Division on the left. There was a small reserve of four battalions and some cavalry, mostly comprising locally drafted Arabs, whose morale was not high, and the Turks had a total of 38 artillery pieces. Townshend's army moved closer in a night march and attacked the Ottoman lines early in the morning of 28 September 1915. By midday, Townshend had broken the Ottoman lines and, moreover, outflanked them in the north. Nurettin committed his tiny reserve, which was defeated, and by nightfall, his army was in retreat. Townshend pursued him, and by 5 October reached Aziziya. Townshend's campaign had been extremely successful for little cost, while Nurettin lost about 4000 men and a third of his guns. The First Battle of Kut was a resounding British victory.

THE BATTLE OF CTESIPHON

The relentless British advance reached Lajj on 21 October 1915. Three days later Townshend was directed to move on Baghdad by 14 November. He was uneasy about this: he had only a single reinforced Indian Army division, and intelligence had informed him that Turkish reinforcements were on the way. In public, however, Townshend exuded confidence. In truth, he had done well thus far and had reason to be optimistic. By early November, Townshend's force, now numbering about 11,000 infantry, reached Ctesiphon (or Selman Pak as it was known to the Turks), which was only about 32km (20 miles) south of Baghdad. It was here that Nurettin chose to make his stand. The ensuing battle would mark the highwater point of the first British offensive in Mesopotamia.

Charles Townshend was the product of the late Victorian British Army and he was schooled in the small wars of the era. He was ambitious, restless and had a somewhat theatrical personality. His successful defence of Chitral Fort in 1895 during a 50-day siege had already won him fame at home. He served against the Mahdi in Sudan and briefly in the Second Boer War. After service in Paris as an attaché, where he became enamoured with French methods, he was posted to Rawal Pindi in command of the 6th (Poona) Division. Typical of his times, he was dismissive of the capability and fighting spirit of the Ottoman Army, and his campaign thus far vindicated these beliefs. His division was a regular Indian Army

Sir Charles Vere Ferrers Townshend (1861–1924)

Townshend was originally commissioned into the Royal Marine Light Infantry, but transferred to the Army. He served in the Sudan and Egypt and won a CB for his defence of Chitral Fort in 1895. To this he added the DSO for his role in Kitchener's expedition against the Mahdi in 1898. With the British declaration of war Townshend was appointed to command the 6th (Poona) Indian Division in April 1915. He won several victories, but after defeat at Ctesiphon, he was isolated in Kut al-Amara. He surrendered in April 1916 and his soldiers went into a harsh captivity. Townshend assisted with the negotiation of the Ottoman armistice at Mudros in October 1918, but his reputation continued to suffer as news of the maltreatment of his force spread. He died in 1924.

Ctesiphon Arch, Iraq. The ancient arch was visible from much of the battlefield at Ctesiphon (Selman Pak). It provided a colourful ancient backdrop for the modern battle fought there in 1915.

one of three brigades, each of three Indian battalions and one British battalion. It was largely untrained in modern conventional operations and had little artillery and few machine guns. There were almost no replacements available when it took casualties, particularly among the officers. Townshend also had the 30th Brigade, the 6th Cavalry Brigade and a flotilla of river gunboats. At Ctesiphon, the meandering river had taken Townshend some 800km (500 miles) from the sea.

Nurettin was the Ottoman Army's counterpart to Townshend. He had a conventional background and had fought guerrillas in Macedonia, the Greeks in 1897, and in the counter-insurgency campaign in Yemen. In 1914 he assumed command of an infantry division. While intelligent (he spoke four foreign languages), like Townshend he was not a graduate of a staff college or a war academy and had no strong political connections, having risen by ability. Unlike

Townshend, he would end his career in command of an army, in the Turkish War of Independence.

While Townshend's army was decreasing in strength each mile it advanced, Nurettin's army grew stronger daily. Over the autumn, the Ottoman 45th Division completed deployment and joined the line. The well trained and combat-seasoned 51st Division (formerly called the 1st Expeditionary Force) arrived on 17 November, with seven fresh infantry battalions and a group of Schneider howitzers. One regiment of the 52nd Division had also arrived at Mosul and the remainder of the division was due shortly. Like its sister division, the 52nd (formerly called the 5th Expeditionary Force) was composed of combat veterans, whose morale and fighting capability was high. Nurettin now had a total effective strength of 20,000 men, armed with 19 machine guns and 52 cannon. He also had a small but capable cavalry force of about 400 men. More importantly, the 45th, 51st and 52nd divisions were some of the best fighting units in the army.

Nurettin selected a defensive position at Ctesiphon, where his right flank rested securely on the Tigris

Turkish prisoners in Mesopotamia. Many of the prisoners taken early on by the British in Mesopotamia were locally conscripted men of Arab ethnicity. They were inadequately trained, and many favoured independence.

River. On 28 September he began to build two defensive lines in depth. The first line was about 10km (six miles) in length with extremely deep trenches, and had 12–15 earthwork redoubts, which were fronted with barbed wire and had overhead cover. The 38th and 45th divisions garrisoned this formidable line. Three kilometres to its rear lay the second Turkish defensive line, which was also strongly constructed. The 51st Division lay in reserve behind this line, and on the left flank of his entrenchments Nurettin positioned his cavalry. On the south side of the river, the 35th Division held similar positions. Although well dug in and possessing a large number of troops, Nurettin was far from confident. He was especially worried about the small number of guns available, as well as shortages of artillery shells. Consequently, he coordinated very detailed and centralized fire plans to maximize his combat power.

TOWNSHEND'S DEPLOYMENT

Townshend organized his force into four columns, one of which was a flying one to outflank the end of Nurettin's line. Townshend knew that he was now outnumbered, but relied on the demonstrated propensity of the enemy to break at the critical moment. He had no idea of the calibre of reinforcements that Nurettin had received in the form of the 45th and 51st divisions. Townshend's plan

massed 9000 Indian and British soldiers against about 3000 Turks at the apex of the L-shaped Turkish line. Although outnumbered overall, Townshend achieved a decisive superiority at the point of his attack, which was on Redoubt 11, or the 'Vital Point' (VP) as Townshend called it.

At 6.30am on the bitterly cold morning of 22 November, the columns of the 6th (Poona) Division began their advance on the Turkish lines at Ctesiphon under the cover of artillery and naval gunfire. The British thought they had achieved surprise and that the Turks were fleeing the lines. Nothing could have been further from the truth as Turkish artillery, machine guns and rifles opened fire by the thousand on the attacking forces. Townshend continued to press the attack all morning, despite mounting losses, which now began to include a number of officers. At 11.30am, he

Nurettin Pasha (1873–1932)

Nurettin (Nur ud Din) Pasha was one of the few Ottoman officers to achieve high command without benefit of a staff college education. He was exceptionally talented and spoke Arabic, French, German and Russian. Nurettin served in the Ottoman–Greek War (1897) and fought guerrillas in both Macedonia (1902) and Yemen (1911–12). He commanded at regimental and divisional level. Selected to command the faltering Ottoman forces in Mesopotamia, he solidified the defences and saved the Ottoman strategic situation there by stopping the British at Ctesiphon. It was Nurettin's campaign plan and vigorous pursuit of Townshend that sealed the fate of the 6th (Poona) Division and enabled the ultimate Ottoman victory. Although relieved by Enver's uncle, Halil Pasha, Nurettin went on to successfully command Ottoman Army corps in 1917–18. Later, in the War of Independence, Nurettin commanded the First Army and played a key role in the expulsion of the Greeks from Asia Minor in 1922. He retired as a lieutenant-general in 1925.

A 2.75in Mountain Gun of the Indian Army. The Indian Army divisions sent to Mesopotamia had almost no organic artillery, save a few mountain batteries. This was a result of the Sepoy Mutiny of 1857 after which the Indian Army had been stripped of its artillery.

ordered his cavalry brigade to attempt to outflank the Turks, but was met by the Turkish cavalry and the 51st Division. Nevertheless, by noon Townshend's men controlled the first line of Turkish trenches and by 1.30pm they held some of the redoubts. Nurettin's 38th and 45th divisions were shattered in this fight. Townshend himself went to the 'vital point' and stood for hours under withering enemy fire, demanding that his brigadiers do the same, which they did.

At this point in the battle, Nurettin ordered the 51st Division under Cevid Bey to counterattack, bringing most of the 35th Division across the river to support it. The fighting continued all afternoon, and as darkness fell the British and Indian advance stalled. Townshend had lost a third of his officers engaged, and 4200 men out of 11,000. His field hospitals, equipped to handle 400 wounded, had to accommodate ten times that number. Nurettin estimated that he had lost some 6100 men, or 30 per cent of his army. That evening both the Turkish and the British commanders were profoundly depressed.

The next day fighting resumed, with Townshend attempting to continue his breakthrough and ordering a second cavalry flanking attack. That morning, a fierce sandstorm blew up, which badly affected the visibility of both armies. The battle continued and Nurettin committed the reformed remnants of the 38th and 45th divisions to a counterattack. Darkness halted the fighting, as both sides sank into exhausted inactivity. A discouraged Townshend began to evacuate his wounded. By 25 November the fighting had ended, and although he still held the first line of Turkish trenches, Townshend knew he could not break through. At midday he decided to withdraw. Simultaneously, Nurettin decided that he too had lost the battle and made preparations to withdraw to the Diyala River. Fortunately for the Turks, his cavalry detected the British retreat and Nurettin was able to reverse his order. The British threat to Baghdad in 1915 was over. Townshend was expected to attack, and his plan was a bold one that maximized the available resources. Given a less capable enemy commander, it might have worked.

Townshend withdrew his battered force down river to Aziziya. As he did so, Nurettin immediately sent the experienced 51st Division and his tribal cavalry brigade on a pursuit operation aimed at encircling and annihilating Townshend's army. The latter had a narrow escape and was brought into camp at Umm at Tubul, where again it was almost encircled. On 1 December Nurettin again outflanked Townshend, forcing him to abandon 500 wounded men, who could not be evacuated in time. With the Turks following close on his heels and having been stung badly, Townshend pulled back to Shadi. There he made the fatal decision to bring his battered army into the dubious refuge of Kut al-Amara. Most of his force arrived there on 3 December.

The town of Kut al-Amara lay in the bend of the Tigris River and contained a total of 7000 Arab residents. General Nixon, the overall British commander in Mesopotamia, approved Townshend's decision, but the general staff had misgivings. From Townshend's perspective, Kut al-Amara offered his army a protected enclave to rest his exhausted army and treat his wounded. Moreover, there were plentiful stores there and he began to fortify the town and offload his supplies from the river steamers. Overall, Townshend's retreat was well handled and skilfully executed. His decision was certainly affected by his own personal experience in defending Chitral Fort and, probably, by his knowledge of the British tradition of successfully enduring sieges that included Lucknow, Rorke's Drift, Ladysmith, Mafeking and

Townshend's advance to Ctesiphon. The initial British offensive against Baghdad enjoyed dramatic success, which was unusual in the first year of the war. However, when first-line Ottoman troops arrived in theatre, the scales tipped against the British.

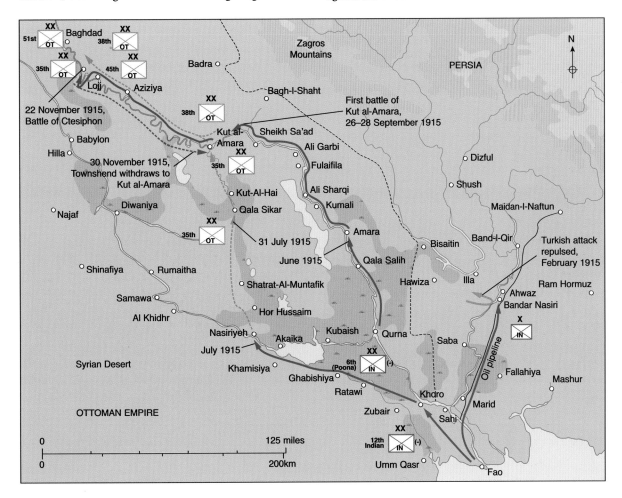

Peking. Moreover, it could be argued that the British had a unique history, in most cases, of relieving encircled forces, Isandhlwana and Gordon's last stand at Khartoum notwithstanding.

On 6 December Townshend sent his cavalry and some of the residents down stream, leaving him with about 11,600 combatants and 3350 non-combatants in the town. He had 60 days of full rations available, along with plenty of ammunition. He also had a powerful flotilla of river gunboats and steamers on the Tigris, and he knew that several additional Indian infantry divisions were arriving at Basra. Therefore, on this day, he was not alarmed about the possibility of being besieged in Kut al-Amara.

Nurettin, in the meantime, began his encirclement of the town by sending a mixed force south of the river and his cavalry east; these forces were to meet 20km

A canvas cloth has turned a hole in the ground into a water supply point for British troops. Large quantities of fresh water were required in climates like Mesopotamia, and moving and storing it became highly important.

(12 miles) down river. He sent the 45th Division to bottle up Townshend, and by the end of 6 December the Turks had completed the encirclement. The next day, he sent the 35th and 38th divisions down river to begin entrenching a defensive line against any relief force. Nurettin had created classic lines of contravallation (facing inward) and circumvallation (facing outward), which were first used by Julius Caesar to besiege Vercingetorix at Alesia in 52 BC. He knew that it was as important to stop the relief force as it was to isolate Townshend, and this act critically shaped the coming campaign. Kut al-Amara was now cut off from Basra, and the Turks began to dig a series of entrenchments across the neck of the bend in the Tigris where the town lay (there was a smaller British enclave across from the town on the southern bank).

Nurettin hypothesized that Townshend had not yet had time to dig in, and so on 10 December he launched an hasty attack on the Old Fort and on a small bridgehead (called Woolpress Village) that the British held on the south bank of the river. However,

The Mesopotamian theatre became a deathtrap for many wounded soldiers, such as these injured British troops. Many who died there might have survived under less arduous conditions.

Nurettin's men were exhausted from their vigorous pursuit, and the no man's land was entirely barren and flat; as a result, these attacks failed. Of equal importance, the Turks had only 50 guns and little artillery ammunition, and so could only conduct a brief bombardment.

On 12 December 1915 the German Field Marshal Colmar von der Goltz arrived at Kut al-Amara to take command in Mesopotamia. Contrary to general opinion, he did not replace Nurettin as army commander but took over as theatre commander. Goltz briefly observed the siege, but left for Baghdad within the week to inspect his forces preparing to invade Persia, which was where his real interests lay. By 23 December, about 25,000 Turkish soldiers ringed the town of Kut al-Amara. Nurettin, irritated by inactivity, launched another attack at night on the town on 24 December, which became known as the 'Christmas Eve attack'. It was characterized by hand-to-hand fighting with bayonets, and was resolved in Townshend's favour by the heroic efforts of the Oxford battalion. The Turks were repulsed with over 2000 casualties. At the end of December minor attacks by the 35th and 52nd divisions met a similar fate.

Despite this, the new year offered positive prospects for the Turks in Mesopotamia. General Townshend was bottled up in Kut al-Amara, and although the British were assembling a relief force at Basra, the 52nd Division had arrived in force. Importantly, the arrival of these divisions shifted the ethnic composition of Nurettin's army from predominately Arabic to predominately Anatolian Turkish, shifting the balance of power in favour of the Turks in the defensive battles ahead. Also, the presence of the 72-year-old but still vigorous Goltz, whose experience with the Turks extended back into the 1880s, gave much inspiration to the Turks. Despite these bright prospects, the Ottoman Empire was unable to provide a steady flow of replacements and the 38th Division was disbanded in late December 1915.

The Turkish and German commander in Mesopotamia, 1916. Very few Germans served in Mesopotamia. The theatre was more or less a strategic backwater for both sides until the very end of the war.

THE SIEGE OF KUT AL-AMARA

The imposing British relief force poised to relieve Kut was led by Lieutenant-General Sir F.J. Aylmer. It was composed of the newly designated Tigris Corps (formerly the Indian Corps), comprising the veteran 3rd (Lahore) and 7th (Meerut) divisions, fresh from the Western Front. In France it had made important contributions to the 'Race to the Sea' and the Battle of Neuve Chapelle, but its overall performance was characterized as 'undistinguished'. Like Townshend's Indian division, the 3rd and 7th Divisions suffered from inadequate modern combined-arms training as well as from a lack of artillery and machine guns. They also suffered badly from a shortage of trained officers and NCOs to replace those lost in France. Unfortunately, these divisions displayed considerable contempt for the Turks, whom they considered as a second-class opponent. The arrival of the Tigris Corps returned the theatre to a relative balance of forces, as the four 12-battalion Indian divisions had 48 infantry battalions while the five nine-battalion Turkish divisions had 45 infantry battalions. Both sides were logistically challenged and, compared to

the situation in France, woefully short of artillery (especially howitzers).

Goltz redesignated Nurettin's Sixth Army as the Iraq Group on 21 December 1915. He did not change Nurettin's order of battle, which divided his army into two parts: XVIII Corps (45th and 51st divisions) encircling Kut, and XIII Corps (35th and 52nd divisions) blocking the British relief force about 30km (18.6 miles) down stream. Oddly enough, there was both river and telegraph traffic between the encircled Townshend and the relief force.

In early January, the British began to probe the Turkish lines and to extend their cavalry around both flanks of the Turkish position. These probes were repulsed, but the British launched a stronger attack on 8 January 1916, which also failed. Nurettin brought his cavalry forward and continued to dig in. On 12 January Aylmer tried to break through the lines of the 52nd Division in a night attack, but his leading brigade was discovered by the alert Turks and was badly mauled. Strong British attacks continued to hammer the 52nd Division from 21 January; the Turks were helped by geography, which rested their right on the river and their left by a salt marsh, thus prohibiting movement. The Ottoman lines were well prepared, which did not deter the British from conducting repeated and costly frontal assaults. Casualties were so

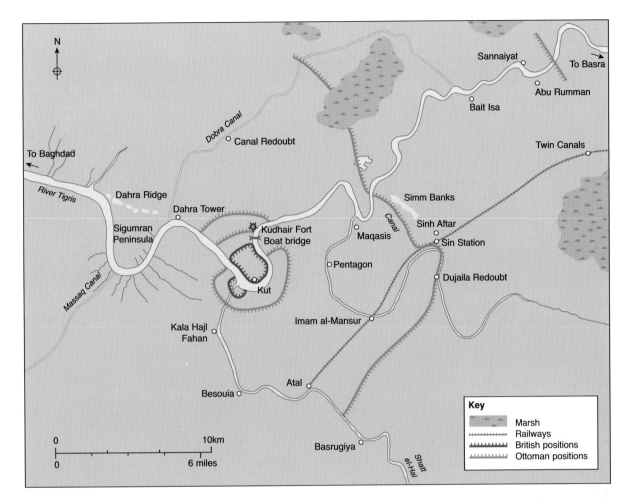

Map labels:

N · To Baghdad · River Tigris · Dahra Ridge · Dahra Tower · Sigumran Peninsula · Massaq Canal · Dobra Canal · Canal Redoubt · Kudhair Fort · Boat bridge · Kut · Kala Hajl Fahan · Besouia · Atal · Basrugiya · Pentagon · Maqasis · Imam al-Mansur · Simm Banks · Sinh Aftar · Sin Station · Canal · Dujaila Redoubt · Sannaiyat · Abu Rumman · To Basra · Bait Isa · Twin Canals · Shatt el-Hai

Key
Marsh
Railways
British positions
Ottoman positions

0 10km
0 6 miles

lop-sided that Aylmer was discouraged from further attacks along the Wadi-Nakhailat and halted his assaults. In Kut al-Amara, Townshend was astonished when news of Aylmer's decision reached him.

Despite his successes, Nurettin would soon be replaced for political reasons. As it became apparent that the empire was about to win a major victory, Enver Pasha decided to replace him with his uncle, Colonel Halil Bey, who was then in command of XVIII Corps (it should be mentioned that Halil was a very capable soldier and had a distinguished combat record). Technically, Goltz remained in command of the entire Mesopotamian and Persian theatres, but he left the daily decision making to his Turkish commanders. The change of command occurred on 20 January, but Halil Bey wisely did not change

The siege of Kut al-Amara. Nurettin created 'lines of contravallation' encircling Kut and 'lines of circumvallation' to thwart any relieving forces. Caesar had used these tactics successfully against Vercingetorix at Alesia in 52 BC.

Nurettin's plans. Fleeing Arabs provided information about the deteriorating condition of the beleaguered British and Indian troops in Kut al-Amara, and Halil Bey decided to starve them out. In the meantime, Halil's gunners lobbed shells into the town, which served to keep everyone inside the British lines on edge. Halil also repeatedly feigned attacks, which further exhausted the British, who were forced to respond as if these were real. In February, Townshend's men went on half rations, while the Ottoman 2nd Division arrived as a reinforcement. Conditions inside the town of Kut al-Amara worsened throughout March. The Turks maintained a more or less continuous artillery bombardment and raided the town with aircraft on a frequent basis.

Aylmer made a single relief attempt on 8 March from the south bank of the Tigris River. Unfortunately, the newly arrived 2nd Division and the 35th Division had established a very strong defensive line about 10km (six miles) east of Kut al-Amara, which was backed by artillery and a strong reserve in each Turkish infantry division sector. By this time, the Kut al-Amara garrison was so weak that Halil was able to bring the 51st Division to reinforce the line. When the British attacks failed, the Turks vigorously counterattacked on 11 March; however, they only managed to achieve small gains.

April brought the final four attempts to relieve Townshend. On 5 and 6 April the British attacked the 51st Division, which had constructed a solid defensive line including minefields. It repelled the attacks, but withdrew to a fall-back position three kilometres (1.86

miles) to the rear. Another major attack followed on 9 April, but this too failed. Aylmer sent a large three-division offensive against XVIII Corps holding the south bank of the Tigris on 17/18 April, and a final push came four days later, which was also unsuccessful. None of these attacks gained ground, while the Turkish counterattacks punished the British severely. As the Turks were solidly entrenched, losses were very one-sided, with the British suffering almost 20,000 casualties and the Turks only 9000. Since these attacks occurred within 10–15km (6–9 miles) of the centre of Kut al-Amara, the noise, smoke and explosions were heard and seen by the beleaguered British. The British relief force continued to probe the Turkish defences throughout the following week, but

Turkish troops with a mortar at Kut al-Amara. This ancient, muzzle-loading mortar demonstrates how poorly equipped the Turks were in Mesopotamia. Such weapons were unheard of in other theatres of war, but the shortage of artillery called for such desperate measures.

Arab prisoners of the British in Kut al-Amara. It is unclear whether these men were a military threat or criminals. It is likely that they were simple thieves who plagued the British lines of communications.

without success. Nurettin's basic operational concept had been clearly vindicated.

In a desperate attempt to help Townshend continue resistance, the Royal Flying Corps and Royal Naval Air Service drew up a plan to drop supplies into the beleaguered town. From 16 to 29 April, British pilots dropped approximately eight tons of supplies, which included food, medicine and even fishing nets. These limited quantities could not materially alter the course of the siege, but they encouraged Townshend and his men to feel that the main army was trying every possible measure to assist them. The missions were not without risk and Turkish anti-aircraft fire and fighter aircraft attempted to thwart these efforts. This caused some missions to be abandoned. To make things worse, other pilots dropped supplies prematurely and into the Turkish lines.

There was one final, sad chapter in the saga of the attempted relief of Kut al-Amara involving the steamer *Julnar*, which was a part of the British flotilla on the Tigris River. It was thought that if Townshend's garrison could be resupplied, he might continue to hold out until the relief of the town. In the words of

General Sir Percy Lake, 'faint as the chance was, the *Julnar*, one of the fastest steamers on the river, had for some days been under preparation by the Royal Navy for an attempt to run the enemy's blockade.' At 8pm on 24 April 1916, with a crew of volunteers from the Royal Navy, the *Julnar* left Falahiyah carrying 270 tons of supplies in an attempt to reach Kut. While nominally under the command of the navy, the ship was in fact captained by a civilian volunteer named C.H. Cowley, who had been commissioned into the Royal Navy Volunteer Reserve as a lieutenant-commander and had spent many years piloting on the Tigris River. The British laid down artillery and machine-gun barrages in the hope of distracting the enemy's attention from the ship's movement. The alert Turks, however, quickly discovered and shelled the *Julnar* on her passage up the river.

Passing the enemy lines astride the river, the *Julnar* drew more and more fire and eventually became

Townshend and his staff. Townshend's initial battles against the Turks were well planned and well fought. At Ctesiphon he was outnumbered two to one. Had he not surrendered at Kut al-Amara, Townshend might have matured into an outstanding battlefield commander.

entangled in cables that the Turks had drawn across the river. By midnight she lay grounded well behind the Turkish lines, where enemy infantry stormed the disabled ship. Townshend reported hearing heavy firing that night down river from Kut al-Amara, which suddenly ceased around midnight. The commander of the enterprise, Lieutenant H.O.B. Firman, was killed and the daring men of the *Julnar* were taken prisoner. The unfortunate, wounded Cowley was recognized by the Turks as a local river pilot, and there is some dispute today whether Cowley, apparently still in his civilian clothing, was summarily executed by the Turks or whether he pulled a pistol and went down fighting. In any event, he died a hero. The next day, British airmen confirmed that the ship was in enemy hands.

By 22 April Townshend knew that further resistance was useless and that he must surrender. Five days later he asked for terms, which, he hoped, would be generous. In particular, both his troops and the local population were completely out of food, and he asked therefore, above all, for immediate assistance in rationing his force and charges. There was much confusion as blindfolded staff officers were passed between the two armies, particularly over the exact terms of surrender. Finally, Townshend himself met with Halil Bey (the elderly, but indomitable, Goltz had died of cholera on 19 April) and attempted to buy his army out of captivity with a promise of a one million pound payment in gold. In fact, Thomas E. Lawrence (later famous as 'Lawrence of Arabia') was a part of this scheme, but it went sour and collapsed. Townshend also attempted to secure some sort of a parole. In the end, the honourable Halil Bey demanded an unconditional surrender, which Townshend was forced to accept. An Ottoman infantry regiment marched into Kut al-Amara at 1pm on 29 April 1916 to receive the surrender. Other than starving men, there was little to capture, as the British had spent two days destroying their artillery, ammunition and military equipment.

The surrender of Townshend's 6th (Poona) Division was the largest of imperial troops between Yorktown in 1781 and Singapore in 1942. It was a terrible embarrassment for British arms, although the total number of soldiers lost was hardly a day's worth of cannon fodder in the big battles then raging in Flanders. Townshend surrendered 13,309 men, including 2864 British, 7192 Indian and 3248 non-combatant troops. Over 4000 of these men subsequently died in Turkish captivity, and it is estimated that 70 per cent of the British prisoners died. Halil and Aylmer exchanged some 1100 sick and wounded British and Indian soldiers for an approximately equal number of unfit Turks. The Turks also recorded capturing 40 artillery pieces, three aircraft, two river steamers and 40 motor cars, almost all of which were damaged. The first Turkish food

supplies arrived by relief boat on 1 May 1916. Townshend and his aides were sent to Baghdad two days later and the Turks began to evacuate their prisoners the following day. The first British to leave Kut al-Amara after Townshend were four generals, 160 officers and 180 of their personal aides, by boat. Townshend's British and Indian soldiers, however, were marched north in columns, often without adequate water, food or medical supplies. As a consequence many died in what some have termed a 'death march'. In the space of just over a year, the British lost 40,000 men in Mesopotamia. Colonel Halil Bey became an overnight hero and received the honorific 'Pasha'. Later, in the Turkish republican era, he would choose the surname 'Kut'. For his part, Townshend went into comfortable captivity on an island in the Sea of Marmara, while his surviving men endured hard conditions in Anatolian POW camps.

British forces captured at Kut al-Amara. The Turks also captured a number of motor cars along with artillery, aircraft and stores. Most were deliberately damaged beyond repair prior to the British surrender.

The heavily armed and sandbagged *Julnar* looks dangerously top heavy in this photo, with two artillery pieces facing forward. She was captured on 24 April 1916.

A shocked British Government demanded to know what had happened, and, since it came close on the heels of the Dardanelles disaster, convened a parliamentary commission. The testimony focused on administrative, logistical and medical problems, as well as the institutional weaknesses of the Indian Army. The report of the commission appeared in 1917 and largely blamed factors internal to the British Army for Townshend's humiliating defeat. In truth, it was Nurettin's aggressive pursuit and lines of circumvallation that defeated him, along with the defensive qualities of the Ottoman Army.

With the surrender of Townshend at Kut al-Amara, the campaign in Mesopotamia entered a period of stalemate. The fighting had exhausted both sides, and without Townshend to rescue there seemed little reason for the British to hurry up river. Halil Bey began to slowly redeploy his forces downstream, carefully fortifying both banks of the Tigris and finally finding enough surplus forces to fortify the Euphrates as well. There was little activity in Mesopotamia for the remainder of 1916 until December, when a renewed and greatly reinforced Imperial force under General Sir Stanley Maude again began the slow march up river.

THE SECOND INVASION OF PERSIA

Despite Goltz's death, Enver Pasha journeyed to Baghdad in mid-May 1916 to confer with Halil Pasha and Colonel von Lossow about the prospects for a renewed offensive against Persia. In the aftermath of the victory at Gallipoli, Enver had troops deploying to Mesopotamia; however, the surrender of Kut al-Amara in April made their presence in the Tigris–Euphrates Valley redundant, and Enver was eager to use them in an offensive capacity. The 2nd Division was already at Kut al-Amara and its sister divisions, the 4th and 6th, were due in theatre by the end of the month. All of these divisions comprised battle-hardened veterans of the Gallipoli campaign.

Enver's ambitious invasion plan called for Halil's XIII Corps to detach the 35th and 52nd divisions to its Sixth Army sister XVIII Corps, and to receive the fresh and rested 2nd, 4th and 6th divisions. An independent cavalry brigade, some irregular units and Persian nationalist volunteers would augment the corps. Lossow also promised German artillery, but this never arrived. Altogether, XIII Corps would total around 25,000 men to oppose a Russian army of several divisions in Persia, but the Russians were widely spread out.

XIII Corps, commanded by Ali Insan Pasha, began its advance in late May after concentrating on the frontier. However, the ever-aggressive Russians

Townshend enters Turkish captivity. He was treated well by the Turks, living in a villa on the Prince's Island at the mouth of the Bosporus. He was accorded free movement in Constantinople, while his men suffered cruelly and died in prisoner of war camps.

attacked the 6th Division and attempted to encircle it together with the XIII Corps headquarters in the border town of Hanikin on 3 June. The Russians came close to succeeding, but their thinly spread infantry battalions were held in check while the centrally positioned Turks crushed the encircling Russian cavalry. Threatened with defeat in detail, the Russians withdrew. Soon after, XIII Corps crossed the Persian frontier, which consisted of rugged mountains with narrow valleys that made offensive operations difficult. General Baratov, the Russian commander, conducted a skilful fighting retreat. The main Turkish force, the 2nd and 6th divisions, advanced through the mountains along the main road to Kermansah. On the Turkish left (or northern) flank, the 4th Division crossed the frontier from Süleymaniye and pushed east towards Sine and Kurve. This division was reinforced with some Persian volunteer battalions and

was now styled the Mosul Group. The main force encountered strong Russian defences near Karind and halted to prepare an attack.

The Turks attacked on 28 June, taking Karind two days later. By now XIII Corps was over 150km (93 miles) beyond the frontier and the Russians continued to retreat. Finally they concentrated for a stand at Hamadan. After a hard-fought, six-day battle, XIII Corps took the town on 9 August 1916. Baratov pulled back another 100km (60 miles) to block key mountain passes while awaiting reinforcements. The distances were too great to sustain Ali Insan Pasha's corps logistically, and his offensive came to a halt. Combat casualties in XIII Corps were very light, but diseases, such as cholera and typhus, had ravaged the corps on the march to Hamadan. With the main body of XIII Corps at Hamadan and the 4th Division forward of the frontier at Süleymaniye, the corps was too spread out for mutually supporting offensive operations. Moreover, Ali Insan Pasha had been told that large numbers of Persian volunteers would join him; however, few actually came to help. For these reasons, he decided that his force was insufficient to continue the conquest of Persia and halted operations. This ended the second invasion of Persia, and XIII Corps limited its activities to a series of patrols to the north and east of Hamadan.

THE CAPTURE OF BAGHDAD

The British made important improvements in their army in Mesopotamia after the disastrous failures before Kut al-Amara in the spring of 1916. Most

Von Lossow was a consummate German general staff officer who spent much of the war serving at the Ministry of War in Constantinople, helping plan the Ottoman war effort.

Von der Goltz, in his role as Governor General of Belgium. The field marshal was the most respected German officer in the Ottoman Empire. He had served with the Turks in the 1880s and 1890s, and had helped train both their staff officers and their army.

importantly, the defeated commanders were relieved and the aggressive General Maude was sent out to assume theatre command. Also, the Imperial force in the Tigris and Euphrates valleys was to increase its strength, by sending two additional infantry divisions (the 13th Division from Gallipoli and the 14th Indian Division) to reinforce Maude. Even the defeated Tigris Corps was renamed I Indian Army Corps. Maude was determined to avenge the defeat of Townshend.

As the summer of 1916 turned into autumn, Maude planned an advance up the Tigris to break Halil's grip on the gateway to Baghdad. He now had a large force concentrated under his direct command, with a total of five infantry divisions, well supported by cavalry, artillery and aircraft. Additionally, he built up a large and capable river flotilla of armed steamers and supply vessels. Maude had a fighting strength of 166,000 men, of whom 107,000 were from the Indian Army. In spite of the high numbers of men and equipment, Maude was determined not to advance until he was fully ready, and resisted political pressure.

Because of strategic diversions elsewhere (such as Persia, Galicia and Salonika) and because of chronic weaknesses in rail communications, the Ottoman general staff did not augment the Sixth Army's strength in the final nine months of 1916. Moreover, Halil Pasha received very few individual replacements for his losses, which grew larger with each passing day. Slow attrition from disease, desertion and occasional British activity continually wore away his army. Thus, while General Maude's army grew in size and capability, Halil's steadily grew weaker. Enver's scheme to invade Persia further reduced his uncle's army. By summer 1916, Halil's force contained only XVIII Corps comprising the 45th, 51st and 52nd divisions.

He also found it necessary to inactivate the unfortunate 35th Division and reassign its soldiers to one of his remaining three infantry divisions.

The Ottoman Sixth Army faced an untenable operational situation, which was exaggerated by the geography of the Tigris and Euphrates River basin itself. There were two avenues of advance into Mesopotamia available to the British. The best route lay north up the Tigris River, along which lay Kut al-Amara, Baghdad and Mosul. The second route followed the Euphrates River, via the ruins of Babylon, to a point about 30km (18 miles) west of Baghdad.

The Second Battle of Kut al-Amara, February 1917. By 1917, General Maude's heavily reinforced army was able to easily outflank Kazim's severely depleted force. Maude made Kazim retreat beyond Baghdad.

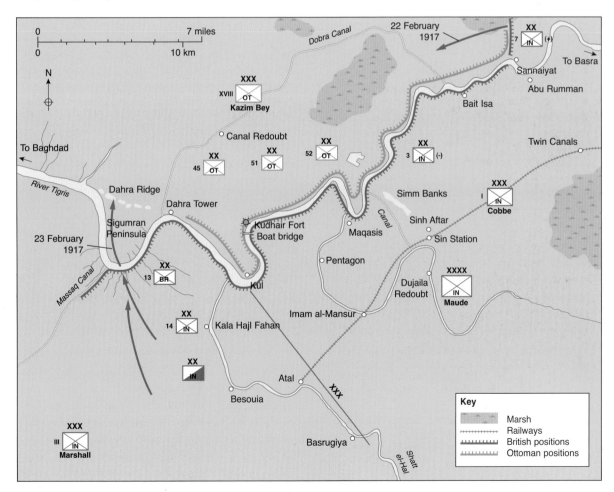

General Sir Frederick Stanley Maude (1864–1917)

Maude was born in Gibraltar and educated at Eton before entering Sandhurst. He was commissioned into the Coldstream Guards and saw service in Egypt and the Second Anglo-Boer War. Maude held a series of general staff positions and in October 1914 he was promoted to brigadier-general and given command of the 14th Brigade. He was seriously wounded in April 1915 in France and promoted to major-general. Maude was assigned to command 33rd Division but instead was reassigned to 13th Division at Suvla Bay. After evacuation from Gallipoli, Maude's division was sent to Mesopotamia in March 1916. With the failure to relieve Townshend, Maude moved up to corps command in July 1916 and overall command shortly thereafter. He immediately set about reorganizing and re-supplying the British and Indian forces in Mesopotamia. His thorough approach to war led to the victory at the Second Battle of Kut al-Amara and the capture of Baghdad in March 1917. Maude died on 18 November 1917 of cholera.

ABOVE Turkish prisoners in British captivity, such as those shown here, usually received better rations and medical care than when active in the service of their own army.

RIGHT British troops entering Baghdad. The Mesopotamian campaigns were never fully resourced by either the War Office or the India Office, and the forces there suffered from inadequate logistical support for most of the war.

However, in the summer of 1916, the British forward positions were located not at this narrow gap, but instead at the widest distance between the two rivers. Halil was thus forced to defend two separate defensive positions with about 100km (60 miles) of desert between them. This invited defeat, because Maude could choose his point of attack, massing superior forces there, before Halil could react. Consequently, Halil faced an almost impossible strategic and operational situation.

In December 1916, Maude began his long-awaited offensive. The Turks were anxious to identify which river approach the British would take as their primary axis of advance. Maude chose the Tigris and advanced with a full-strength corps on either side of the river towards Kut al-Amara. Rains slowed his advance, but by 17 February 1917 his army had reached Sannaiyat, about 20km (12.4 miles) downstream from Kut al-Amara, where Aylmer's relief force was defeated. Maude's deliberately slow pace made it possible for Halil to shift most of his meagre forces to reinforce XVIII Corps, which held the line there. Thus, by mid-February 1917 the Turks had the entire XVIII Corps, commanded by Colonel Kazim Bey, in the old defensive positions originally established by Nurettin. Kazim Bey also commanded the River Group, equivalent to a division in combat power. As a percentage of his available strength, Halil

was able to mass over 75 per cent of his small army to oppose Maude.

Almost all of Colonel Kazim's corps deployed on the north bank of the Tigris in an attempt to defend the most likely approach to Kut al-Amara. However, Maude unexpectedly shifted both of his corps to the

British troops on the march. The campaign season in Mesopotamia effectively lasted from October through April, when the temperatures permitted active field operations. Low water in the rivers impeded summer operations as well.

south bank and began to mass on the Turkish right flank towards Kut al-Amara. Halil was unaware of the true situation and sat in his lines waiting for Maude to move. The first attacks began on 17 February, and five days later Maude initiated demonstrations at Sannaiyat and at Kut al-Amara to further confuse Halil. On 23 February Maude began a divisional-size assault crossing of the Tigris up river from Kut al-Amara, and by the end of the day had a pontoon bridge across the river. Local Turkish counterattacks were unsuccessful in dislodging the bridgehead. Most of Halil's strength and his reserves remained in now useless positions down river from Kut al-Amara and by nightfall he realized that his corps was threatened

with encirclement from the north. He reacted promptly and ordered an immediate withdrawal. XVIII Corps began to pull out of its defensive positions that very night. Desperate rearguard actions bought enough time for Halil to evacuate most of his infantry, but he was forced to abandon most of his artillery and supplies. Halil withdrew up river for the final defence of Baghdad. Maude's campaign, long in coming, was brilliantly executed and showed great agility at the operational level. He understood that it was almost impossible to force the Turks out of their strongly held trenches, and he used manoeuvre to render Halil's position untenable.

Halil withdrew to the Diyala River line, along a small tributary entering the Tigris about 15km (nine miles) below Baghdad, where he tried to make a stand. He inactivated the 45th Division, which was far below strength and without artillery, and assigned its survivors along with two newly arrived infantry regiments to form the 14th Division. This division became part of XVIII Corps to assist in the defence of Baghdad. Maude resumed his relentless march up river on 4 March and attacked the tired and dispirited Turkish troops along the Diyala. After several days of hard fighting, it was clear to Halil that he could not hold the Diyala or Baghdad itself. Although reluctant to surrender this city with its great political, cultural and religious significance, Halil made the bitter decision to abandon Baghdad and continue his retreat up river. On 11 March 1917, Maude took Baghdad and avenged Kut. His victory came at a time of stalemate in other theatres, and cheered the British public. In contrast, it was a new low point for the Turkish Army and one that could not easily be remedied.

Halil took his now tiny army about 60km (37 miles) up the Tigris. His right flank lay at Ramadiye on the Euphrates and his left flank extended along a weak line into Persia. Halil then moved himself and his army headquarters far up the Tigris to Mosul. His total force, at this time, amounted to little more than 30,000 men and was spread over 300km (186-mile) front. In April the 2nd Division returned from the poorly advised Persian expedition; however, this was too little too late and did not alter Halil's position. For the Turks, the overall strategic situation in Mesopotamia, in the late spring of 1917, appeared hopeless.

Then, surprisingly, General Stanley Maude stopped advancing. Maude's supply lines stretched back to Basra and were getting longer with each mile he advanced. Moreover, the summer season of disease was upon the region. Maude was also concerned over how and when the Russians might support him in Persia and he possessed intelligence that the Turks were preparing a massive counter-offensive with a new force (the Yildirim Army) aimed at the recapture of Baghdad. He requested but was denied reinforcements. As a consequence, Maude decided to remain on the defensive in Baghdad and renew his offensive in the autumn. His decision was, in retrospect, cautious and it is doubtful whether the Sixth Army could have prevented further British attacks, or held Mosul, had

Maude continued his advance. Indeed, considering the huge disparity in combat power and logistics, it is remarkable that Halil held the British back for as long as he did. In the end, it was Maude's understanding that it was Townshend's fatal overextension at Ctesiphon, under political pressure to advance, that had led to the disaster at Kut al-Amara. He was determined not to repeat this error, and the war in Mesopotamia stabilized in March 1917 with the British in possession of Baghdad.

In Persia, casualties and unreplaced losses forced an operational pause on both the Turks and the Russians, which lasted from August 1916 into the winter. XIII Corps did receive a trickle of replacements and reinforcements, including some battalions of Muslim North African deserters from the French Army. In February 1917, Halil made the difficult decision to recall Ali Insan Pasha's corps and over the next month it withdrew over 400km (250 miles) through the mountains in winter conditions. By mid-March, XIII Corps had been evacuated from Persia and its forward elements were arriving along the Diyala line. Meanwhile, the events of 1917 overtook the Russians, as discontent and revolution swept through their army. XIII Corps now took up the task of the defence of Mesopotamia.

THE END IN MESOPOTAMIA

The summer of 1917 passed uneventfully, as the torrid heat prevented active operations. In the autumn, Maude began minor operations, but remained in place. Then, unexpectedly, he died on 18 November 1917 of cholera in Baghdad. Maude's death ended any real possibility of continued offensive operations in Mesopotamia and it remained a quiet backwater of the war. The Turks were more than happy not to disturb the status quo. Maude's replacement was General Marshall, who finally launched an offensive in March 1918 to outflank the Turks at Khan Baghdad. This offensive failed, but Marshall managed to inflict severe losses on the Turks.

However, events took a different turn as the great Ludendorff offensives on the Western Front in March 1918 made a dramatic impact on the British posture in the Middle East. The German Spring Offensives were aimed at knocking the BEF back to the Channel and isolating it from the French. During these battles, the British took heavy casualties and experienced a shortage of infantry on the front (although replacements were available in Great Britain, political pressures kept them at home). In any case, the Imperial general staff directed General Allenby in Palestine to send about 60,000 trained British soldiers to France. In all, Allenby sent two full divisions, 23 infantry battalions, nine cavalry regiments and artillery and machine-gun units, causing his army's strength to fade. However, some 'Easterners' in London felt that Allenby's campaign had great potential politically and wanted it to continue as a priority effort. In the end, Marshall's army in Mesopotamia became the bill payer and was forced to send two Indian Army divisions to Palestine (the 3rd and 7th) to replace the men Allenby had sent to France. Moreover, the replacement flow of men from India was diverted to Allenby rather than Marshall. This drained Marshall's strength and drew his army down to something of a caretaker garrison for Baghdad. Throughout the summer of 1918, the British in Mesopotamia did nothing.

All of this changed with Allenby's great victory at Megiddo and the collapse of the Salonika perimeter. On 2 October 1918, Marshall received instructions to gain as much ground as possible should the Ottoman Empire ask for an armistice. Marshall began to push up river, again meeting the divisions of XVIII Corps, and on 23 October the British attacked over the Little Zab River. Outflanking the Turks, Marshall's cavalry encircled the surviving men of Ismail Hakki's Tigris Group, which surrendered on 30 October. On the same day, an Ottoman delegation signed the armistice ending the war in the Middle East. Marshall, under pressure from London to gain control of the important oil fields at Mosul, put his fast-moving cavalry on the

> '*With the failure of the Julnar there was no further hope of extending the food limit of the garrison of Kut.*'
>
> Sir Percy Lake, dispatch, 1916

road the next day (in violation of the armistice agreement). On 1 November 1918, British cavalry rode into the undefended city of Mosul and took control of it (along with the vital oil fields). The Ottoman Sixth Army remained in being as did XIII Corps, but they were shadows of their former selves and could not stop Marshall's occupation of the city. With this episode, the war in Mesopotamia came to an end.

THE CAUCASUS IN 1916

While 1916 was a year of triumph for the Turks at Gallipoli and Kut al-Amara, it was a year of disaster in the Caucasus. In truth, the victories over the British came as an unexpected surprise to the general staff, and it was unprepared to deal with the consequences of success. At the end of the Gallipoli campaign a large surplus of infantry divisions became suddenly available and many, including Mustafa Kemal, thought that the empire should remain on the defensive and use them as a reserve. Enver Pasha, however, remained committed to offensive operations, and instead of keeping these formations concentrated and available, he sent them off to distant theatres in penny packets.

In the Caucasus in January 1916 the front was quiet, and the Ottoman Third Army stood on the defensive along the frontier northeast of Erzurum. The army was understrength and its three corps contained an average of about 12,000 men. Overall, the Turks had about 125,000 men, while the Russians had over 200,000 available. The Turks believed that the harsh winter precluded offensive operations and were surprised when General Yudenich attacked on 10 January 1916. Yudenich's main effort was a frontal attack on XI Corps, which held a series of strongpoints

A British officer wearing a gas mask in Mesopotamia in 1917. Although gas was never used in Mesopotamia, it was used by the British during the Gaza battles. The results were ineffective and it was never used again in the Middle East in World War I.

A British gun barge. Command of the rivers was an important consideration and both sides employed riverboat flotillas. Because of the swampy nature of the terrain, both sides used barges as mobile field artillery firing platforms.

rather than a line of continuous trenches. This allowed the Russians to infiltrate the Turkish positions and push them out of their lines. The disorganized Third Amy retreated in disarray and fell back to the fortress of Erzurum, losing some 10,000 men (mostly from XI Corps). Erzurum was heavily fortified and well armed with over 200 cannon, and was the third most powerful fortress complex in the Ottoman Empire. It had kept out the Russians in previous wars, and was believed to be secure.

To the surprise of the Turks, General Yudenich closed on the fortress at the end of the month and continued his offensive. Simultaneously, the Russian launched supporting offensives in the north towards Trabzon and in the south towards Malazgirt, while Yudenich brought his artillery forward. On 11 February 1916, he unleashed an intense bombardment on two of Erzurum's forts and then launched a night attack with infantry. The fighting inside the forts, hand-to-hand, ended with small groups of survivors holding isolated tunnels and gun positions. As dawn broke the Russians held a deep salient, which was immediately (but unsuccessfully) counterattacked by the Turks. A final Russian push of five columns on different axes led to the fall of the city on February 1916. This was a disaster for the Turks as the fortress was the lynchpin of the entire defence of eastern Anatolia. Third Army managed to conduct a fighting retreat saving most of its infantry, while Yudenich's army captured hundreds of guns, stores and the hospitals of Erzurum.

In fairness, the understrength army corps of Third Army held frontages of over 30km (18.6 miles), while their counterparts at Gallipoli held six. This diffused the Turk's ability to concentrate combat power on the front lines. Enver relieved the commander and sent

Vehip Pasha out to take command of the defeated army, which was now reduced to about 50,000 men and 84 guns.

Belatedly, Enver recognized that the strategic posture of the Caucasus resembled a house of cards waiting to collapse. He directed the general staff to start sending 10 of the Gallipoli divisions east on 1 March. His intent was not to reinforce the defeated Third Army and retake Erzurum. Rather, Enver wanted to form a new Second Army in the east and conduct a counter-offensive to push the Russians entirely out of Anatolia. It was wildly optimistic and he expected to be able to do this by June 1916. Unfortunately, the abysmal and antique Ottoman railway system did not reach into the Anatolian hinterlands and, furthermore, Enver dispatched the divisions slowly and individually. It was a terrible

mistake and illustrated the inexperience of Enver in matters regarding higher strategy. Over the spring and early summer these forces arrived in penny packets in Caucasia along the Black Sea and along the southern flank, while none went directly to Third Army holding the vital centre.

The relentless Yudenich continued his offensive in July 1916 and rapidly took the city of Bayburt, before capturing the key city of Erzincan. These defeats essentially destroyed the Third Army as an effective fighting organization. Meanwhile, in the midst of these disasters, the Gallipoli divisions made their way eastward and were held inactive over the summer as

Although the Russian armies in Caucasia contained some Cossack regiments, such as this one, cavalry was of little real use in the heavily mountainous region. Most of the Ottoman cavalry stationed there was redeployed to Palestine.

ABOVE **The Russian Army conscripted men locally, and there were a number of Islamic regiments on its rolls in the Caucasus. This photo depicts the regimental colours from an Islamic and a Christian regiment.**

the new Second Army formed on the long southern flank of the Anatolian front. It grew slowly into a powerful force of 12 infantry divisions and one cavalry division. Finally, the long-awaited Second Army offensive began on 2 August 1916, commanded by the capable Ahmet Izzet Pasha. Because of Russian weakness, instead of concentrating his army, he formed three operational groups on separate axis of attack. This was possibly the best army the empire had put together during the war, composed of veteran formations, and Ahmet Izzet launched it northeast towards Erzurum. Unfortunately, the slow deployment gave plenty of notice to the Russians, who planned accordingly and while the Turks enjoyed localized success, overall they met with failure. Well prepared defences and heavy Russian counterattacks defeated Ahmet Izzet's three groups in detail. By the end of September the offensive was finished with 30,000 casualties out of 100,000 who went forward. This was one of the worst mistakes made by the Ottoman Empire in the war. Had the divisions of this army been fed into Third Army as they arrived, the tactical balance would certainly have been altered in the Turks' favour. Enver's gamble on offensive

operations resulted in the loss of huge amounts of territory and the destruction of two armies.

As the cold weather set in in the autumn of 1916, a lull in the fighting occurred that gave both sides the opportunity to regroup their hard-pressed forces. For their part, the Turks formed the Anatolian Army Group and started to reconstitute their Caucasian armies, which by now had grown to a substantial 25 divisions. However, all of these divisions were worn down to half strength and, in many cases, to a quarter of their authorized strength. The Third Army commander, Vehip Pasha, was convinced that his Third Army's morale was so battered by nine months of defeat that it needed to be rebuilt from the ground up; Enver approved a radical plan to do so. As there were simply no replacements available to stand in for losses, Vehip dissolved eight entire infantry divisions and distributed the men to his remaining divisions. However, even this extreme action only brought them up to two-thirds of their normal authorizations.

Vehip then created what he styled 'Caucasian divisions' and reorganized them into two new 'Caucasian corps' (he also dissolved the unfortunate IX, X and XI corps). Typically, Vehip immediately started an intensive training programme and quickly erased the stigma of defeat. It was a remarkable turn around that returned Third Army to an effective force. The Second Army also inactivated three divisions and sent two more to Palestine, becoming a shell of its former self.

By the end of 1916, the situation in the Caucasus was stable, but the Turks had lost the critical Erzurum fortress, the cities of Bayburt and Erzincan and the key coastal port of Trabzon. Over the course of the year they suffered several hundred thousand casualties, including almost 70,000 killed and 27,000 POWs. It was a disaster, but fortunately for the Ottomans, Russia was about to enter a year of revolutions and strife that would paralyse the offensive capacity of its Caucasian armies. The year 1917 in the Caucasus would prove to be one characterized by almost total inactivity, as both sides observed something of an informal truce.

STRATEGIC DIVERSIONS IN 1916

At the end of the Gallipoli campaign, the Ottoman Army was left with a surplus of 20-odd infantry divisions clustered around Constantinople. During the spring of 1916, Enver Pasha responded to this situation by promising his German and Austrian allies assistance in the Balkans. Over the year, he would send seven infantry divisions deep into Europe on campaigns of marginal value to the strategic interests of the Ottoman Empire.

In early October 1915, a two-division Anglo-French expeditionary force landed at Salonika, Greece (which was then neutral), in a vain attempt to drive up the Vardar Valley to relieve Serbia, then collapsing under a combined attack by Austria, Bulgaria and Germany. This endeavour, like the Dardanelles operation, was the result of a hotly contested decision by 'Easterners' and 'Westerners' in London and Paris, and reflected to a great degree the increasing frustration with the

BELOW **The Russians captured a considerable number of Ottoman prisoners of war. However, both food rations and medical care were inadequate for these men, and many did not survive captivity.**

stalemate on the Western Front. There was probably more enthusiasm in France for the Salonika expedition, but it was too little too late and the Central Powers easily crushed their tiny opponent. However the Serbs refused to surrender and their army retreated to the Adriatic coast where it was evacuated by the Allied navies and reconstituted in the Salonika entrenched camp, where it again joined the Allied ranks. To assist in containing the Allied perimeter, Enver sent XX Corps, composed of the

Turkish troops in Salonika practise firing at enemy aircraft in 1917. The Vietnamese used this World War I tactic of anti-aircraft defense in the Vietnam War against American aircraft. It was occasionally successful in both conflicts.

46th and 50th divisions, to Macedonia in the autumn of 1916. These divisions saw little hard fighting, and were withdrawn in the spring of 1917.

To the north, the Brusilov Offensive of June 1916 had a crushing effect on the Austro-Hungarian Army by inflicting a defeat of huge scale. This created a manpower shortage on the Eastern Front that the Germans attempted to fill. However, they were then engaged on the Somme and at Verdun and were unable to completely solve the problem. General Erich von Falkenhayn asked the Turks to assist by sending as many men as possible. Enver Pasha responded by ordering XV Corps, comprising the veteran 19th and 20th divisions from Gallipoli, to

prepare for movement to Galicia. XV Corps was well equipped by Ottoman standards and the Germans augmented it when it arrived in August 1916. Over the next year, the corps fought in many defensive actions, but managed to hold its sector intact along the Zlotalipa River. For the first time, Turkish soldiers were exposed to poison gas shells, but the Germans had provided them with gas masks and they weathered the barrage with few casualties. As the Russian war drew down in the summer of 1917, the general staff brought the corps home before sending it to Palestine.

ROMANIA ENTERS THE WAR

By far the largest commitment of Ottoman divisions in Europe after Gallipoli came when Romania entered the war on 27 August 1916. Although the Romanians opened the war with an attack on Austria-Hungary, the Germans and their allies were well prepared for this contingency and conducted an attack of their own. This involved an enveloping offensive by General Erich von Falkenhayn from the northwest and by a joint German–Bulgarian–Ottoman army group commanded by General August von Mackensen from the south. Enver sent VI Corps (15th and 25th divisions), which began combat operations on 18 September, against the Romanians. The Turkish operations were characterized by well conducted attacks and by vigorous pursuits of the battered enemy forces. As winter set in, Enver dispatched the 26th Division to bring the corps up to full strength, and by mid-January 1917 the Romanian Army was decisively defeated and had been ejected from its own country. The Turks lost about 20,000 men in this campaign; however, they maintained VI Corps in Romania until the spring of 1918, when it was finally brought home.

Altogether in 1916 (counting the residual Gallipoli front at Cape Helles), the Ottoman Empire fought on seven active fronts (eight if the Arab Revolt is considered). In his zeal to be an equal partner of his allies, Enver Pasha sent his soldiers to places that were not critical to the Ottoman Empire's war effort. This had unfortunate consequences and contributed to the disasters in the Caucasus, Mesopotamia and Palestine.

Erich Georg Anton Sebastian von Falkenhayn (1861–1922)

Falkenhayn was born in West Prussia and served as a military instructor to the Chinese Army. He attended the Prussian War Academy and became a general staff officer. During the Chinese Boxer Rebellion (1900) he saw action in the relief of Peking. Falkenhayn continued to serve on the German general staff, and was appointed Prussian Minister of War in 1913. In September 1914 the Kaiser dismissed Moltke from his post as chief of the general staff and replaced him with Falkenhayn. He believed that France could be defeated by an attritional strategy and was responsible for the planning of the Verdun campaign, which was as disastrous for Germany as it was for France. Consequently, he was replaced by Hindenburg and sent to command against the Romanians in the autumn of 1916. There Falkenhayn recovered some of his reputation and was next sent to Palestine to command the Ottoman forces in early 1917. After losing Gaza and Jerusalem he was replaced by Liman von Sanders in February 1918. Upon his return to Germany he retired.

Falkenhayn is shown here on the left.

CHAPTER 5

The Arab Revolt

In 1916, the leader of the Arab nationalist movement entered into an alliance with Great Britain and France. This led to the dispatch of a young captain named Thomas Edward Lawrence to aid the Arabs in their revolt against Turkish rule. The resultant campaign would tie down thousands of Turkish troops in the theatre, and eased the threat posed to the vital Suez Canal by the Ottoman Army.

The remaining months of 1915 were quiet in Palestine, following the withdrawal of Cemal Pasha's defeated expeditionary force from the Suez Canal. When the British failed to pursue him, or even advance beyond the waterway, the theatre lapsed into stasis. As a result, the general staff stripped many of Cemal Pasha's experienced units and personnel from his order of battle and sent them to more active theatres. Fortunately, the British were quiet throughout this time and contented themselves with running railways and logistical lines out into the Sinai to facilitate future operations. In the absence of

Austrian troops marching up Mount Zion, Jerusalem. Austria-Hungary sent heavy artillery and support troops to Palestine in very limited numbers. These fresh-looking and well equipped soldiers have probably just arrived in theatre.

161

A Turkish train on the Damascus–Medina railway at el-Kasr station. The Ottoman railway system in Palestine was an essential lifeline for their armies deployed there. Its purpose was to connect Damascus to Mecca and Medina.

fighting, the Fourth Army's main effort in 1915 was directed against the rebellious Armenians, in large-scale counter-insurgency operations north of Antioch.

Along the front, Cemal reorganized his forces into the Desert Force Headquarters, which would command and control the forces in the Sinai. This headquarters was located at Beersheba and Cemal placed the German Colonel Friedrich Kress von Kressenstein in command. The headquarters was organized into two components: the GHQ Desert Force, which was charged with operational and tactical matters, and the Desert Lines of Communications Inspectorate, which was tasked with logistics and communications. As 1915 wore on, the Ottoman 8th, 10th and 25th divisions, by now combat hardened and experienced, were sent to the Gallipoli Peninsula. Most of the machine guns and field howitzers went with them. The Ottoman Army in Palestine was left unable to renew offensive operations.

THE REVOLT BEGINS

In February 1916, Enver Pasha made an extended tour of the Fourth Army area. He was more concerned with the political situation regarding the Arabs than with military matters. Like the Armenians, many Arabs, especially among the elites, were increasingly resentful of the policies of the Young Turks, and were becoming more attracted to the idea of pan-Arab nationalism. Active nationalist committees were at work, the most famous being Ahad and Fatah, which were dedicated to the independence of the Arab lands. By 1914, these organizations even included Ottoman Army officers of Arab ethnicity. Indeed, for hundreds of years, some part of the Ottoman's Arab lands had been in revolt on a more or less continuous basis. When war broke out in 1914, the Turks were in the process of suppressing a violent rebellion in Yemen.

Enver and Cemal met with several Arab leaders in an attempt to alleviate the increasingly tense situation. They were particularly concerned about the continued Turkish control of the holy cities of Mecca and Medina, as well as the continued security of the railway system. Sharif Faisal, who was then on friendly terms with the Turks, was wooed into compliance.

However, dealings with Sharif Hussein ibn Ali, the Hashemite king of the Hedjaz, were quite different, and negotiations quickly broke down. In fact, he was then in the early stages of raising his rebellion against the Turkish yoke, which began in the spring of 1916. Hussein's followers proceeded to take Mecca and several Red Sea ports, and Hussein appealed to the Allies for support. The British in Egypt were quick to respond and began to send weapons and gold to help Hussein, and soon advisers followed to coordinate operations, one of whom was a junior officer named Thomas Edward Lawrence.

T.E. Lawrence went on to became widely known as 'Lawrence of Arabia', although there were a number of other British and French advisers in Arabia doing much the same thing at the same time. Lawrence was an archaeologist and academic, who had spent time in

Syria studying Crusader castles before the war. He was an ascetic, spoke passable Arabic, and became enamoured with Arab culture. Because of his regional expertise, when war broke out Lawrence was commissioned and sent to Cairo to work in the intelligence division and later in the Arab Bureau. He wrote reports, but his restless nature drove him to volunteer for the dangerous mission of being an adviser to the Arabs, and he found himself in Ottoman territory working with Hussein. Along with Lawrence the British sent around 1000 Arabic former prisoners of war of the Ottomans, and an ex-Ottoman Army officer named Ja'afar al Askari. The British intended

Kress and Baron Lager, the chief Austrian commander. Kress spent almost three years in the Syrian and Palestine theatres. He was relieved after his failure to hold Gaza and Beersheba, and was replaced by Ottoman generals.

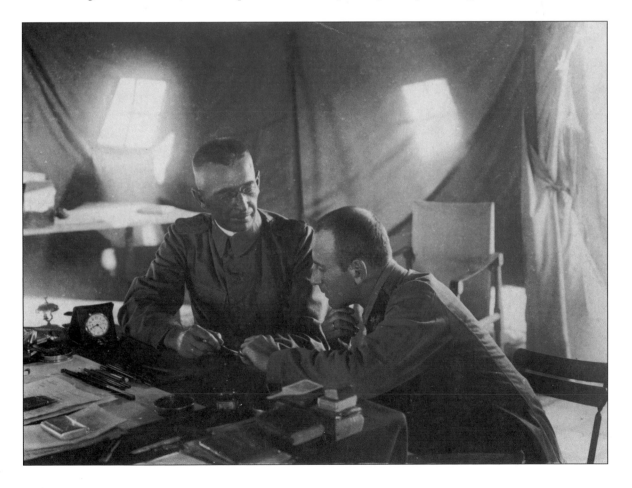

Thomas Edward Lawrence (1888–1935)

Lawrence was born in Wales, the illegitimate son of Thomas Chapman. He was educated at Oxford and in the summer of 1909 he began a walking tour in Syria and Palestine studying Crusader castles for his thesis. In 1910 Lawrence obtained a first-class degree in history and the next year he participated in an archaeological expedition excavating the Hittite site of Carchemish. Lawrence acquired a working knowledge of Arabic and the customs of the Arab people. At the outbreak of the war, he was assigned to the intelligence staff in Cairo as an Arab expert. In 1916 he volunteered to go into Arabia and raise a rebellion against the Turks. Lawrence soon became an influential figure in the Arab forces and became an advocate of guerrilla warfare. He took part in the capture of Aqaba in July 1917. After the war Lawrence accompanied the Arab delegation to Paris in 1919 but failed to influence the outcome. Disgusted by politics, Lawrence resigned and enlisted in the RAF under the name of Ross, but he was discovered and joined the army calling himself Shaw. In 1925 he returned to the RAF as Shaw and moved to a cottage named Clouds Hill where he lived out the remaining years of his life. He died in a motorcycle accident. His book about the Arab revolt *The Seven Pillars of Wisdom: a Triumph* (1927), is considered a classic on guerrilla warfare. Lawrence remains one of the most enigmatic and complex personalities to emerge from World War I.

this group of trained and seasoned soldiers to become the hard nucleus around which Hussein could build an effective regular army. Originally clothed in British uniforms, the Arabs soon reverted to traditional garb.

Hussein's chief of staff was an ex-Ottoman officer named Major Aziz al-Masri, who had come over to the rebels when Hussein called for volunteers. Aziz al-Masri evolved a strategic plan for the revolt, which was taken up and became the signature characteristic of the operations of the Arab army. He envisioned a hard core of regulars (8000 in total) supported by a large number of irregular Arab tribesmen (20,000 altogether), which would avoid sustained combat by conducting raids and destroying the railway system. The constant pin-prick attacks reinforced by the cutting of rail communications would eventually bleed the Ottoman garrisons to death. In late 1916, to accommodate this strategy, the Sharifian Arab Army was reorganized into a Northern Army under Emir Faisal and a Southern Army under Emir Ali. Both contained a regular brigade, several artillery batteries and a varying but larger number of tribesmen. Faisal was sent up the railway towards Damascus, and Ali went south to take Medina. The Turks for their part were determined to hold on to their Arab provinces, and when Sharif Hussein's revolt broke out that spring, Cemal appointed Fahri Pasha to take command of Medina and to maintain control of the Hedjaz railway. With only a handful of Turkish battalions, this officer performed outstanding service in defending the city and, for the remainder of 1916, the Turks managed to keep the railway open on a more or less regular basis.

1916 IN THE SINAI

Significant German and Austro-Hungarian military assistance began to arrive in April in the form of German aircraft and Austro-Hungarian howitzers. The German airmen and machines were immediately employed on reconnaissance missions over the Suez Canal. The British, now commanded by General Sir Archibald Murray, began to advance slowly along the Mediterranean coast. Most of Murray's divisions had been evacuated from Gallipoli and were experienced in fighting the Turks. Many of the men, however, were struck down by malaria and assorted tropical diseases.

Cemal decided to resume offensive operations in mid-April, and the Turks pushed forward towards the unsupported British outpost at Katia in the Sinai. On 23 April 1916, Kress sent his cavalry forward to pin the British reserves near Kantara while a small infantry force of two battalions supported by a four-gun artillery battery successfully encircled a British cavalry unit at Katia. In a classic encirclement operation, Kress captured most of a British cavalry regiment and its commander. It was a small defeat, but alerted the British to the dangers of forward deployment.

In late April, the first reinforcements from the victorious Gallipoli army arrived in Palestine. This was the experienced 3rd Division, full of hardened and disciplined combat veterans. Concerned about British offensive preparations along the coast, Cemal and Kress decided to launch a second expedition against the British. They intended to keep the British off-balance by conducting a limited attack, which would again encircle the forward British units. The attack

force was built around the 3rd Division and in addition this contained four batteries of German and Austrian artillery, a machine-gun battalion and two anti-aircraft gun sections, totalling some 12,000 men. At the beginning of July 1916, this force closed with the British at Katia and Bir Romani. On the evening of 16 July 1916, the Turks pressed an infantry regiment forward to fix the British front-line troops, and began to prepare their attack. Kress planned to pin down the British 52nd Division in its defences forward of Bir Romani and then to swing a left hook around it in the hope of cutting it off. The British were vulnerable to this by being spread out along their newly built railway and deployed in divisional clusters stretching back into Egypt. The attack began at 5.15am on 4 August

British-led forces in the Battle of Katia, 1916. Kress's capture of a large part of a British cavalry regiment provided a limited but welcome victory for Ottoman forces.

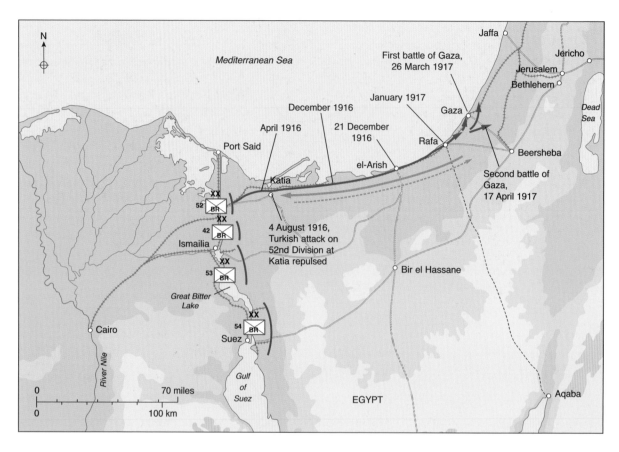

The British advance across the Sinai, April 1916–April 1917.
The Turks relied on camels and oxen for logistics support in
the Sinai Desert. The British, who were much more reliant
on material, built a railroad and a water pipeline to support
their eastward advance.

1916 and as the 31st Infantry Regiment went forward
to pin down the British, Kress swung his 32nd and
39th Infantry regiments around their left flank and
into the British rear. At 2pm, effective British
counterattacks halted Kress. His follow-on attacks
stalled later that day, and on the next day British
reserves hammered his troops to a halt. Kress
recognized failure, and began to pull back his forces
on 7 August. The Turkish losses were light, but failure
put an end to offensive action, and thereafter the Sinai
front lapsed into a period of stasis for several months.

As British strength grew, Murray began to advance
his forces along the coast to exploit the weakening
Ottoman posture. His first attack came at Magdhaba

on 23 December 1916 against an isolated Turkish
position held by two battalions of the 80th Infantry
Regiment. The British threw the 1st and 2nd
Australian Light Horse brigades, the New Zealand
Mounted Rifles and the Imperial Camel Corps against
the Turks. At 6.30am, 11 Australian aircraft began to
strafe and bomb the enemy, thus exposing their
positions. At dawn the attack began and immediately
it ran into heavy fire that halted it for the next six
hours. About 2.30pm a determined Australian bayonet
attack breached the defences, causing a Turkish rout.
Within two hours a cavalry encirclement brought
victory, from which very few Ottomans escaped.

The British brought up more men and worked on
extending their water pipelines and coastal railroad.
On 9 January 1917, the British launched another
encircling attack on the Turkish outpost in the old fort
at Rafa. Like their position at Magdhaba, Rafa was
weakly held and isolated. The Anzac Mounted

Division conducted a similar attack that resulted in a similar triumph from which few Turks escaped. This victory brought Murray's army to the gates of Palestine and positioned him to conduct further advances. The twin victories of Magdhaba and Rafa encouraged both London and Murray to consider a major offensive towards Jerusalem. Unfortunately, Gallipoli and Kut al-Amara notwithstanding, these victories also encouraged the British to interpret their success as a sign of Ottoman weakness and lack of fighting spirit. This underestimation of Ottoman combat effectiveness would have serious repercussions, as Murray's generals began to plan operations against Gaza.

THE FIRST AND SECOND BATTLES OF GAZA

The British Army in the Sinai grew substantially in 1916 and was renamed the Egyptian Expeditionary Force (EEF). Tired divisions withdrawn from Gallipoli arrived as reinforcements, but later Territorial and cavalry units from England were sent as well. Murray spent the summer improving his logistics and constructed rail lines and a water pipeline towards el-Arish in late 1916. Kress recognized the vulnerability of el-Arish, which he abandoned in mid-December 1916, falling back to a line on the old frontier. It was

apparent to the Ottoman Fourth Army staff that this position could not be held either and Cemal Pasha ordered the establishment of a new defensive position at Gaza. Kress began withdrawing, and by mid-March 1917 the Ottoman Fourth Army was in position in its Gaza defences. The Turks also received important reinforcements, in the form of the 3rd Cavalry Division – which finally gave them a mobile mounted capability. In the vicinity of Gaza, Kress now had some 18,000 men.

The British attacked Gaza with an infantry division on the morning of 26 March 1917. Murray sent two cavalry divisions to bypass the city itself and take it from the rear, and he retained his remaining two infantry divisions to shield his ever-lengthening and open right flank. This was a prescient decision, as Kress was planning to envelop the British with forces he had positioned in the desert. The well dug-in Turks held in the face of repeated British assaults, but by the end of the day British cavalry had nearly cut off the city. However, by this time Kress's 3rd and 16th

divisions and 3rd Cavalry Division were well under way and advancing to cut off Murray's army from its water points and rail heads. With victory in sight, but learning of the Ottoman envelopment, Chetwode and Dobell, the corps commanders, decided to withdraw from Gaza. Since Murray was 70km (43.5 miles) to the rear at el-Arish, he was unable to stop the withdrawal. Overall, however, it is hard to criticize the decision to withdraw, which was made by the men on the spot. Had Murray been closer to the front, he might have been able to use aircraft to discover Kress's intent.

The 26 March battle came to be known as First Gaza, and it was the best chance that Murray had to break the Turkish line without committing major forces to the region. The Gaza–Beersheba line was the finest natural defence line between the frontier and Jerusalem. The city of Gaza lay on the Mediterranean Sea and Beersheba sat at the foot of the rugged Judean Hills. At the First Battle of Gaza, three full-strength British infantry divisions and two full-strength Imperial cavalry divisions were stopped by three understrength Turkish divisions. Murray's failure earned the Turks enough time to reinforce the Palestine front, and the British would eventually commit seven infantry divisions and four cavalry divisions to Palestine.

Political pressure on Murray intensified and he was pushed prematurely into attacking again. He rebuilt his army into the Eastern Force (of three infantry divisions), under General Dobell, to attack Gaza. Murray brought up additional infantry and mounted formations as well as 4000 poison gas shells and eight tanks (in the desert for the first time in history). Importantly, the EEF deployed over 170 artillery pieces as well. Murray's attack began on 17 April 1917, and continued ineffectively for three days. This was because the Ottoman 53rd Division had been brought into the Gaza defences, now considered by the Turks

A regimental standard presented to the defenders of Gaza during the First Battle. All Ottoman Army regiments were numbered and had regimental colours called *sanjacklar*. Carefully picked men guarded them and carried them into combat. As in Britain, Ottoman colours were awarded distinctions based on campaign participation.

as something of a fortress, contributing several thousand rifles to the defence. Moreover, in the time since First Gaza the Turks had dramatically increased the depth and scale of their fortifications (particularly by increasing overhead cover). A British two-hour artillery attack was followed by infantry being launched directly into the Turkish front. Tanks were employed for the first time in the Middle East (but were shot to pieces), wind dissipated the poison gas, and the infantry was stopped by well emplaced machine guns. Two days later, after sustaining about 6500 casualties, Murray called off the attack. The Turks lost about a third of this number, but they still held Gaza. Murray and Dobell were relieved of command and sent home to England. Turkish sources record that the British left three of their eight tanks within the Turkish trench lines. The gas attack was scarcely noticed at all. Murray's army was not inexperienced (many of his infantry were Gallipoli veterans) and it is hard to understand why the British, two full years after Gallipoli, still attempted frontal assaults (with inadequate artillery support) on strongly prepared Ottoman Army positions.

THE OTTOMAN ARMY IN PALESTINE

In May 1917, the Ottoman Fourth Army was organized into five army corps, two of which garrisoned the Gaza–Beersheba line. Facing the British on the Gaza line were XXII Corps, composed of the 3rd, 7th, and 53rd divisions, and XX Corps, containing the 16th and 54th divisions (the 3rd Cavalry Division was in reserve). With these troops, the Turks continued to improve their defensive lines. By July, the Fourth Army had grown to 151,742 rifles, 354 machine guns and 330 artillery pieces (its highest recorded strength). However, the defensive lines had also been extended, now almost encircling the oasis town of Beersheba, and stretching continuously for almost 50km (30 miles).

Encouraged by success, Enver Pasha began to toy with the idea of taking the strategic initiative by forming a combined Turkish–German field army. This was a logical outcome of the evolving favourable levels of cooperation between the Germans and the

The main Turkish base of Hafir el-Aujar. Ottoman Army logistics units were modelled on the German Army system and formed a conveyor belt to the front. Most of the supplies were hauled to the front by animal cart.

Turks. On the German side the idea of a large Turkish–German army group was encouraged by General Erich von Falkenhayn, the victor of the Romanian campaign. In any case, sometime after the fall of Baghdad and before the arrival of Falkenhayn in Turkey for staff discussions on 7 May 1917, Enver was seized with the idea of retaking Baghdad. He intended to accomplish this by forming what he styled the Yildirim Army (or the Thunderbolt Army Group). Enver envisaged this force concentrating in upper Mesopotamia to retake Baghdad. From there it would either complete the reconquest of lower Mesopotamia or perhaps invade Persia. Unfortunately for the Turks, the elements of grand strategy appealed to Enver and, once again, overwhelmed his common sense. The Yildirim Army would comprise two main elements: Halil's Sixth Army and a newly formed Seventh Army. The two Ottoman armies, reinforced by Germans, would regain the strategic initiative for the empire. The new Seventh Army was to be formed by divisions returning from the European fronts in Galicia, Romania and Macedonia. These experienced divisions represented Enver's last strategic reserve and could not be replaced. However, with the Caucasian, Palestine and Mesopotamian fronts stabilized for the summer of 1917, a momentary window of opportunity appeared on the strategic horizon wherein the initiative might be regained in one theatre of war.

Enver met his senior commanders in Aleppo on 24 June 1917 to discuss his plans. Attending this meeting were Ahmet Izzet Pasha, Mustafa Kemal Pasha (now in command of the Second Army), Cemal Pasha, Halil Pasha and Bronsart von Schellendorf of the Ottoman general staff. Enver unveiled his plan to create a new Seventh Army on the upper reaches of Mesopotamia using the divisions made available by the conclusion of the European operations. It would attack southeast along the Euphrates River, while Halil's Sixth Army attacked south along the Tigris River. Then the armies might encircle and destroy the British at Baghdad.

Cemal Pasha thought that the Turks should concentrate their dwindling number of fresh divisions in the vicinity of Aleppo as a centrally positioned strategic reserve. This force might then respond to threats in the Caucasus, in Palestine or in Mesopotamia. He also put forth the idea of maintaining troops in the Adana region as insurance against an amphibious landing by the Entente powers. Cemal concluded his summary of the strategic

A German Mauser Gewehr 98 rifle. The Ottoman Army stressed rifle marksmanship and trained its men well at regimental depots before assigning them to combat units.

situation by stating that an all-out offensive against Baghdad was dangerous for the Turks because failure would destroy the last strategic reserve. Enver, however, had already decided upon this course of action but promised that his German ally would provide significant assistance. He told Cemal that the Germans would provide a light division, heavily laden with a large number of machine guns, and that Falkenhayn himself would come down to command the combined armies. Izzet Pasha and Mustafa Kemal were uncomfortable with the plan, but were also overruled. Cemal Pasha then cabled the government in Constantinople directly to express his reservations over the plan. However, the decision had already been made and planning was well under way to begin the deployments. In fact the Grand Vizier had personally requested that the Germans send Falkenhayn himself.

The unhappy Cemal went to Constantinople in mid-August to argue his case in person. Another council of war was held, in which Cemal and his chief of staff presented their appreciation of the weakness of the Palestine front along the Gaza–Beersheba line. Their conclusion reaffirmed their belief that a large theatre reserve in Syria was more necessary than an attack in Mesopotamia. Enver and Falkenhayn began conversing in fluent German and conducted an animated discussion at the map boards. Much to Cemal's

Ottoman Stormtroops

As the war progressed, the Ottoman high command keenly followed the tactical developments on the Western Front and attempted to implement new ideas in the army. In the summer of 1917, the Ottomans began to move towards the new German *stosstruppen* (stormtroop) doctrine. Initially a local initiative of Kress von Kressenstein in the 7th Division, the activity was spurred by the arrival of the 19th Division from Galicia, which had already formed a stormtroop battalion. On 1 September 1917, Enver Pasha ordered the formation of three assault troop battalions (*hucum tabur*), composed of young, fit and aggressive men. The troops were put through a four-week assault course and equipped like their German counterparts with bags of hand grenades and light machine guns. Pamphlets explaining the latest German tactics were written and distributed as well. The battalions were never used in offensive operations, but were mostly used for the remainder of the war as counterattack forces or as immediate tactical reserves. They were instrumental in repelling Allenby's Trans-Jordan raids in the spring of 1918.

surprise, Enver explained that Falkenhayn agreed with Cemal about the vulnerable condition of the Fourth Army. Moreover, Falkenhayn now advocated using the Yildirim Group to throw the British back across the Suez Canal, before attempting to retake Baghdad. Cemal was uncomfortable with this new proposal, preferring instead to simply abandon the Baghdad scheme and maintain a theatre reserve. In the end, Cemal was relieved of responsibility for the Palestine front and was reduced to providing logistical support to Falkenhayn. Unhappy with this turn of events, but willing to continue to serve in a diminished capacity, Cemal settled into a new headquarters in Damascus. There he observed the destruction of Falkenhayn's army during the next year. Cemal noted later in his memoirs that there were continuous disputes between Mustafa Kemal and Falkenhayn over command and

Members of the Turkish Machine-Gun Corps on the Tel el-Sheria–Gaza line. The Ottoman Army set up a tactical schools system in Palestine to maintain its fighting proficiency. In addition to a machine-gun school, it had courses for staff officers and for throwing hand grenades.

policy issues in the Yildirim Group. Cemal further stated that, were it not for Falkenhayn, the Turks could have held the Gaza–Beersheba line for years.

Falkenhayn arrived in July 1917 to command what the Germans called Army Group F (or the Yildirim Army, as the Turks called it). The army was almost entirely Turkish, while Falkenhayn's army staff was mostly German. This soon became a sore point with the Ottoman officer corps, who became aware that Falkenhayn did not trust them to carry out complex staff procedures. The Germans also sent the German Asia Corps, which was in reality only a brigade-sized force, to help the new army. The Turks had expected to see some kind of light German infantry divisions, but instead received three infantry battalions, and three machine-gun and three cavalry detachments. Accompanying the Asia Corps were an artillery battalion, artillery-spotting aircraft, communications experts and motor transport. Of particular value was a small aviation group of about 30 modern German aircraft and pilots.

Enver began to send troops to Aleppo, and by September substantial forces were assembling there. In

The German aerodrome at Huj. Four *flieger abteilung* (squadrons) participated in the campaigns in Palestine. These squadrons enabled the Ottomans to establish air parity until late in the war.

July, XV Corps' headquarters arrived from Galicia followed in August by the 19th Division and the 20th Division in September. A new III Corps was activated and deployed, as were its subordinate units, the 50th Division from Macedonia and the 59th Division from Aydin. Four or five trains a day ran south to bring these formations into Syria. Eventually the German Asia Corps also arrived after an arduous journey from its staging area in Silesia. Given the abysmal condition of the Ottoman rail network in 1917, the Ottoman concentration of troops in Syria was remarkable.

As the new armies gathered there, Enver made his final choices regarding the Ottoman strategy. Based on reports coming from the Gaza–Beersheba front that indicated a significant British offensive was in the works, Enver cancelled the proposed plan to retake Baghdad. Embracing Falkenhayn's ideas, Enver decided to reinforce the Gaza–Beersheba line with the Yildirim troops. On 26 September 1917 he split the old Fourth Army area, giving Cemal both Syria and West Arabia, and ordered the Yildirim Army Group and the Seventh Army to Palestine. In subsequent orders, given on 2 October, Enver activated the new Eighth Army in Palestine, appointing Kress to command it. Falkenhayn's newly formed Yildirim Army Group now controlled the Sixth Army in Mesopotamia and the two armies in Palestine.

Dissent over the Ottoman Empire's strategic direction continued. The newly appointed Seventh Army commander, Mustafa Kemal, sent a strongly worded letter to Enver Pasha advocating a return to a defensive military policy based on large, centrally positioned reserves able to respond to any threat by the British. Unfortunately, Kemal also bitterly condemned German influence in Turkish strategy and expressed his concern that Turkey was becoming a 'German colony', which led to his resignation several weeks later.

The infantry divisions near Aleppo began to move south, but not all went to Palestine. Recognizing the need to reinforce Halil Pasha with additional troops, the 50th Division was sent eastwards to Mesopotamia, while the 59th Division was deactivated and its troops used to fill out the other divisions departing the Aleppo staging area. To make up for these lost forces, Enver dispatched two infantry divisions and a cavalry division to the theatre. However, it would take quite a while for these formations to arrive in the Syria–Palestine area of operations and ready themselves for battle, and time for the Ottoman

Cemal Pasha inspecting Austrian troops entering Jerusalem. Cemal lost control of the Palestine front in the autumn of 1917. The newly formed Yildirim Army, commanded by Erich von Falkenhayn, took command of the Gaza–Beersheba line.

defenders ran out at dawn on 31 October 1917, when Allenby's long-awaited offensive began.

THE BRITISH ARMY IN PALESTINE

After the relief of General Murray, the imperial general staff sent out General Sir Edmund Allenby as the new British commander in June 1917. Allenby came from France where he had successfully commanded Third Army against the Germans. He was a large and imposing man and was nicknamed 'the Bull'. He was known throughout the army as an able trainer of soldiers, although his curt and abrupt manner often irritated his subordinates. More importantly, he thoroughly understood the dynamics of modern warfare and was especially aware of the need to carefully integrate infantry and artillery operations. Allenby would spend the summer of 1917 preparing his great offensive aimed at breaking the Gaza–Beersheba line.

The British Lee-Enfield Mk II rifle. The British Army lowered the rifle strength of its infantry divisions in 1917. However, the divisions grew in combat power as Lewis guns and grenade launchers were added in lieu of riflemen.

Most of Allenby's divisions were Territorials mobilized at the outbreak of the war, including the 52nd, 53rd and 54th divisions, which had fought against the Turks at Gallipoli. He also had the 10th, 60th, 74th (Yeomanry) and 75th divisions, which likewise had combat experience against the Turks. Moreover, his Desert Mounted Corps comprised three mounted or cavalry divisions. He requested and received over a hundred additional heavy artillery pieces, extra divisional artillery, and thousands of replacements to bring his battalions to full strength.

However, it was not in material terms that Allenby made the greatest changes in his army. In truth, the army he inherited from Murray was something of an ad hoc construct within which infantry divisions were combined with cavalry divisions in composite army corps. Allenby immediately deconstructed Murray's army and reorganized it into two conventional infantry corps (XX and XXI) and a cavalry corps. This mirrored standard British Army organizational architecture and aligned the EEF with its counterpart BEF in France.

In doing this, Allenby enabled the most current British tactics and doctrines to take root in Palestine. In particular, he provided his army with an infantry-based capability that stressed fire and manoeuvre built around the Lewis light machine gun. In parallel, Allenby reorganized his corps-level artillery, consisting mostly of his heavy guns and howitzers. Coming from France, he recognized that simply adding more guns did not alter the tactical equation and that control of artillery was an essential element of gaining battlefield superiority. To accommodate this, in the summer of 1917 Allenby put his heavy guns together in heavy artillery groups, which supported his two infantry corps. These artillery groups were tasked with counterbattery operations designed to knock out the Turkish artillery. Thus a coherent and complementary system of artillery support appeared in Palestine, light divisional guns directly supporting the infantry and heavy guns suppressing the enemy's artillery. Finally, and of great importance, Allenby's strength of character and personal presence visibly improved the morale of the EEF. He exuded confidence and he visited his men often to set the example.

Allenby was also fortunate to inherit a capable command team composed of seasoned officers familiar with the theatre and their opponents' capabilities. However, he reassigned them to new positions that he thought were suited to their talents. Sir Edward Bulfin was promoted to command XX Corps; Sir Philip Chetwode, one of the best-known cavalrymen in the army, was given XXI Corps; and the Australian Sir Henry Chauvel received command of the Desert Mounted Corps. Allenby also replaced Murray's chief of the general staff with Sir Louis Bols, who had served with Allenby in Third Army. The professional and conventional Bols then received the brilliant and desert-wise Guy Dawnay as his assistant.

Sir Edmund Henry Hynman Allenby (1861–1936)

Allenby began his military career with the Inniskilling Dragoons in 1882 following an education at the Royal Military Academy (Sandhurst). He served in South Africa and in the Second Boer War from 1899 to 1901. He was a staff college graduate of Camberley and served in successive staff positions. In the British Expeditionary Force on the Western Front, Allenby commanded the 1st Cavalry Division. After the First Battle of Ypres, he was promoted to command the Third Army. He was nicknamed 'the Bull' and was prone to fits of anger and quietude. At times he clashed with his superiors and in 1917 he was sent to command the Egyptian Expeditionary Force (chiefly because of a disagreement with Haig over tactics used at the Battle of Arras). He captured Gaza and then Jerusalem in December 1917. His most famous victory at Megiddo in September 1918 was one of the most decisive victories of the war. In 1919 he was created a field marshal and ennobled. He served as High Commissioner to Egypt until 1925, before retiring.

It was a sweeping change for the EEF, but it made the army in Palestine Allenby's army.

The British plan envisaged an envelopment of the Turkish left flank at Beersheba by XX Corps and the Desert Mounted Corps. Using carefully orchestrated plans, Allenby's logisticians proposed to support seven divisions far out in the desert. The major problem, especially for the cavalry, was one of ensuring an adequate supply of water. To this end, pipelines were laid and depots were built, but the plan hinged upon the seizure of the historic wells at Beersheba before the Turks could destroy them. Surprise was paramount and Allenby's intelligence staff devised a plan to deceive the Turks. This turned on the Ottoman intelligence estimate that the British main attack would centre on the coastal city of Gaza while a single division hit Beersheba. This was the result of the Turks' analysis of British logistics (mainly railways and pipelines laid along the coast road). Their estimates and suspicions were confirmed on 10 October 1917 when an intelligence bonanza dropped into their laps. This was the famous 'lost haversack' episode hatched by Major Richard Meinertzhagen of the intelligence

The 94th Heavies, which shelled the Turks in capturing Jerusalem. Allenby's reorganization of his heavy artillery and its employment in Western Front-style roles was a critical element in the success of his army.

staff. Meinertzhagen set up a phoney front-line reconnaissance, during which he appeared to drop a blood-stained haversack while fleeing from Turkish cavalry. The haversack contained personal letters, sandwiches and false operational documents relating to an impending British attack. These documents revealed that the British would attack Gaza while landing simultaneously on the coast north of the city. Moreover, the plans confirmed that a single division would be sent against Beersheba as a diversion. Although some histories claim that Meinertzhagen was a fraud and that the Turks were not fooled by his ruse, it is a fact that between 10 and 28 October 1917, Kress moved the 7th Division to the coast north of the city to guard against an amphibious attack while placing the fresh 53rd Division in the Gaza fortress. Moreover, he placed the 24th Division in a reserve position to support Gaza and he moved the 19th Division away from Beersheba and closer to the city of Gaza. It is clear from these movements that Kress believed, for whatever reason, that a British plan mirroring Meinertzhagen's false documents was about to unfold.

BEERSHEBA AND THE THIRD BATTLE OF GAZA

Falkenhayn held the Gaza–Beersheba line with the strongest forces yet assembled by the Ottomans in Palestine. Many of the Ottoman divisions were

composed of veterans of Gallipoli or the European fronts. Kress von Kressenstein's Eighth Army held Gaza and was composed of XXII Corps (with the 3rd and 53rd divisions) in Gaza and XX Corps (26th and 54th divisions) stretching eastward toward Beersheba. A newly activated army, the Seventh, continued the Ottoman line into the town of Beersheba. The line was thinly held by the 16th Division, but the town of Beersheba itself was garrisoned by III Corps (27th Division and 3rd Cavalry Division), commanded by Ahmet Izzet Pasha. The 27th Division was composed almost entirely of Arabs and was thought to be unreliable. British preparations were highly visible, but the Turks believed that Allenby could only move a division and cavalry on Beersheba because of logistical constraints. The Ottoman defensive layout relied on strongly dug-in frontline forces and counterattacks, but the towns of Gaza and Beersheba acted as anchors at each end of the line. Because of the previous British attacks, Kress ringed each with entrenchments for an all-around defence. In Beersheba there were 4400 riflemen, 60 machine guns and 28 artillery pieces (about a single brigade equivalent in the British Army). The Ottoman chain of command informed III Corps that the British could be expected to attack with a force of two divisions, and Ahmet Izzet Pasha felt that he could defend the important town, with its important water wells, with the troops on hand.

On 31 October 1917, after a carefully concealed night movement, Allenby's army attacked Beersheba at dawn. However, instead of one or two divisions he moved two entire British corps to execute his attack. The British XX Corps (with four infantry divisions) attacked from the west and the south, while the Cavalry Corps enveloped and attacked Beersheba from the east. XX Corps' attack drove into the mostly Arab regiments of the Ottoman 27th Division and the Arabs surprisingly held the British off for the better part of the day. This attack was designed to pin down Ahmet Izzet's reserves while the Imperial cavalry enveloped the town from the east, which was almost undefended. In desperation, Ahmet Izzet Pasha sent the 3rd Cavalry Division into action to hold open the road to the north. Although the Arabs and Turks fought stubbornly, by

Meinertzhagen and the Lost Haversack

One of more controversial personalities of the war in the Middle East was Major Richard Meinertzhagen (1878–1967), who was born to a wealthy London Jewish banking family. Joining the army in 1905, he spent his early years fighting natives with the King's African Rifles and acquiring a reputation for eccentricity and self-aggrandizement. Meinertzhagen was an expert ornithologist who wrote diaries wherever he went. Early in the war he was appointed to a military intelligence post in Palestine. In hatching the lost haversack episode, Meinertzhagen created a compelling scenario that convinced Kress von Kressensein to move his scant reserves to oppose the presumed landings and attacks that the documents in the haversack revealed. After the war he became an ardent advocate for the Zionist movement and worked to establish the new state of Israel. He was sacked from the army in 1926 for insubordination. He published four books about his experiences. Opinions are mixed today regarding some of his claims to have been a force in the making of the modern Middle East.

the end of the day the battle was all but over. Famously an Australian light horse regiment charged the Ottoman defences on the eastern perimeter, seizing a key hill controlling access into the town. Recognizing that his defence was untenable, Ahmet Izzet ordered his corps to withdraw from Beersheba. Although the Turks had demolitions plans in place to destroy the wells, the defence collapsed so quickly that Allenby's troops captured them intact. Given that the Turks expected a divisional attack, a concentric attack by seven full-strength British divisions caught them by surprise, and the fact that III Corps was able to withdraw successfully was a minor miracle.

Allenby's army then hit Gaza, with a deliberate attack by XXI corps (of three British infantry

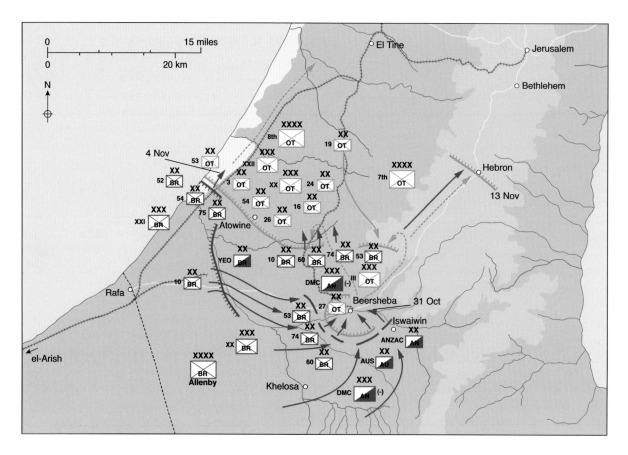

The Third Battle of Gaza–Beersheba. The Turks expected Allenby to move a single division against Beersheba. To their surprise, Allenby massed two entire army corps of six divisions on the Ottoman positions there. They never recovered from this mistake.

divisions). The Gaza garrison was twice the size of that in Beersheba and was more strongly dug in. Allenby conducted a coordinated bombardment from artillery on land and from naval gunfire from the sea. However, the British were unable to break through, and Ottoman counterattacks were able to restore the situation. Kress was able to hold most of the line and British progress was slow, disappointing some officers. However, the attack on Gaza was never more than a supplementary attack to pin Kress in the city. Allenby's main effort was the seizure of Beersheba, from which point his cavalry would collapse the Ottoman left wing and envelop Gaza from the east. By 6 November, Allenby's cavalry was pushing towards the city.

The Yildirim Army staff recognized that the battle was lost and Falkenhayn ordered his battered forces to conduct a fighting withdrawal to new defensive positions about 10km (six miles) to the north. Kress and Fevzi Pasha, the Seventh Army commander, began to disengage, leaving rearguard detachments to delay the British. These detachments were sacrificed to allow the main body of troops to escape. The 3rd Cavalry Division, fortunately preserved by Ahmet Izzet after the debacle at Beersheba, retained enough combat power to successfully screen the army's open flank. By 9 November, the Eighth Army had withdrawn 20km (12.4 miles) north while the Seventh Army fell back more slowly under less British pressure. Falkenhayn moved his headquarters to Jerusalem, where he began to restore his communications and re-establish control of his forces. Although the British captured many Ottoman soldiers and guns in the retreat, every Ottoman division survived to fight another day.

However, Allenby and his army were now inside Palestine itself.

THE FALL OF JERUSALEM

Allenby relentlessly continued his attack, driving Kress's Eighth Army back even more on 11 November. The attacks continued along the coast and had the effect of making the forward position of the Seventh Army, now commanded by Fevzi Pasha, vulnerable to a flanking attack. Fearing encirclement, Fevzi was forced to withdraw. Maintaining his cavalry as a screen, he pulled his scattered infantry formations tighter around Jerusalem. Between 19 and 21 November, the British wheeled again and attacked east towards Jerusalem. On 25 November, Kress executed a counter-offensive with the 3rd and 7th divisions, driving the British back and restoring the tactical situation along the coast. During the next week, the British shifted their main effort towards the capture of Jerusalem, but

Fevzi's Seventh Army fought them to a standstill. For the first seven days of 1918, Fevzi's XX Corps held out. Nevertheless, by dusk on 7 December, the British were in the outskirts of the holy city. That night, the battered but intact XX Corps abandoned the city and withdrew to new defensive positions 4km (2.5 miles) to the east of Jerusalem. The defenceless civil administration then sent out emissaries to arrange for the peaceful turnover of the city. On 11 December 1917, Allenby entered the city on foot through the Jaffa Gate.

British attacks continued from 13 to 17 December. The New Year found the Turks battered, but holding a solid line anchored in the east on the Dead Sea and in the west on the Mediterranean Sea. Every Turkish

Turkish troops awaiting a British attack at Beersheeba. The Turks had a single understrength cavalry division in Palestine. Its horses were under-fed and under-watered. Allenby's cavalry arm, by comparison, was massive: four full-strength divisions that were well mounted and well trained.

ABOVE **The two British sergeants who met the flag of surrender at Jerusalem, pictured outside the city. Because of the religious significance of the city to Muslims, Jews and Christians, the Ottomans decided to surrender Jerusalem intact. It fell on 8 January 1918.**

LEFT **General Allenby leaving Jerusalem after reading of the Proclamation. Allenby's triumphal entry into Jerusalem was a huge propaganda victory for the British. However, the city had little, if any, military significance.**

infantry division that had begun the fight on 31 October on the Gaza–Beersheba line was intact and still fighting (although some were reduced to cadre strength). Screened by the Dead Sea and the Jordan River, the Turks still held the railway from Dera to Medina, although this line was constantly being harassed and cut by Lawrence and his Arab army. As 1917 came to an end, so too did Allenby's offensive. Exhausted and living on lean logistical support, his army ceased offensive operations and the Turks earned yet another respite.

Casualties for the Turks had been severe during the period from 31 October to 31 December 1917, with the Yildirim Army Group losses approaching 26,000 men killed, wounded, captured or missing. Allenby lost about 18,000 men, but these would be replaced, while the Turks received few new men. According to British historian Cyril Falls, 'considering that he [Allenby] had odds of well over two to one in infantry and eight to one in cavalry, his achievement may not seem so remarkable. In fact, it was hard and costly to turn Turkish troops out of defensive positions in this hilly, rocky country'. Falls's tribute does not include the massive artillery superiority that Allenby enjoyed, or the huge logistical support that he amassed, nor does it attribute any advantage to the Royal Navy. Considering all of these factors in combination, it is remarkable that any Turks survived the onslaught at all. Indeed, not only did they survive, but the divisions of the Turkish Army retired in fair order to continue the fight.

THE ARAB REVOLT CONTINUES

By 1917, the Arab Revolt was in full swing, financed and aided by the British. There were four principal bands of armed Arabs, which operated mainly against the Dera–Medina railway. In the north, Prince Faisal conducted large-scale raids on 25 January and on 23 July 1917 against the garrison towns of Tafile and Fulye, respectively. Farther south, the Emir Ali operated against Tebuk, Abdullah operated against el-Ala, and Sheriff Hussein attacked the fortified city of Medina itself. Most of these Arab bands numbered between 3000 and 4000 men. While these Arabs could not (and would not) hold ground, they were capable

of repeatedly cutting both the rail and the telegraph lines extending south.

One of the most dramatic moments in the Arab campaign came when T.E. Lawrence and Faisal made a daring approach across the desert to attack Aqaba. They swept into the port city and took it almost without a fight on 6 July 1917. Nevertheless, this was an important victory because it unleashed Faisal's army to move north. Moreover, the capture of the port enabled the British to begin regular supply convoys, which provided important logistical support to the Arab armies.

While these raids were bothersome, they were not significant in the military sense. Nevertheless, larger and larger numbers of Turkish soldiers were called upon to guard the lines of communications south to Medina. Consequently, Liman von Sanders (then still in Constantinople) urged the Ottoman general staff to abandon entirely the Hedjaz. However, the importance of the retention of the holy cities of Mecca and Medina made this politically unthinkable (especially after the loss of Baghdad and Jerusalem later that year).

Lawrence, pictured here during the Arab Revolt, often clad himself in the robes of an Arab sheik. Many regular army professional officers found his unconventional appearance, and thinking, very disturbing.

CHAPTER 6

Armageddon

The string of British victories in
Palestine in the closing months of 1918
led to Erich von Falkenhayn's replacement.
The Palestine front was now brought under
a single Ottoman commander, but the
Allied advance was relentless. At Megiddo,
the British smashed through the Turkish
defences. In the Caucasus, by contrast,
Ottoman forces made considerable gains.

In Palestine, Allenby's offensive finally ground to a
halt north of Jerusalem. This was a result both of
torrential rainstorms in the last week of 1917 and
the exhausted condition of his soldiers. This
temporary respite allowed the Turks a brief period in
which to recover their operational effectiveness.
However, in February 1918 Allenby renewed his
offensive by ordering an attack on Jericho, hoping to
force the Ottoman XX Corps back across the Jordan
River. The attack began on 19 February and the
battered Turks were once again forced to withdraw.
However, they were now behind the east bank of the
Jordan River, which offered them a fine natural
defensive obstacle, and were able to dig in.

**German officers head a line of Ottoman prisoners captured
near Jericho in July 1918. Desertion and the willful surrender
of soldiers in combat were a major problem in Palestine.**

Despite this small success, the string of Ottoman defeats that began at Gaza led to the relief of General Erich von Falkenhayn. The Turks were becoming increasingly dissatisfied with his advice and command style. Although most of the blame for the defeats at Gaza and Beersheba could be laid at the feet of Kress, Falkenhayn was held responsible. Part of his troubles were also caused by his contempt for Ottoman officers and by his refusal to allow them to participate in planning important combat operations. Falkenhayn's reputation as a commander of multi-national armies that he had established in Romania was coming undone as his efforts to stop Allenby failed again and again. It became fashionable in Constantinople to remember Falkenhayn's disastrous handling of the Verdun operation and his failure to hold the Gaza–Beersheba line, rather than for his success in Romania.

Following the exit of Falkenhayn, the problem remained of who to appoint as theatre commander. Despite their frequent disagreements about the war and the treatment of Armenians and Greeks, Enver Pasha valued the fighting abilities of Liman von Sanders, who had won the Gallipoli campaign. Enver approached Liman von Sanders on 19 February with an offer to command the Yildirim Army Group. The German, tired of being sidelined in Turkish Thrace, eagerly accepted his offer several days later. Enver also took the opportunity to separate the Mesopotamian theatre from the Yildirim Army Group, which simplified its responsibilities. Enver also ordered Cemal's Fourth Army in Syria to coordinate its operations with the new command, which finally brought the Palestine front under a single commander. On 8 March, after a difficult railway journey, Liman von Sanders and his staff arrived in Syria; he consulted the departing Falkenhayn about the defensive strategy for Palestine. There were significant differences of tactical and operational opinion between the two

generals. Falkenhayn was an advocate of a flexible defence, which allowed for both retreat and for the surrender of ground. Liman von Sanders, based on his personal experiences on the Gallipoli Peninsula, was an advocate of a theory of static tactical defence, which dictated that ground should be retained at all costs and if lost, immediately retaken by counterattacks. Liman von Sanders was unhappy with the Yildirim Army's dispositions and plans, and he immediately began to reverse the operational and tactical direction of the defence of Palestine.

THE TRANS-JORDAN RAIDS

The British conducted another offensive shortly after Liman von Sanders's arrival, with the objective of establishing a bridgehead on the east bank of the Jordan. Famously, this offensive was conducted in concert with large-scale Arab raids on the Dera–Hedjaz railway and was preceded by diversionary attacks across the entire front. The main attack began on 21 March; the British launched two infantry divisions and two cavalry divisions across the river, breaking the back of the Ottoman lines on the Jordan River. Allenby wanted to seize Amman, cut the railway and then 'probably withdraw'. He hoped to outflank the main Turkish lines and perhaps break loose from the deadlocked trenches. By 30 March, the British had pushed the 48th Division back into the city of Amman, on the Hedjaz railway. However, for reasons that remain unclear Allenby called off the attack and withdrew the next day. Certainly, the stated reason that the Turks had brought up substantial reserves, which offset the numerical advantage of the British, is not true. The possession of the city of Amman would

> 'The policy of Falkenhayn was defence by manoeuvre; that of the Liman defence by resistance in trenches.'
>
> Cyril Falls, *Military Operations*, 1926

RIGHT **The mayor of Jerusalem, Hussein Effendi, meets men of the 2/19th Battalion, The London Regiment under the white flag of surrender on 9 December 1918 at 8am. Relations between Ottoman civil servants in occupied areas and the British were generally correct, as this photograph suggests.**

Bodies of Turkish troops after an attempt to capture the city of Jerusalem on night of 26/27 December 1917. Ottoman counterattacks in late 1917 restored the situation and stabilized the lines once again. It is possible that these dead men were from a stormtroop detachment.

cut, once and for all, the Dera–Hedjaz railway and also offered the opportunity to outflank the strong Ottoman main defensive lines. It was an important objective for the British, and the abandonment of their attack was probably due to the fact that Allenby had been ordered to send troops to France. The Turks conducted a vigorous pursuit and compressed the withdrawing British into a bridgehead in the Jordan River valley. After a bloody repulse on 11 April, the Turks halted their counterattacks and began to dig in. This engagement became known as the First Battle of the Jordan.

On 30 April the Second Battle of the Jordan began, when the British again launched an attack toward

Amman from their bridgehead on the east side of the Jordan. In the intervening two weeks, the Turks managed to bring up strong forces (24th Division and 3rd Cavalry Division), which were available to conduct a flank attack on the advancing British. These divisions, along with Ottoman stormtroop battalions, conducted strong counterattacks between 2 and 4 May that swiftly halted the British offensive. Fighting along the Jordan died down until mid-July 1918, when brief (though bloody and inconclusive) attacks were conducted by both sides.

THE SUMMER OF 1918

Palestine was relatively quiet during the spring and summer of 1918 (with the exception of the skirmishing along the Jordan River). The understrength Ottoman Army did not have sufficient combat power, while Allenby's army was stripped of experienced formations for reinforcements for the BEF in France, which was reeling from the heavy Ludendorff offensives in the spring of 1918. Allenby was ordered to send to France, beginning in March, two infantry divisions, nine yeomanry (cavalry) regiments, 24 British infantry battalions, five heavy artillery batteries and five machine-gun companies. To maintain his strength, the India Office sent him two Indian Army infantry divisions from Mesopotamia, and a number of Indian cavalry regiments and infantry battalions as well as thousands of individual replacements. Allenby lost a significant portion of his trained and experienced British Army combat power, and in return received inexperienced and less well trained Indian troops. These events forced Allenby to spend the summer engaged in a complete reorganization and retraining of his army.

The British were still left with seven full-strength infantry divisions in Palestine, but the national character of these formations had changed significantly. Only a single all-British infantry division remained (the 54th Division); four other 'British' divisions were actually the 2nd/3rd Indian (the 10th, 53rd, 60th and 75th divisions), and the final two divisions were Indian Army infantry divisions (3rd and 7th Indian divisions). Only in mounted strength did Allenby's situation actually improve, gaining one division, for a total of four mounted divisions.

Allenby still commanded a large and well equipped army with which to renew the offensive against the Yildirim Army Group. Unfortunately, many of the newly arrived Indian soldiers were untrained or unseasoned in combat. Of 54 incoming infantry battalions, 22 had combat experience but had given up a company of men, 10 were composed of combat veterans who had not trained together, and 22 had seen no active service whatsoever. This situation forced the EEF to begin a long training programme that lasted throughout the summer as Allenby prepared his army for offensive operations. Fortunately for the British, the EEF had in Allenby one of the finest trainers in the army.

Allenby's training programme was vigorous and comprehensive. He began with the careful integration

of the incoming Indian Army battalions into the gutted divisions by linking one British infantry battalion with three Indian battalions to form new brigades. Moreover, some of the remaining individual British officers and NCOs were earmarked to receive elementary training in Indian languages to assist in the integration process. The staffs enlarged the available system of tactical schools that existed in Egypt and in the rear areas of the army. This included heavy machine-gun, Lewis gun, rifle grenade, signals and small-unit tactics courses and the incoming Indians received allocations and were programmed into the training cycles. There were also courses for company commanders and staff officers as well as individual training for raw recruits.

The reorganized Ottoman Gendarmerie in Barracks Square, Jerusalem, 1918. The gendarmerie (*Jandarma*) was a paramilitary organization that fell under the Ministry of the Interior in peacetime and the Ministry of War in war.

Importantly, Allenby also ensured that the latest 'lessons learned' from the Western Front were integrated into his training programmes. The EEF reprinted pamphlets that brought the most recent developments in tactics to the army in Palestine. These were supplemented by frequent lectures at brigade level by experienced staff officers, who updated Allenby's officers regarding current trends and tactics. These lectures were followed by tactical demonstrations and conferences. Allenby himself visited his divisions and also held conferences to ensure that every bit of practical information was reaching his soldiers. He also ordered mock Ottoman trenches to be constructed, which would allow his soldiers to rehearse combat operations before an attack. Allenby was very aware of contemporary British tactical thought and ordered his companies to begin combined-arms training in open warfare

tactics, thus bringing the infantry together with artillery, machine guns and engineers.

In August 1918, the Yildirim Army Group had 12 understrength divisions available for the defence of a 90km (56-mile) front. The Ottoman Amy in Palestine had grown progressively weaker over the course of the year. This was a combination of losses (which had never been replaced), inadequate numbers of replacement soldiers and a higher than normal rate of desertion. By mid-summer, morale in the Ottoman divisions was at an all-time low, and supplies of all types were very limited. Moreover, many of the Arab conscripts were enthused with the idea of Arab nationalism and willingly deserted to the British. The strength of some infantry divisions dropped to a front-line rifle strength of 2000 men. Even in the army's premier divisions (such as the 19th Infantry Division) infantry battalions, which at Beersheba had numbered 600 men, now numbered 200 men or less. Some regiments tried to keep a company at full strength, but this affected the remaining companies.

A group of Turkish prisoners. Although unkempt and motley in appearance, these Ottoman POWs retain much of their military bearing. This reflects the Spartan-like discipline of the army and its training regimes.

To make matters worse for the regular infantry establishment, the Ottoman Army in 1917 began to form assault battalions modelled on German stormtroops. The best officers and the most fit and aggressive soldiers were selected for these units and then sent to intensive battle training courses. Several of the assault battalions saw active service during the battles along the Jordan River in April. Although the need for such a specialized offensive capability had passed, the Turks retained their assault battalions in most of their divisions in Palestine. This practice concentrated the cream of the divisional infantry strength into a single battalion and had the effect of weakening the regular line infantry battalions. Exaggerating the situation, the flow of replacements and recruits dried up in the summer of 1918 and the line infantry regiments received men who were mostly

Indian lancers bringing in Turkish prisoners, Jericho, 15 July 1918. Over half of Allenby's cavalry force was composed of Indian Army regiments. He would unleash them at the Battle of Megiddo on the Turkish rear.

deserters or criminals from the empire's jails, hardly the most promising raw recruits to replace combat losses. This situation greatly reduced the effectiveness of Liman von Sanders's army.

According to late 1918 Ottoman Army doctrine, Liman von Sanders should have had 18 divisions in the line to defend his 90km (56-mile) front, plus an additional seven divisions in a deeply layered arrangement of reserves. Of course, these templates were based on full-strength Ottoman divisions numbering some 12,000 men; Liman von Sanders's divisions operated at about a sixth of that number. In reality, the Yildirim Army was attempting to hold the front with about 15 per cent of the troops required by the army's tactical doctrine.

THE OPPOSING PLANS

Allenby intended to inflict a decisive defeat on the Turks at the strategic level. His plan was the reverse of the Gaza–Beersheba plan of 1917. Instead of feigning to attack near the sea and attacking inland at Beersheba, in 1918 Allenby chose a feint near the Jordan River (scene of his spring and summer offensives) and then to smash his way through the Turkish defences on a narrow avenue next to the sea. Achieving a breakthrough, Allenby intended to pass his cavalry corps through the breach and rupture the Turks' lines of communications. This accomplished, Allenby would envelop the remaining Turkish forces. Probably the best-known aspect of his plan was the attention paid to an elaborate deception scheme

encouraging the Turks to believe that he intended to strike his main blow along the Jordan River front. Allenby's intelligence staff sent out phantom wireless units, constructed elaborate dummy positions and moved small numbers of troops frequently, all of which were designed to make the enemy think that the EEF was massing for a main effort in the east. Particular attention was given to aerial superiority operations that denied the Turks and the Germans the opportunity to conduct aerial reconnaissance over the British lines. Importantly, Allenby's new plan was different from his previous ones in that he called for the destruction of the enemy army by disruption and envelopment rather than for the occupation of important geographic features, foreshadowing the blitzkrieg operations of World War II.

At the tactical and operational level the EEF developed very sophisticated plans that focused on the

120mm Krupp Howitzer M1905, in Turkish service. The Ottomans increased their artillery inventory as the war progressed. By the end of 1918 the Germans had sent the Turks 559 artillery pieces of various calibres.

A Turkish VIII Army Corps camp. This photograph was probably taken during pre-war manoeuvres and reflects the professionalism that the army was capable of when it could put its best foot forward.

coordinated use of artillery in support of the infantry. A short creeping barrage was planned for the divisional artillery while counterbattery targets were selected and registered for the corps artillery (two-thirds of the heavy guns were allocated to this task). Senior commanders, who in the past had remained well behind the lines, were brought forward to closely control operations. Detailed coordination instructions and rehearsals were drawn up to ensure that the exploitation force of cavalry would be able to execute the difficult task of the passage of lines through the infantry. The infantry was trained to move forward bypassing strong points of resistance. Finally, procedures for close air support were developed and plans laid for aircraft to support the cavalry with deep raids into enemy territory. Overall the EEF's mature plan of operations mirrored the latest tactical techniques that the BEF had used at Amiens in August (minus, of course, the tanks).

Liman von Sanders, on the other hand, had no real plans at the strategic or operational level other than a determination to hold every inch of ground. This was not a function of his tactical belief but reflected the relative immobility of his army. Indeed, by the summer of 1918, the Ottoman Army in Palestine did not have enough draft animals to transport its artillery, ammunitions and supplies. The animals on hand, moreover, were weakened by inadequate quantities of fodder and grain, which made their usefulness as draft animals problematic. While the infantry retained some measure of tactical mobility, the rest of Liman von Sanders's army was almost incapable of movement. The result of this was that the army was ordered to fight for every position. The few reserves that were available were small in number and were controlled at corps and divisional level. Once the battle began, Liman von Sanders had almost nothing with which to influence the battle.

This situation made it imperative for the Yildirim Army's staff to predict where Allenby might strike his main blow. While the extant historiography maintains that Allenby achieved complete surprise, the Turkish record indicates that this is untrue. In fact, several days before the attack, both Cevat Pasha and Mustafa Kemal requested permission to withdraw to a more defensible position 20km (12.4 miles) to the rear because they believed an attack was imminent. The Turks concentrated their best divisions in the

threatened coastal sector and these were supported by the bulk of the army's heavy artillery. Liman von Sanders's only large reserve formation was also positioned directly behind the Ottoman XXII Corps, which held the coastal sector. Finally it must be noted that the front-line Ottoman regiments were warned several days in advance of the impending attack. Moreover, no Ottoman Army reserves were drawn to the Jordan River valley, thus nullifying the elaborate deception measures.

Cevat's Eighth Army defended the coast with XXII Corps (the 7th and 20th divisions) and the Left-Wing Group, a corps-sized formation commanded by German Colonel von Oppen (the 16th and 19th divisions and the German Asia Corps). The line continued eastward with Seventh Army (of which Mustafa Kemal took command on 17 August) consisting of III Corps (1st and 11th divisions) and XX Corps (26th and 53rd divisions). The Fourth Army defended the Jordan front with VIII Corps (48th Division and several provisional divisions), the Sheria Group (3rd Cavalry Division and 24th Division), and II Corps (62nd Division). By early September 1918,

British artillery in action. By the standards of the Western Front, artillery combat in the Middle East was all but derisory. Barrages were of short duration, and ammunition expenditure numbered in the tens of thousands of projectiles rather than in millions.

the evidence of an impending British offensive was undeniable, and Liman von Sanders maintained his best forces in the coastal plain. Consequently, although the Yildirim Army Group remained spread along the entire front in static defensive positions, it managed to concentrate in the threatened sector.

THE BATTLE OF MEGIDDO (NABLUS PLAIN)

Allenby concentrated four full-strength infantry divisions (the 60th and 75th divisions and 3rd and 7th Indian divisions) on a front of about 12km (7.5 miles) opposite the Ottoman XXII Corps. Unlike the nine-battalion British divisions then fighting in France, Allenby's EEF divisions maintained the 12-battalion organization. Altogether he planned to throw 24,000 infantrymen supported by over 40 guns against XXII Corps (a further 8000 infantrymen lay in immediate reserve). Poised directly behind this were the 4th and

5th Cavalry Divisions and the Australian Mounted Division. Opposing this force were some 3000 Turks in the trenches of XXII Corps supported by about a hundred guns (a further 5000 Turks were assigned to Oppen and in reserve).

The British offensive began with the Arabs and Colonel T.E. Lawrence conducting raids cutting the railway between Dera and Amman on 16 September. On 17 and 18 September the British XX Corps began a diversionary attack in the centre of the Turkish front. These operations were designed to fix the Turks in place and to deceive them as to the true location of the main attack. The main attack began at 4.30am on 19 September 1918, with a short bombardment followed by a creeping barrage that screened the advancing British infantry. Turkish resistance was sporadic and uneven along the front. In most places Allenby's Indians and British overran the enemy trenches in a very short time. The attacking troops used the most current British fighting methods, including the bypassing of enemy strongpoints.

Because of Liman von Sanders's tactical guidance, the Turks prepared to fight to the death for their positions. Initially, very heavy British artillery fire pounded the front-line positions of the regiments of the 7th and 20th divisions. Allenby's tactics mirrored those in France and the bombardments were relatively brief. Then, as the infantry came forward, the artillery shifted its fire to conduct a creeping barrage in front of the assaulting troops. These creeping barrages were timed to shift the curtain of fire closer to the enemy every couple of minutes, with the infantry following about 75m (82 yards) behind the bursting shells. It was dangerous, but it kept the Turks off their machine guns long enough for the British and Indians to close with the enemy trenches. By 5am, the British artillery firing had ceased and by 5.50am all local Turkish reserves had been committed to the fight. Reports indicating an imminent collapse poured into the Turkish XXII Corps Headquarters.

By 7am, the British had broken cleanly through the Turkish defences and were waiting to pass the cavalry through the breach into the Turkish rear. The first real reports about the conditions in the breakthrough area

Lawrence and Guerrilla Warfare

Lawrence has achieved wide contemporary notice as a prophet of the tactics of insurgency. However, modern Turkish histories show that the Ottoman Army was able to deal with the mobile Arab rebel armies by largely ignoring them. Lawrence's bands raided isolated outposts and, more frequently, destroyed the Ottoman railway line to Medina. These losses were pinpricks to the Turks and the broken rail lines were easily repaired within days of their destruction. Even in the final campaigns in Syria the Turks deployed few military assets against the Arabs. Moreover, they never worried about an actual Arab uprising behind their lines as the rebels had little interaction with the civilian population in either Syria or Palestine. On the British side, Allenby was often disappointed by the Arab failure to assist him on his right flank. As a matter of record the Arab Revolt was never a movement that was broadly supported by the Arab population. While associated with guerrilla warfare and insurgency, in truth the glamorous Lawrence was more of a practitioner of what might be termed 'irregular warfare'.

reached Liman von Sanders at 8.50am from the Eighth Army, indicating that the 7th Division was all but destroyed and the situation was very bad. Additionally, the XXII Corps artillery had been lost. The army also reported that the adjacent 19th Division was now under heavy attack. The report ended with an urgent request for assistance. Liman von Sanders responded immediately, sending his few available reserves (an infantry regiment and some army engineers) forward to help the Eighth Army. It was too little too late. By 10am, the British had passed two entire cavalry divisions through the huge hole blown open in the Turkish defences. These cavalry divisions were ordered to ride hard and straight towards the Turkish rear. The cavalry were assigned deep objectives, including the towns of Nazareth (containing Liman von Sanders's

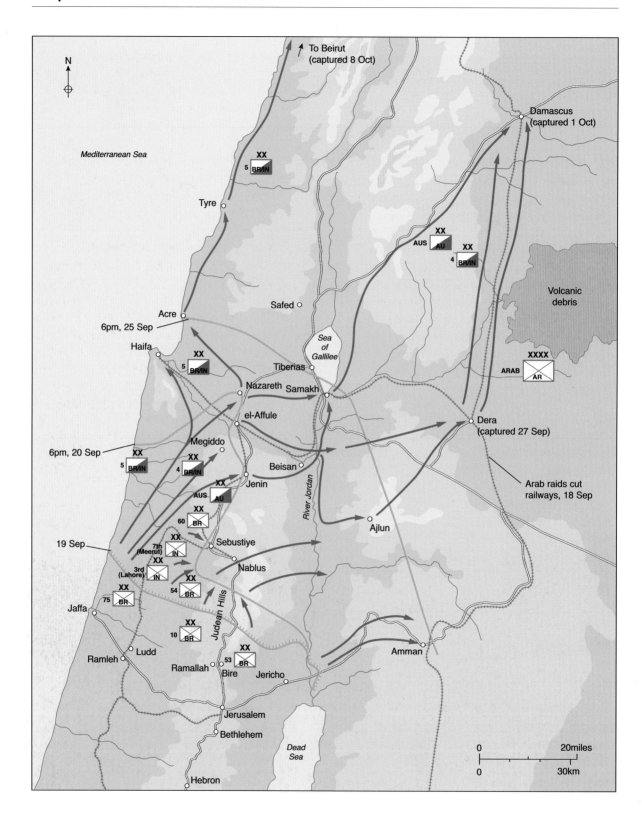

N

Mediterranean Sea

To Beirut
(captured 8 Oct)

Damascus
(captured 1 Oct)

Volcanic
debris

Tyre

XX
5 BR/IN

XX
AUS AU

XX
4 BR/IN

Safed

Acre

6pm, 25 Sep

Haifa

Sea
of
Gallilee

XX
5 BR/IN

Tiberias

Samakh

XXXX
ARAB AR

Nazareth

el-Affule

Megiddo

6pm, 20 Sep

XX
5 BR/IN

XX
4 BR/IN

Beisan

Dera
(captured 27 Sep)

Jenin

XX
AUS AU

Arab raids cut
railways, 18 Sep

XX
60 BR

River Jordan

Ajlun

19 Sep

XX
7th
(Meerut) IN

Sebustiye

XX
3rd
(Lahore) IN

Nablus

XX
75 BR

XX
54 BR

Jaffa

Judean Hills

XX
10 BR

Ramleh   Ludd

Amman

XX
53 BR

Ramallah   Bire   Jericho

Jerusalem

Bethlehem

Dead
Sea

0   20miles

0   30km

Hebron

The Battle of Megiddo and the pursuit to Damascus, 19 September–8 October 1918. Liman von Sanders had almost no reserves behind the Megiddo line. When Allenby's infantry ruptured the Ottoman lines, it led to one of history's greatest cavalry exploitation and pursuit operations.

headquarters) and Megiddo, and the northern exits of the Plain of Esdraelon. It was hoped that the cavalry would be able to capture Liman von Sanders himself.

Reports from the centre and the left wing began arriving at Liman von Sanders's headquarters early, but ceased almost entirely later in the day. He interpreted the devastating news correctly: his right wing was destroyed and his flank exposed. He reacted promptly and ordered the Seventh Army to begin withdrawing to the north in order to prevent the British from conducting a short envelopment to the Jordan River. Liman hoped that the Fourth Army might hold firm and provide a solid anchor for his rapidly disappearing army. The next day Allenby's cavalry took Nazareth, almost capturing the surprised Liman von Sanders in bed early in the morning. The following day the British and Indian cavalry reached the shores of the Sea of Galilee and the upper Jordan River. Unlike in previous battles, the Ottoman Army in Palestine disintegrated. For all practical purposes, the

Turkish XXII Corps and its divisions was destroyed in two days. On 21 September the Eighth Army itself ceased to exist and its commander, Cevat Pasha, fled to the safety of Mustafa Kemal's headquarters.

It was an impossible strategic and operational situation for Liman von Sanders, who was totally incapable of preventing Allenby from destroying his army piecemeal. From 21 to 23 September, the famous Ottoman III Corps fought a gallant rearguard action from Tubas to the Jordan River. This allowed the Turks to block the developing British encirclement. Together, these units bought enough time for the surviving units to pull back behind the Jordan River. By 25 September, the coastal cities of Haifa and Acre had fallen, as had Meggido. By 27 September, the relentless cavalry had broken the Jordan River line and pushed the Turks back towards Dera. The British had now entered Syria and the Battle of Meggido, or the Nablus Plain as the Turks call it – in reality a series of battles within a campaign – finally ended.

In spite of the great victories in Armenia and in Azerbaijan, it was now apparent to all but the most

Serving rations to Turkish troops in the desert. Ottoman soldiers were authorized rations in the amount of 3149 calories per day, including 600g of bread and 250g of meat. To receive even half of this amount was a rarity for them.

diehard nationalists in the Turkish General Staff that Turkey was now in an indefensible condition, which could not be remedied with the resources on hand. It was also apparent that the disintegration of the Bulgarian Army at Salonika and the dissolution of the Austro-Hungarian Army spelled disaster and defeat for the Central Powers. From now until the armistice, the focus of Turkish strategy would be to retain as much territory as possible.

Liman von Sanders's defeat was inevitable. First, the terrain was favourable for the attack, at least in comparison with Gallipoli or Caucasia. Second, there was room for Allenby to shift corps-size formations around the battlefield to achieve deception and concentration. Third, and without doubt most importantly, the British Army had made significant and effective changes in its fighting methods and tactical doctrines in 1918. It is doubtful whether Liman von Sanders entirely grasped how quickly, and in which ways, the British Army had changed. In truth, his plans might have prevailed against the tactically clumsy British Army of 1915, but not against the highly mobile army of 1918.

Whether the outcome of these battles would have been different had Falkenhayn's ideas about a flexible defence been retained will never be known. However, it is likely that a more flexible Turkish defence would not have resulted in the total destruction of division-level Turkish formations. The British would have advanced in any case, but the orderly fall back of the infantry divisions on the coastal plain might have prevented the ruptured lines that enabled the great British cavalry breakthrough, which led to the annihilation of the Eighth Army.

> ‘The army will attack with the intent of inflicting a decisive defeat on the enemy and driving him from the line.’
>
> General Sir Edmund Allenby, Force Order 68, 1918

AIR OPERATIONS

Aerial operations reached their high point in the Middle East with Allenby's offensive at Megiddo. By 1918 substantial numbers of aircraft had made their way to the theatre, although not in the huge numbers then seen in France. Allenby had organized his airmen into the Palestine Brigade, Royal Flying Corps in 1917 and expanded it as more aircraft and pilots arrived. He used it at Third Gaza primarily to destroy Kress's aircraft on their airfields in an attempt to deny him the use of air assets. As the campaign developed, Allenby's airmen became very proficient in their jobs. Of particular note was the rapidly developing capability in aerial photography, which mapped almost every square inch of Palestine. This was linked to a very effective mapping service that, in turn, produced high-resolution tactical maps for the army. As the war entered 1918, Britain's highly efficient aircraft industry enabled the air staff to send the latest aircraft to Palestine, including DH-9s, Bristol Fighters and SE-5as. This gave Allenby an edge in quality and quantity over the Germans and Turks.

For their part, the Turks languished at the end of a long and problematic logistical chain that reached through Anatolia and the Balkans to Germany. The Turkish air service was entirely reliant on German military assistance packages to provide aircraft and spare parts. By 1918, most of their available air squadrons were deployed to Palestine and Gallipoli, but these were under-equipped and poorly manned. However, the Germans also sent four active air squadrons to Palestine under the terms of the Yildirim Agreement's protocols (Flieger Abteilung 301–304), which were popularly called the ‘Pasha squadrons'. These aircraft were very valuable to Liman von Sanders, who came to rely on them for reconnaissance and aerial mapping. Unfortunately for the Ottomans their numbers were too small to allow them to be used to a great extent in active combat missions against enemy ground forces. Importantly, by 1918 most of the Turco-German squadrons were equipped with aircraft (Albatros D.IIIs, for example) that were a generation behind the most current the British employed in Allenby's squadrons.

The air campaign waged in support of Allenby's offensive at Megiddo ranks as one of the most important factors in his victory. In a carefully orchestrated campaign, the Palestine Brigade established air superiority in September 1918 to deny the Turks the opportunity to conduct reconnaissance flights over the British lines. This had the effect of blinding Liman von Sanders as to the locations of British troop concentrations and movements, enabling any attacks to achieve complete surprise. Allenby's airmen then prepared a carefully crafted plan that located the key defiles, road junctions, enemy headquarters and communications centres, and then targeted them for destruction. Communications procedures were developed, including radio, flares and dropped messages that enabled Royal Flying Corps liaison officers

accompanying the leading cavalry detachments to communicate directly with aircraft overhead.

On 21 September 1918, Allenby's air chief, Sir John Salmond, unleashed his airmen on the Turkish rear areas. While Allenby's artillery supported his attacking infantry, Allied aircraft prepared the way for Allenby's cavalry. The Turkish telephone exchanges were quickly knocked out and enemy headquarters were attacked as well. Missions were flown against enemy reserves, road junctions and logistics sites. Additionally, a counter air campaign was successfully waged against the enemy's airfields to keep the Turkish and German aircraft pinned to the ground. With almost no situational or

An air reconnaissance photo taken over Jerusalem. Allenby's Royal Air Force squadrons brought the art of aerial photography to a high level. As a result his army enjoyed superb maps and real-time intelligence.

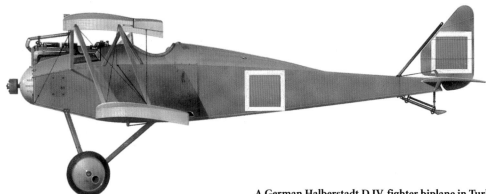

A German Halberstadt D.IV, fighter biplane in Turkish service. The Germans sent over 300 aircraft to the Turks during four years of war. Most of these were two-seater reconnaissance or fighter aircraft.

spatial awareness and confronted with the massive disruptions caused by attacking aircraft, the Turks were unable to mount a coherent defence. When Allenby's cavalry began its great drive into the Turkish rear, it was supported by aircraft that provided immediate intelligence on enemy locations. It was a brilliant and effective effort by a thoroughly professional air–ground team.

Probably the most famous and best-known event of the air campaign came on 21 September 1918, when Australian airmen caught the retreating Ottoman Seventh Army in the Wadi el-Far'a defile. In this narrow chokepoint, the Australians of No. 1 Squadron

found the Turks unsupported by either friendly aircraft or anti-aircraft guns and conducted carefully orchestrated aerial attacks coordinated by wireless with six aircraft arriving to bomb and strafe the Turks every half hour. Thousands of men and animals died in these attacks. After the battle, the ground forces counted over a hundred cannon, 59 motor lorries and over 900 horse-drawn wagon and carts in the defile.

END GAME IN SYRIA

Liman von Sanders and his commanders fought to keep the Ottoman armies intact. Allenby, however, maintained relentless pressure and ordered his fast-

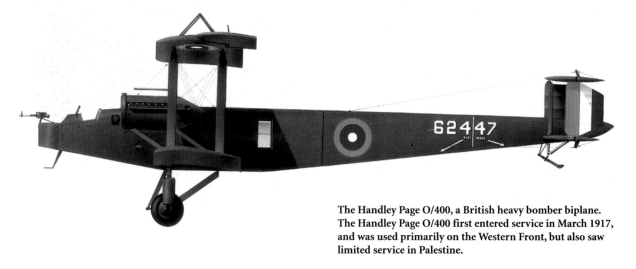

The Handley Page O/400, a British heavy bomber biplane. The Handley Page O/400 first entered service in March 1917, and was used primarily on the Western Front, but also saw limited service in Palestine.

moving and powerful cavalry to seize Damascus. Liman von Sanders shifted some of his few remaining combat formations northwards to deal with this threat and assembled the 24th, 26th and 53rd divisions and the 3rd Cavalry Division under the command of III Corps for the defence of the city. However, these units were badly worn down by combat and retreat, and could not hold Damascus, which fell on 1 October 1918. The 3rd Cavalry Division was destroyed in a desperate rearguard action, which allowed the remainder of the Turkish forces to escape northwards.

An impossible strategic situation confronted Liman von Sanders in early October 1918. The Eighth Army had been destroyed and its headquarters captured. III Corps, with the 1st and 11th divisions, was still intact and conducting a fighting retreat, as was XX Corps, and the 48th Division. Many of these divisions were very short of cannon as the Yildirim Army Group had

lost most of its artillery. In early October, the 43rd Division arrived as reinforcement but was immediately committed to the defence of Beirut. The British tempo was unrelenting, and they took Beirut on 8 October. On 16 October, the Fourth Army headquarters was encircled and destroyed in the city of Humus. The 48th Division attempted to set up blocking positions at Hama, south of Aleppo, but lost the city on 19 October. On 25 October, Allenby's army entered Aleppo. Almost simultaneously, Lawrence and Faisal Hussein arrived in Damascus in an attempt to establish an independent Arab presence in Syria. The campaign for Lebanon and Syria lasted a month.

On 26 October 1918, Liman von Sanders's headquarters fell back to the Anatolian city of Adana. The

The Allied entry into in the Hedjaz. The Turkish force present there, out of communications with the homeland, held out until after the signing of the Mudros armistice.

The Allied entry into Damascus. After Megiddo the Turks tried to fight a delaying action back to Damascus. Allenby's cavalry constantly outflanked them and rode them down. The city fell on 1 October 1918.

army still had combat capability with the 23rd Division at Tarsus and XV Corps in Osmaniye (41st and 44th divisions). Mustafa Kemal's Seventh Army was located in Raco with III Corps at Alexandretta (11th and 24th divisions), and XX Corps near Katma (1st and 43rd divisions). While badly worn down, Liman von Sanders prepared his army for a final defence of the Ottoman heartland.

At the armistice, the newly installed Turkish Minister of War, Ahmet Izzet Pasha, recalled Liman von Sanders to Constantinople on 30 October 1918. In his place Mustafa Kemal was appointed to command the Yildirim Army Group, and he reported for duty the next day. Liman von Sanders's farewell message to his armies praised the Ottoman performance at Ariburnu and Anafarta (in Gallipoli) and in Palestine. He expressed how proud he was to command Ottoman forces from the first time he set foot in Turkey, and he thanked the Turks for their hospitality. The tireless Mustafa Kemal immediately began to energize the defence of the Anatolian heartland.

It is uncertain today how many casualties the Ottoman armies sustained in these campaigns. General Wavell, in his biography of Allenby, states that the British took 75,000 prisoners and 360 guns in the six-week campaign from 18 September to 31 October. Indeed, the Turkish official history of the campaign quotes these British figures, possibly as a result of the loss of records caused by the destruction of the Fourth and the Eighth Army headquarters. The cost to the

British was about 6000 men. Allenby's lop-sided victory was one of the most complete in a war that was almost bereft of such achievements. However, the Ottoman Army was still in the field and actively preparing its defence of southeastern Anatolia when the armistice was signed. Further British operations in the winter of 1918 would have come up against determined men under Mustafa Kemal in mountainous terrain.

1918 IN THE CAUCASUS

From May 1917, the Caucasian front was quiet as the Turks enjoyed a Russian strategic pause. On the Russian side, war weariness and the effects of the revolution continually eroded troop morale. They maintained four army corps guarding their conquests in Anatolia, but none were in any condition to fight. In a sense, the Russian army in the Caucasus 'self-demobilized' in the autumn of 1917 as troop strength evaporated. As the Russians withdrew the remnants of their army, a loosely organized federation composed of the newly independent states of Armenia, Azerbaijan and Georgia was left behind to face the Turks. Unfortunately for these peoples, the Russians were focused on salvaging their nation from the grasping German negotiators at the ongoing peace talks at Brest-Litovsk. None of the infant Caucasian republics were represented at the peace table, nor did the Russians evince any interest in ensuring their safety. In January 1918, when the Treaty of Brest-Litovsk came into effect, the continued existence of these states was not guaranteed, nor were the Turks obliged to honour their territorial integrity. This created a serious power vacuum in the Caucasus, and although these new states had small armies, they were not nearly as powerful as the Ottoman forces that remained in the region.

As the Russians reduced their armies in the Caucasus, the Turks were also able to draw down their Caucasian armies as well. The Caucasian Army Group was inactivated on 16 December 1917 with the unlucky Second Army soon following. The IV Corps, with the 5th and 12th Infantry divisions, was absorbed into the Third Army, which assumed the frontage and the responsibilities of the inactivated Second Army. The Third Army commander, Vehip Pasha, had carefully husbanded the strength of his army for more than a year. His creative reorganization of his army into what he styled 'Caucasian corps' and 'Caucasian divisions' was successfully completed during the previous year (in reality these were merely reduced-strength divisions), and the rebuilt units were rested and combat ready. Indeed, having no significant or active enemy opposing it, the general staff requested that Vehip send some of his infantry divisions to more active fronts. Vehip, however, successfully fended off most of these requests, losing only the 2nd Caucasian Cavalry Division to the Palestine front. Vehip's army was actually very weak, which was reflected in his strength returns. On 1 January 1918, the total strength of the combined I and II Caucasian corps was 20,026 men, 186 machine guns and 151 artillery pieces – a total barely exceeding the combat strength of a single British infantry division fighting on the Western Front. The I Caucasian Corps on 11 February 1918

Members of the Army of Islam operating a heavy mortar in 1918. The Caucasus front in 1918 was the single bright spot in the Ottoman war effort. The Army of Islam captured the oil port of Baku on the Caspian Sea on 15 September 1918.

reported about 12,000 soldiers present for duty. Additionally, the corps returns showed a total of only 98 machine guns and 46 artillery pieces present on the same date. Under most circumstances, the Ottoman Third Army would be considered incapable of offensive action.

However, throughout 1917 Enver Pasha had been watching the situation in the Caucasus, and in December he seized on a tactical report from the Third Army written by a Captain Hüsamettin stating that the Russians were incapable of maintaining the front for very much longer. Enver was also alarmed by Third Army reports of British and French involvement in the Tiflis region and by the formation of large Armenian and Greek military units. Furthermore, there were rumours of massacres of Muslim Turks and Azerbaijanis by Armenians. Ottoman intelligence had also received information that Armenian Dashnak

committees were preparing to establish a breakaway republic centred on Erzurum in the Caucasus.

After analyzing these reports, Enver Pasha and the Ottoman general staff began to consider the possibilities of a renewed offensive in the Caucasus, one that would reclaim the frontiers lost in 1877. Enver decided to reinforce Vehip's army and issued official orders to the Third Army on 23 January 1918 to begin planning and preparations for offensive operations. The 15th Infantry Division (recently returned from operations in Romania), 120 motor driven trucks, three Jandarma battalions and the full-strength 123rd Infantry Regiment were earmarked for service with the

Kress and German staff officers attending a funeral in Georgia. The Germans were furious at Ottoman attempts to invade Georgia in violation of the Treaty of Brest-Litovsk. They sent troops there to oppose the Turks, thereby ensuring the survival of the Georgian Republic.

Third Army. These forces were put on fast steamers on 9 February, and they began to arrive in the small Black Sea port of Giresun three days later (the Russian Navy, by now, being reduced to inactivity).

As the Third Army was brought to a condition of combat readiness, the I and II Caucasian corps received orders assigning them objectives deep within the territory occupied by both the Russians and the Armenians. In concept, the plan envisioned a three-pronged drive into Russian-held territory. The II Caucasian Corps would drive along the northern Black Sea coast, with the 37th Division, to reclaim Trabzon. The I Caucasian Corps would seize Erzincan and then drive on towards Erzurum. The IV Corps received orders to seize Malazgirt.

Opposing the Third Army was an Armenian army of about 50,000 men, equipped mostly with cast-off Russian equipment. They were organized into two rifle divisions, three brigades of Armenian volunteers, and a cavalry brigade. The rifle divisions were made up of veteran soldiers from the Druzhiny units, which had fought alongside the Russians for almost four years. These were augmented by volunteers from the surviving local Armenian populations of Erzurum, Van and the Eliskirt Valley. The Armenian National Army (as it was called) was actually well equipped, since it was allowed to recover the best of the equipment left behind by the departing Russians. The definitive Western history of the Caucasian campaign reported that the combat strength of the Armenian National Army did not exceed 16,000 infantry, 1000 cavalry and 4000 volunteers. These small numbers of Armenians were greatly outnumbered by Vehip's Third Army.

On the morning of 12 February 1918, Vehip's troops went forward. Erzincan was seized in short order and with it the Turks took tons of supplies, artillery pieces and large quantities of munitions. The Armenian population in the area began immediately to flee towards the east, while the Armenian Army began a delaying retreat towards the rear. The Turks retook the important Black Sea port of Trabzon on 25 February and sea-borne reinforcements immediately began to debark.

A view of the port of Batum from the city's fort. The collapse of Russia's Black Sea Fleet in 1918 enabled the Ottoman Navy to conduct operations in the Black Sea with impunity.

Despite adverse weather and occasional Armenian resistance, Vehip Pasha urged his troops forward. The Armenians attempted to hold the fortress of Erzurum, but after several days of fighting I Caucasian Corps reclaimed the city on 12 March. There they discovered that the retreating Armenians had massacred many Muslim inhabitants in retaliation for the massacres inflicted on the Armenians in 1915. By 25 March, the Turks were advancing across the entire front.

Vehip reorganized his army in April 1918 to configure it for offensive operations deep in the Caucasus. He formed what would be called in modern terminology an 'operational manoeuvre group' by transforming II Caucasian Corps into a Group Command. Under this new command, Vehip assigned the entire I Caucasian Corps and 5th Caucasian Infantry Division. Reinforcements arrived in the form of VI Corps Headquarters (from Romania), brought by fast steamers to the Third Army. In the centre the new group was ordered to drive on Kars (lost to the Russians in 1878) while VI Corps would drive along the coast toward Batum. To the south IV Corps would liberate Van and Bayazit. The scope of the operation was ambitious, and it was a remarkable undertaking to reorganize the entire command structure on such a short and unannounced basis. In spite of potential problems, the Turkish commanders moved ahead and made it work.

Vehip's troops took the city of Sarikamis on 5 April, avenging the defeat of 1914, and then began advancing on Kars. The long-held city of Van was liberated on 6 April and Dogubeyazit fell on 14 April. The IV Corps continued its attack and took the frontier town of Saray. However, it did not stop, and drove into Persia, taking Kotur (last held in the spring of 1915 by the Van Jandarma Division) on 20 April 1918.

Along the coast, Armenians and local Greeks attempted to defend Batum, but VI Corps' attacks pushed them back and Batum fell on 14 April 1918. Again, the Turks captured quantities of war material, particularly much-needed transport including two locomotives, cars and wagons. In the coastal regions, the Turks also discovered many Muslim villages that

Russian naval cadets in Batum. The Turks lost Batum to the Russians in 1878, but briefly held it again in 1918. The port reverted to Soviet control shortly after the Turkish withdrawal from the Caucasus.

were reduced to piles of burnt debris, their residents now nothing more than dismembered corpses. The Turks attributed these atrocities to the local Christian inhabitants rather than to the Russians.

In the centre, the Armenians attempted to hold the fortress city of Kars, which had fallen to the Russians in 1878. The Russians had heavily fortified the city and turned the defences over to the Armenians intact. It was defended by 10,000 Armenians and the fortress contained over 200 artillery pieces.

The Turks advanced on the city in early April 1918. By 24 April they had almost encircled Kars and laid siege to it. It was clear to all concerned that Vehip had the means and the determination to take the city and the Armenian leaders frantically tried to negotiate a truce. Vehip demanded the surrender of the fortress intact as the price for a peaceful withdrawal, and the Armenians had no choice but to accept. The following morning the Turks entered the intact fortress of Kars with its abundant storehouse of supplies and large quantities of weapons. The

artillery park was captured in its entirety and added significant combat power to the Turkish Army. Vehip's men continued eastwards, and by the end of April 1918 the Third Army had arrived at the old 1877 frontier.

Turkish offensive operations continued into May 1918 with IV Corps pushing deeper into Persia from Dogubeyazit and taking the city of Moko. Vehip then pushed beyond the 1877 frontier on a broad front, conducting offensive operations along the railway line towards the Caucasian city of Tiflis. The political situation continued to deteriorate and became very confusing. The Turks, Russians and delegates from the Trans-Caucasian Federation had been trying to reach an agreement since 23 February, at a conference in the port city of Trabzon. The Russians were hoping for an end to Turkish expansion into the Caucasus while the Georgians, Azeris and Armenians sought to gain legitimacy for their fledgling national states. In the middle of these negotiations, Georgian nationalists in Tiflis proclaimed the complete independence of the Trans-Caucasian Federated Republic. Soon

Russian soldiers photographed at Tabriz. The Russian occupation of parts of Persia was short lived, as the army dissolved in the chaotic aftermath of the revolution.

afterwards, the new state proclaimed its commitment to a continued state of war with the Ottoman Empire, and the Trabzon talks collapsed.

Peace discussions resumed in Batum on 11 May 1918, but Vehip Pasha simply issued an ultimatum demanding the occupation of much of what is now Georgia. While the delegates bickered, the Third Army continued its relentless advance.

The Germans were particularly bothered by the Turkish demands and were not at all happy with the continuing Turkish drive into former Russian territory (they regarded Ottoman expansion into the Caucasus as a serious violation of the Treaty of Brest-Litovsk). Unfortunately for the Germans, alliance politics required the maintenance of effective relations with the Turks, and the Germans resorted to devious methods to stop the Turkish incursions. Colonel Kress von Kressenstein, having been released from his assignment commanding the Turkish Eighth Army,

Troops in the Caucasus 1918. The identity of these men is unclear, but with their signature heavy personal arms and ammunition bandoliers, they are probably Armenian.

was sent to Tiflis, along with German diplomat Count von Schulenberg. These two Germans hastily conferred with the alarmed leaders of the Trans-Caucasian Federated Republic to arrive at an unusual yet enormously creative solution to the problem.

On 27 May, the Georgian members of the republic announced the creation of a separate Georgian state. Simultaneously, Kress and Schulenberg announced the creation of a German protectorate for the newly independent Georgian state. The Turks were furious, with Vehip calling for an immediate invasion of Georgia. Almost immediately signs of German influence appeared in Georgia, with German and Georgian flags flying together everywhere. The German Army even sent some companies of infantry by sea from the Crimea to the Georgian port of Poti. Alarmed by the growing rift between the allies, Enver Pasha and his new chief of staff, German General Hans von Seeckt, went to Batum for discussions aimed

at easing the tensions. Conceding to German pressure, the northward expansion of the Turks into Georgia was temporarily halted.

However, Enver refused to relinquish his cherished dream of a pan-Turanic empire and once again reformed his Caucasian forces. From the units of the Third Army, Enver formed a new Ninth Army. To coordinate the activities of these two armies, Enver formed the new Eastern Army Group commanded by Vehip. In orders issued to all formations on 8 June 1918, Enver now reoriented the strategic direction of his Caucasian forces to the east and to the south, towards Azerbaijan and Persia. The new command structure of the Eastern Army Group accommodated this change in strategic direction by establishing two separate armies, which could operate on a wide front, with new missions and objectives. The Ninth Army was directed to attack into Persia and to seize Tabriz. The Third Army was directed to continue the drive eastwards towards the Caspian Sea. The Third Army staff hurried to move troops and equipment around the theatre to support the new command structure.

On 29 June, Enver ordered Vehip home to Constantinople and directed Halil Pasha, the hero of Kut and commander of Sixth Army, from Mosul to replace him as the commander of the Eastern Army Group. By mid-June 1918, the Third Army was making good progress, with a renewed advance eastwards along twin axes towards Baku. The Armenians and Azeris counterattacked the advancing Turkish columns and attempted to establish a defensive line in the vicinity of Kurdamir. However, Halil's 5th Division pushed onward towards Baku, and by 27 July occupied positions overlooking the city.

The rest of the Third Army laboured to catch up with the 5th Division's swift movements and there was a temporary lull in the tempo of operations. In July 1918, Enver began to put together the idea of an 'Army of Islam'. Built around a hard core of Turkish divisions, this force would mobilize Islamic supporters and sweep down through Persia to retake the Shatt al-Arab, where it would trap the British forces in

Mesopotamia. Enver's agents went to work to establish ties with and support from the Pahlevi family in Persia. On 10 July 1918, Enver activated the new Army of Islam (composed only of the 5th Caucasian Infantry Division and the 15th Division and some independent regiments).

THE MARCH TO BAKU

One of the more interesting vignettes of World War I occurred as the Turks conquered Azerbaijan and approached Baku. In early January 1918, the British became concerned about Turkish inroads into the Caucasus and, in particular, about a possible threat to British interests in Persia. Consequently, they decided to send an expedition to Baku. Major-General L.C. Dunsterville, who was a boyhood friend of Rudyard Kipling and the model for 'Stalky' of Kipling's 'Stalky and Co.', was appointed to lead an armed military mission to the Caucasus. Dunsterville began organizing his expedition, now called 'Dunsterforce', at Baghdad in the spring of 1918. His

Georgian troops. German occupation and assistance assured the preservation of Georgian independence for a brief time. Soviet forces took control of the republic when the Germans returned home at war's end.

The Ottoman advance to Baku and Petrovsk in mid to late 1918 demonstrated that, despite massive casualties, their army still retained combat effectiveness and cohesion at this late date in the war.

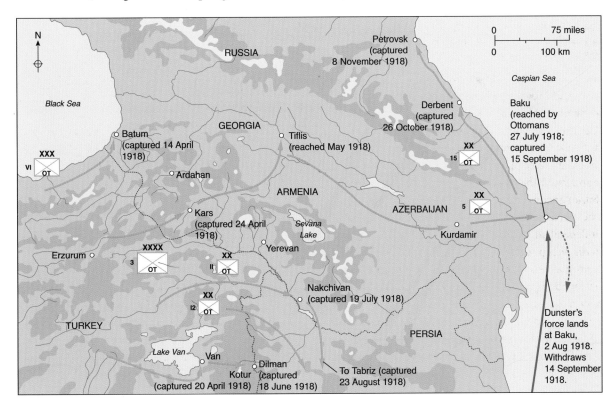

Baku's rich and productive oil fields became a strategic objective for British, Ottoman and Soviet forces in 1918. Ultimately, the Soviets regained control of them.

rather fuzzy mission was to proceed into Persia and enter the Caucasus via the Caspian Sea. Typically, Dunsterville was well supplied with money and advice but was short of troops and equipment. By mid-February he had reached Enzeli on the Caspian coast and there he formed a small army of Cossacks, Russians and Azeris. These men were not particularly reliable and Dunsterville narrowly escaped ambush several times, finally retiring to Hamadan. There, he began training his ragtag army with British officers and NCOs and awaited events as they unfolded in Enzeli. Because of the developing Ottoman threat to the Baku oil fields, the British began to send reinforcements to Dunsterville in June 1918. Dunsterville then began to fight his way back to Enzeli, where he could coordinate future combined operations with Bicherakov's Cossacks. By early July, Dunsterville had built a small flotilla on the Caspian

and landed the Cossacks at Alyat. Encouraged by this he began to land the main body of Dunsterforce on 2 August in Baku.

THE ARMY OF ISLAM ATTACKS

In the meantime, the Army of Islam started its attack on the city on 31 July. Several serious assaults were waged over the following week, but the Azeris and Armenians held firm. Reinforcements arrived and Halil prepared to renew the attacks. However, he received the first reports that 300 British soldiers had arrived in Baku on 5 August and that a further 5000 were awaiting transportation in Enzeli. Halil's worried staff now thought that they would need an additional 5000 fresh troops and several batteries of heavy artillery to take Baku. By 17 August, Dunsterforce had three battalions of British infantry, some field artillery and three armoured cars in Baku. However, Dunsterville was becoming more discouraged every day as the Azeri and Armenian defence force began to fall apart from the lack of dynamic leadership. Halil began to plan for the final assault on Baku, with the 15th Division coming in from the north and the 5th Caucasian Infantry Division attacking from the west. The attacks began at 1am on 14 September 1918 and the Turks made rapid progress against crumbling defences. The disenchanted Dunsterville was ready and had planned a withdrawal reminiscent of the Gallipoli evacuation. He quickly recognized that the defence was failing and decided about 11am that he must withdraw his forces. While his rear guards protected the evacuation, Dunsterforce loaded its personnel and equipment and by 10pm on 14 September had set sail for Enzeli.

With the withdrawal of the British, chaos broke out amongst the Azeris, the Cossacks and the refugee Armenians. Throughout the night, as the Turks drove at the remaining defences, fires, pillaging and massacres broke out in Baku. The Turks continued their artillery bombardment of the town throughout the night. By the next day, perhaps as many as 6000 Armenians were dead, many of them refugee civilians slaughtered by the Azeris. The Turks took the town on 15 September 1918. The Turks were stunned by the internecine massacre of the Armenians, but many regarded it as just punishment for the massacres of Turks in Erzurum province when the Armenians pulled out in March 1918.

Halil pushed the 15th Division northwards along the Caspian Sea to the town of Derbent, where, on 7 October the advance was halted by determined resistance. Under heavy naval gunfire from Russian fleet units, the Turks continued their attacks on 20 October. A running battle lasted for six days until the Turks shattered all remaining resistance. The 15th Division then continued to drive northwards along the Caspian coast, arriving at Petrovsk on 28 October. The division launched several attacks in early November, finally taking the city on 8 November 1918. This was the last Turkish offensive operation in World War I (occurring after the armistice) and marked the northernmost point of the Turkish advance into the Caucasus Mountains. In the south, the Ottoman Ninth Army initially had six infantry divisions assigned to its rolls when it received the mission to invade Persia and conquer Tabriz, but by the end of June 1918 two divisions had been taken away for other theatre requirements. Nevertheless, the 12th Division attacked, taking Dilman on 18 June. By 27 July, the division had beaten its way down to Rumiye. In the north, the Turks attacked and took Nachivan on 19 July 1918. Continuing down the railway towards Tabriz, the 11th Division took Tabriz on 23 August, but faced with an increasing British presence in Persia the Ninth Army's offensive now ground to a halt.

In September, the Turks had consolidated their grip on northern Persia and held a line reaching from Astara on the Caspian Sea to Miane in Persia, about 60km (37 miles) southeast of Tabriz, and on into the Ottoman Empire near Süleymaniye. The Turks held this territory until the armistice.

Lionel Charles Dunsterville (1865–1946)

Lionel Charles Dunsterville (1865–1946) was a classmate of Rudyard Kipling at the public school Westward Ho!, and became the basis for Rudyard Kipling's character 'Stalky'. He was commissioned into the British infantry and transferred to the Indian Army. He served on the Northwest Frontier, Waziristan and later in China. Dunsterville's World War I service saw him initially posted to India prior to his appointment at the close of 1917 to lead a force across Persia in an effort to aid in the establishment of an independent Trans-Caucasia. He was turned back by 3000 Russian revolutionary troops at Enzeli, but was then charged with the occupation of Baku. Here he was also unsuccessful, but proved to be a resourceful and steady commander in difficult circumstances.

CHAPTER 7

Turkey's Surrender

In October 1918, the Ottoman leadership began to explore the possibility of exiting the war by means of an armistice with the Allies. The Ottoman Army was still in the field, fighting to defend the Anatolian heartland and seeking to secure the gains in the Caucasus. Moves soon began, though, to demobilize its forces and return the number of troops to peacetime levels.

Some historians credit Allenby's victories in Palestine and in Syria as the proximate cause of the Ottoman decision to quit the war. This is untrue and it was the collapse of the Salonika front and the advance of General Milne's army on Constantinople that finally convinced the Young Turks of the hopelessness of the situation. In fact, by late 1918 Constantinople was all but undefended because the Turks had sent most of their available reserves to Palestine or Caucasia. While there were troops on the Gallipoli Peninsula, these were dedicated to coastal defence. On 5 October 1918, Talaat Pasha's cabinet decided to explore the possibility of an armistice.

After the war the Allies consolidated their dead on battlefield sites and constructed formal war grave cemeteries. The Turks left their soldiers in common, unmarked graves.

Eight days later, the Ottoman chargé d'affaires in Madrid sought Spanish assistance in requesting American help to take the Ottoman Empire out of the war. Neither Spain nor America was at war with the Ottoman Empire and the Turks felt that President Woodrow Wilson's '14 Points' indicated an apparent magnanimity towards the people of the Central Powers. These efforts failed, and as Milne approached Edirne the Turks resorted to sending Major-General Charles Townshend, the defeated commander of Kut al-Amara, to the island of Lemnos to announce their intention to seek an armistice. However, by this point in the war, the unfortunate Townshend was reviled in

A military parade at the Jaffa Gate. The British had approximately one million soldiers in the Middle East after the Mudros armistice. Churchill urged caution over their demobilization.

his own country, and his mission on behalf of the enemy embarrassed both the British and the Turks. Nevertheless, this act galvanized the British and provoked the French. The Allies and the Turks then entered into negotiations, which took place in the harbour of Mudros. The preliminary discussions centred on the occupation of strategic points such as the Dardanelles and the Pozanti and Amanus tunnel complexes. Although there was dissent between the British and French, since the British had carried the weight of the war in the Middle East, the final conditions favoured them. On 30 October 1918, an armistice was signed on the deck of the battleship HMS *Agamemnon*.

The Ottoman Army, however, was still in the field and fighting. It comprised over 25 infantry divisions as well as numerous fortresses. Moreover, the

command and control structure of the army was intact and retained the ability to carry out combat operations. The Ottoman Army held large tracts of land including the Anatolian peninsula and Arabia. Significantly, it held nearly all of Russian Caucasia including the oil city of Baku. Although the Ottoman Army was clearly at the edge of collapse, with desertion a huge problem (perhaps over 300,000 men by 1918), it was still a force to be reckoned with.

DEMOBILIZATION

The armistice found the Ottoman Army in the middle of three ongoing operations. The Yildirim Army was preparing for a determined defence of the Anatolian heartland immediately to the north of Aleppo, the Ninth Army was withdrawing forces from Caucasia for redeployment to Constantinople, and a reactivated Third Army was establishing itself in the Catalca Lines to defend the capital. These endeavours ended, and the

Australian cavalry troops leaving Jerusalem for demobilization camp, 12 October 1918. In less than a year the British had drawn their forces in the Middle East down to less than 300,000 men. This left them unable to direct the course of events as rebellions and Turkish nationalism threatened regional stability.

Ottoman general staff went immediately to work to demobilize the troops and return the army to its peacetime garrisons.

In November 1918, the Ottoman Army did not simply quit the war, as Lenin remarked about the Russian Army, by 'voting with its feet'. Unlike Germany, which had to immediately surrender 25,000 machine guns and 5000 artillery pieces, the Turks were under no such obligation. Nor did the armistice oblige them to demobilize their armies quickly. The actual schedule of demobilization was dictated by British Vice Admiral Sir John de Robeck on 26 November 1918, whereby older men would be released first in year-group increments;

for example, the men of year groups 1897–99 began to muster out of service on 6 January 1919. The process went quickly in some areas and slowly in others, but by the end of March 1919 the Ottoman Army had only 61,223 officers and men on active duty.

As planned, the re-established post-war Ottoman Army was set at 20 infantry divisions (down from a 1914 peacetime total of 36 infantry divisions). Most of the surviving infantry divisions were composed of ethnic Turks from the Anatolian heartland and these divisions were not dissolved. Although this left the

SMS *Goeben* of the Imperial German Navy on 1 January 1914. Memorabilia from this ship can be seen today at the Turkish Naval Museum in Istanbul, Turkey.

SMS *Goeben*

Winston Churchill characterized the SMS *Goeben* as the ship that brought Turkey into the war, and, in many ways, he was correct. The 23,000-ton *Moltke*-class battlecruiser was launched in Hamburg in 1911. She carried ten 11in guns and twelve 5.9in guns and could steam at 28 knots carrying over a thousand sailors. The *Goeben* was transferred to the Ottoman Navy on 16 August 1914 and renamed the *Yavuz Sultan Selim*. The ship participated in the Black Sea raids that brought Turkey into the war and fought several engagements against the Russian fleet over the next two years. The *Yavuz* emerged from the Dardanelles on 10 January 1918 to sink two British monitors, but was badly damaged by mines returning from her sortie. She survived the war to become the flagship of the new Republican navy. The ship was modernized in 1936 and finally decommissioned in 1954. The *Yavuz* was the sole surviving battlecruiser from World War I and was offered for sale in the 1960s. Unable to sell the ship the Turkish Government sent her to the scrap yard in 1973 where she was broken up by 1976. She outlived almost all of the men whose fate she had altered in 1914.

Turks with divisions scattered from Edirne to Baku, the hard core of tough combat infantry divisions remained intact. Within the post-war infantry divisions, every infantry regiment maintained one battalion at 50 per cent strength and two battalions at 25 per cent strength. The divisions also maintained four artillery batteries each and 36 machine guns.

By 27 January 1919, the Turks were simultaneously demobilizing and implementing the new force structure, much to the dismay of the British commanders trying to occupy the key strategic points of the empire. These smaller divisions gave the Turks a force of about 40,000 infantrymen under arms with 240 cannon. There were additional men assigned to the Gendarmerie and to the supply services. Altogether 48,000 men carried rifles. However, there were 791,000 rifles, 4000 machine guns and 945 artillery pieces stored in depots deep in the Anatolian

heartland, which allowed them to mobilize the 20 cadre divisions at full strength as well as arm 10 additional divisions if needed. The garrison cities of the post-war army were spread more or less evenly throughout what is now modern Turkey. Also differing from the treaty restrictions covering the Germans, the Turks were not forced to disband their general staff nor to disenfranchise the tough core of emerging leaders seasoned in the cauldron of war.

THE COST

The human cost of World War I in the Middle East remains hard to calculate, and there are a variety of contradictory figures. This is true concerning the number of civilian casualties as well, especially among the Ottoman Armenians. A total of 325,000 Ottoman military dead (from wounds and disease) is the number most commonly cited. This total seems to have originated in Commandant Larcher's 1926 book, but is considerably lower than the totals listed in the modern Turkish official histories. In fact, the Ottoman Army lost around 426,000 military dead or about 17 per cent of the 2.6 million men mobilized. Of course, these figures only present military losses, to which must be added the huge loss of life and productivity of the Muslim, Armenian and other Ottoman civilians killed or injured during the war.

In geographic terms, the Turks began the war with 2,410,000 square kilometres (930,500 square miles) of territory inhabited by 22 million people; after Mudros they retained 1,283,000 square kilometres (495,370 square miles) of territory inhabited by 10 million people (most of whom were Turks). Substantial parts of the most productive area of the empire were occupied by foreign powers. The economy was ruined, coal production had fallen to almost nothing, and the empire's former enemies and neighbours began to take even more territory from her.

Allied casualties are equally hard to assess. Britain sent about 1.5 million Britons, Indians, Australians and New Zealanders against the Turks and suffered 264,000 casualties. Russian casualties surely equalled this, while the French suffered probably fewer than 50,000. Moreover, the British Army was forced to keep a number of infantry divisions in the Middle East, which proved costly in both financial and political terms and led to a crisis in government in 1922. Field Marshal Lord Carver, writing in 1999, thought that the war against the Turks was a terrible waste of effort and diverted scarce resources from the French theatre.

A British funeral procession in the Middle East, with the soldiers bearing reversed arms. This common military practice is thought to have first occurred at the Duke of Marlborough's funeral in 1722.

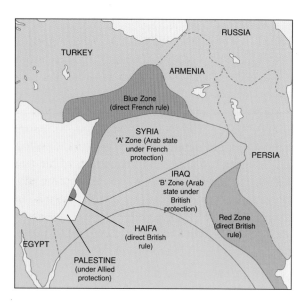

The proposed divisions according to the Sykes–Picot Agreement of 1916. This secret agreement between Great Britain and France, with Russia's assent, broadly divided up Ottoman territory, allowing the controlling powers to decide on state boundaries within these areas. With a few casual strokes of a pencil on the map of the Middle East, Mark Sykes and François Picot altered forever the geopolitical balance of the region. The unanticipated consequences of their work still linger today.

A PEACE TO END ALL PEACE

The treaties that formally ended World War I established what has been called 'a peace to end all peace'. This is an accurate assessment that reflects the many problems that afflict the modern world as a consequence of the destruction of the Ottoman Empire. The Ottoman Empire lay at the heart of the 'Eastern Question', which centred on the balance of European power in the Near East. However, the outcome of the war as framed by the various treaties was incompletely developed and led to a series of events that defined the world of the late twentieth century. The 'Eastern Question' is still with us, and one has only to look to Bosnia, Kosovo and the Balkans; Georgia, Armenia and the Caucasus; Iraq, the Kurds and the Tigris-Euphrates basin; Israel, Lebanon and Palestine; and the resurgent Islamic fundamentalism coming out of the Arabian peninsula, to understand the degree of instability wrought in 1919.

To a large degree, the problems began in 1915 when a series of letters were exchanged between Sir Henry McMahon, the British High Commissioner in Cairo, and Hussein ibn Ali, the Sharif of Mecca, promising independence in return for revolt against the Ottomans. The activities of the Arab Bureau in Cairo and those of T.E. Lawrence further inflamed Arab nationalism. However, in May 1917 Sir Mark Sykes of Britain and François Georges Picot of France arrived at a diplomatic agreement, which today is regarded as watershed benchmark in the history of the modern Middle East. The agreement, termed the Sykes–Picot Agreement, envisioned a post-war settlement that divided the Ottoman provinces between the two nations. In general, France claimed Syria and Lebanon, while the British (who were engaged on the Turkish fronts to a much greater degree) took just about everything else (including Mesopotamia, Arabia and Palestine). The Sykes–Picot Agreement became the basis for the division of spoils at Paris in 1919. Compounding this in November 1917 was the ill conceived British Balfour Declaration that pledged a future Zionist homeland for Europe's Jews while simultaneously promising not to displace or penalize the Arabs. There were also French promises made to the émigré Armenians to reconstruct an Armenian state in the eastern Ottoman provinces. Added to these layers of proclamations, Colonel T.E. Lawrence became a self-proclaimed advocate of Arab nationalism and further inflamed the Arab leaders by suggesting to them that independence would be bestowed upon them at Versailles. Lawrence even accompanied the Arab leaders to Paris dressed in the flowing robes and burnoose of a desert sheik, much to the discomfort of the British delegation.

The peace in the Middle East was a multi-stage process. The Treaty of Versailles in 1919, while not affecting the Ottoman Empire directly, established the League of Nations mandate system, which was aimed at the administration of the ex-German colonies. It was extended to include the Ottoman territories occupied by the Allied armies. Later, at the Conference of San Remo in April 1920, the British and French agreed to honour the Sykes–Picot Agreement and divide the Ottoman Empire along the lines discussed in 1917. The Treaty of Sèvres, signed on 10 August 1920, formally ended the Ottoman war and was as harsh and punitive as its predecessor signed at Versailles. In the treaty, the Ottoman Empire lost almost all of its non-Turkic provinces, including Arabia, Mesopotamia, Palestine and Syria, which then became mandates of the British and French. However, the treaty went much further and dismembered Anatolia by creating the independent states of Armenia and Kurdistan. The important city of Smyrna and most of the Aegean islands were promised to Greece. The rump Ottoman Government was forced to sign the treaty in the face of great public opposition from the Turkish people.

In many ways, the Treaty of Sèvres was a causal agent in the rise of Turkish nationalism in 1921–22.

Mustafa Kemal and others were so incensed by the harsh terms of the treaty that they formed a nationalist government and raised a nationalist army. Kemal and his army went on to expel the invading Greeks from western Anatolia and forced the Italians and French from the south and southeast, as well as making it impossible for Britain to remain in control of Constantinople and the Dardanelles Straits. By late 1922, Kemal had carved out the borders of modern Turkey. The unhappy Allies returned to the conference table and hammered out the Treaty of Lausanne in July 1923. The new treaty annulled the Treaty of Sèvres and established most of the current borders of the modern Republic of Turkey.

The signing of the Treaty of Sèvres on 10 August 1920. The treaty would later be annulled following the Turkish War of Independence (1919–23).

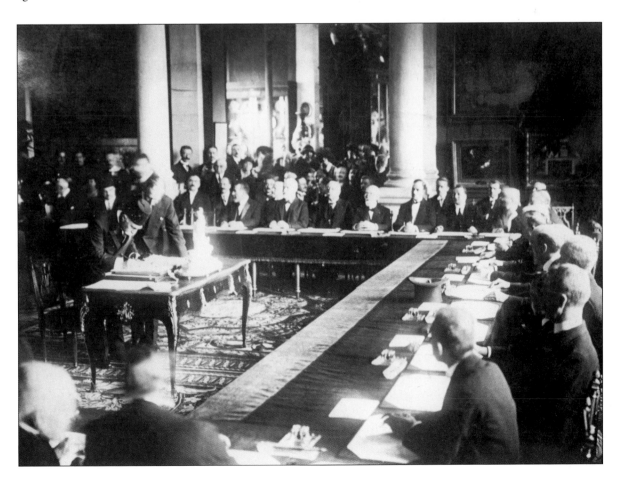

FURTHER READING

Allen, W.E.D. and P. Muratoff, *Caucasian Battlefields: a History of the Wars on the Turco-Caucasian Border 1828–1921* (Cambridge, Cambridge University Press, 1953)

Carver, Field Marshal Lord, *The Turkish Front 1914–1918* (London, Sidgwick & Jackson, 2003)

Cassar, G.H., *Kitchener's War: British Strategy from 1914 to 1916* (Washington, DC, Brassey's Inc., 2004)

Erickson, E.J., *Ordered To Die: a History of the Ottoman Army in the First World War.* (Westport, Greenwood Press, 2000)

—— *Defeat in Detail: the Ottoman Army in the Balkans 1912–1913* (Westport, Praeger, 2003)

Falls, C., *Armageddon: 1918* (Philadelphia, J.B. Lippincott Company, 1964)

Fromkin, D., *A Peace to End All Peace: the Fall of the Ottoman Empire and the Creation of the Modern Middle East* (New York, Henry Holt and Company, LLC, 1989)

Hickey, M., *Gallipoli* (London, John Murray, 1995)

—— *The First World War: the Mediterranean Front 1914–1923* (Oxford, Osprey Publishing, 2002)

Hughes, M., *Allenby and British Strategy in the Middle East 1917–1919* (London, Frank Cass, 1999)

James, R.R., *Gallipoli* (New York, Macmillan, 1965)

Lawrence, T.E., *Revolt in the Desert* (Garden City, Doubleday, 1927)

—— *Seven Pillars of Wisdom: a Triumph* (Stockholm, Alb. Bonniers, 1946)

Meinertzhagen, R., *Middle East Diary 1917–1956* (London, The Cresset Press, 1959)

—— *Army Diary 1899–1926* (London, Oliver and Boyd, 1960)

Millar, R., *Death of an Army: the Siege of Kut 1915–1916* (Boston, Houghton Mifflin, 1970)

Moorehead, A., *Gallipoli* (New York, Harper & Row, 1956)

Morgenthau, H., *Ambassador Morgenthau's Story* (Garden City, Doubleday Press, 1918)

Muhlmann, C., *Der Kampf um die Dardanellen 1915* (Berlin, Drud und Berlag von Gerhard Stalling, 1927)

Perrett, B., *Megiddo 1918: the Last Great Cavalry Victory* (Oxford, Osprey Publishing, 1999)

Sanders, L. von, *Five Years in Turkey* (London, Bailliere, Tindall & Cox, 1928)

Sheffy, Y., *British Military Intelligence in the Palestine Campaign, 1914–1918* (London, Frank Cass, 1998)

Steele, N. and P. Hart, *Defeat at Gallipoli* (London, Macmillan, 1994)

Strachan, H., *The First World War: vol. I, To Arms* (Oxford, Oxford University Press, 2001)

Townshend, Sir, C.V.F., *My Campaign in Mesopotamia* (London, Thornton Butterworth Ltd., 1920)

Travers, T., *Gallipoli 1915* (Charleston, Tempus Publishing Inc., 2001)

Wavell, A., *Allenby: a Study in Greatness* (New York, Oxford University Press, 1941)

Weber, F.G., *Eagles on the Crescent: Germany A ustria, and the Diplomacy of the Turkish Alliance, 1914–1918* (Ithaca, Cornell University Press, 1970)

Westlake, R., *British Territorial Units 1914–18* (London, Osprey Publishing Ltd, 1991)

Wilcox, R., *Battles on the Tigris: the Mesopotamian Campaign of the First World War* (London, Pen and Sword, 2006)

Wilkinson, S., *The Brain of an Army: a Popular Account of the German General Staff* (Westminster, Archibald Constable & Company, 1895)

Woodward, D., *Hell in the Holy Land: World War One in the Middle East* (Manhattan, KS, University of Kansas Press, 2006)

INDEX

PICTURE CREDITS

AKG Images: 35, 120(bottom)

Art-Tech/Aerospace: 57, 72(top), 79, 142, 144, 192

Art-Tech/MARS: 14(bottom), 15, 89, 115(bottom), 141, 162

Australian War Memorial: 209

Bridgeman Art Library: 11(Art Museum of Ryasan, Russia), 103(National Army Museum), 123(right, Archives Charmet)

Cody Images: 6, 72(bottom), 80, 81, 93, 108, 131, 150, 154, 164, 181, 199, 200

Corbis: 64(bottom), 115(top), 117, 123(left), 121, 124, 130, 148(top), 219

Nik Cornish @ Stavka: 201, 202, 204, 207

Mary Evans Picture Library: 22, 94, 111

E. W. W. Fowler: 41, 59(bottom), 61, 85, 86, 95, 96, 101, 104, 107, 110, 112, 128, 129

Getty Images: 100, 118, 136, 205, 208

Getty Images/Popperfoto: 48, 133

Greatwardifferent.com: 98

Imagestate/Heritage Images: 31, 38

Library of Congress: 1, 12, 14(top), 17, 20, 26, 27, 28, 30, 32, 40, 43, 44, 45, 47, 60, 62, 64(top), 66, 82, 84, 91(top), 120(top), 125, 132, 146(both), 148(bottom), 159, 160, 163, 165, 167, 168, 171, 172, 173, 174(top), 176, 179, 180(both), 182, 185, 186, 187, 188, 189, 191, 195, 197, 203, 210, 212, 213, 216

Bertil Olofsson/Krigsarkivet: 68

Photos 12: 10, 69, 137, 155, 156, 157

Photoshot: 56

Public Domain: 36, 102, 122

RIA Novosti: 37

Suddeutsche Zeitung: 8, 13, 21, 25, 50, 51, 52, 53, 54, 65, 67, 126, 138, 140, 143, 145, 153, 158, 214

TopFoto: 59(top), 74, 76, 77, 116, 149, 206

Artworks

Amber Books: 18

Art-Tech/Aerospace: 134, 174(bottom), 198(both)

Art-Tech/John Batchelor: 19, 170, 190

Art-Tech/De Agostini: 24, 71, 91(bottom), 114